THE AMERICAN AUTOMOBILE

The American

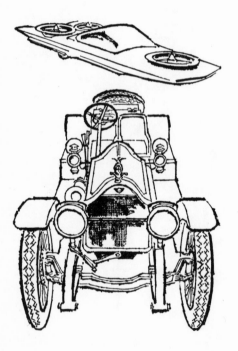

THE CHICAGO HISTORY
OF AMERICAN CIVILIZATION
Daniel J. Boorstin, EDITOR

Automobile

A BRIEF HISTORY *by John B. Rae*

 THE UNIVERSITY OF CHICAGO PRESS
CHICAGO & LONDON

Library of Congress Catalog Card Number: 65-24981

The University of Chicago Press, Chicago & London
The University of Toronto Press, Toronto 5, Canada

To Florence, Helen, and Jim, who all helped

Editor's Preface

The automobile has been the great vehicle of American civilization in the twentieth century. Seldom has a people found in technology so appropriate, so versatile, and so pervasive an expression. Originating in Europe, the automobile acquired novel forms in the United States. Here within a half-century, although it still remained in most of Europe a toy for the few, it had become a new social force touching everybody—an expression of and an instrument for speedy movement around and across the continent and up the social scale.

When before has a civilization found so powerful a catalyst? The automobile was peculiarly well suited to reinforce the characteristic tendencies of American civilization. A providential instrument for a people with much space and little time, the automobile has diffused and leveled and stirred and homogenized a continent-civilization. It has spread the freedom to travel among all classes and at the same time has helped remove the very differences between parts of the country, between kinds of landscapes which were once an incentive to travel. The automobile has brought farmers to the city and the city to the farm; it has siphoned city-dwellers to the suburbs and has made suburbs more city-like. More than any other device, it has been responsible for transforming large tracts of America and the dwelling places of most Americans into an environment neither urban nor rural, not properly to be called landscape. Dominated by superhighways and motels and drive-ins and parking areas, much of America can now be called motorscape.

If we are an automobile-riding, we are also an automobile-ridden people. Despite the daily offerings that Americans insert in parking meters, and the grand new parking temples rising in the centers of our cities, we seem unable to appease the motor goddess. She remains wayward and voracious, every year more independent in her demands, more unpredictable in her needs, until all we can confidently forecast is that her power is not likely to decrease. The yearly births of automobiles have for some time now been exceeding those of the human population.

The story of the automobile—so recent that we have hardly begun to think of it as history—touches nearly every aspect of the American economy and of American culture in this century. As Mr. Rae reminds us, the whole American economy has been crucially involved with the automobile. It is the story of booms and depressions, of the rise of industrial unionism, and of the national effort in two world wars. We cannot understand what we mean in America by competition or by monopoly, by advertising, by industrial leadership, or by know-how, unless we have understood the role of the automobile. It touches the most intimate regions of our life—courting practices and the family and a man's feelings about his place in the social scale—and the most public. It touches the history of American taste. And, not least important in the perspective of history, the automobile industry, through its decisive role in the Second World War, has helped develop the know-how and the machinery by which we move into the age of the airplane, without yet having left the age of the automobile.

The automobile, then, has long ceased to be only an instrument of technology and has become a characteristic American institution. But its history has been neglected in favor of more conventional and more traditional subjects. In this book, Mr. Rae helps us discover the automobile as a touchstone of our civilization. He admirably serves the purpose of the "Chicago History of American

Civilization," which aims to make each aspect of our culture a window to all our history.

The series contains two kinds of books: a chronological group, which provides a coherent narrative of American history from its beginning to the present day, and a topical group, which deals with the history of varied and significant aspects of American life. This book is one of the topical group, which includes, among others, John F. Stover's *American Railroads*.

DANIEL J. BOORSTIN

Contents

Illustrations

MAPS

PLATES

Tables

CHAPTER I

The Birth of the Automobile

The automobile is European by birth, American by adoption. The internal-combustion engine, upon which most automobile development has been based, is unmistakably of European origin, and both the idea and the technique of applying it to a highway vehicle were worked out first in Europe. On the other hand, the transformation of the automobile from a luxury for the few to a convenience for the many was definitely an American achievement, and from it flowed economic and social consequences of almost incalculable magnitude. The American automobile industry has grown into the largest manufacturing operation in the world, its annual performance is the most important single indicator of the condition of the American economy, and American life is organized predominantly on the basis of the universal availability of motor transportation. All this would have been an impressive accomplishment over a period of centuries: as it was, it took place in two generations.

EARLY EXPERIMENTS

The dream of a self-propelled vehicle goes far back into history. Roger Bacon wrote in the thirteenth century that "cars can be made so that without animals they will move with unbelievable rapidity," and he evidently thought that the scythe-bearing chariots of antiquity had some kind of mechanical propulsion. Three

hundred years later Leonardo da Vinci revived the idea, specifically for a military vehicle analogous to the modern tank. For both
Bacon and Leonardo these had to be speculations, since in neither
age was a feasible power plant available.

The first real step toward making the dream a reality was taken
by an eighteenth century French artillery officer, Nicholas Joseph
Cugnot. In 1769 he built and ran a three-wheeled carriage mounting a steam engine of his own design, with the idea that it might be
used for pulling guns. It was a clumsy contraption that left the road
the first time it had to take a curve at its top speed of three miles an
hour, and it offered no improvement whatever over the horse; but
it was indisputably the first self-propelled highway vehicle.

Following Cugnot there was a long lapse while the steam engine
was undergoing refinement so that it could meet the eternal demand
made of any locomotive engine: more power for less weight. In the
early years of the nineteenth century Richard Trevithick, a British
mining engineer, and the versatile American genius Oliver Evans
made crude but workable steam vehicles. Evans's machine, which
he called the *Orukter Amphibolos*, was actually a dredge for use in
the harbor of Philadelphia. He put it on wheels to get it through the
streets of the city (1805)—and incidentally to demonstrate the
practicability of the "steam waggon"—but he still failed to persuade the Pennsylvania legislature to let him use steam power on the
state's highways.

In Great Britain, although Trevithick abandoned his experiments, others carried on. The first half of the nineteenth century
witnessed several impressive English experiments with steam omnibuses. Some of these vehicles operated for lengthy periods on
regular routes with excellent records of punctuality and safety.
Their success, indeed, brought about their downfall, because railway and stagecoach companies joined forces against them. They
were harassed by discriminatory tolls and fees, and their operation
became impossible with the passage of the "red flag" law in 1865,
which limited self-propelled vehicles on public highways to a
maximum of four miles an hour and required that each be preceded

by a man on foot carrying a red flag. This law remained in force until 1896. It was a short-sighted piece of legislation whose only perceptible consequences were to cut off a promising development in highway transportation and retard the growth of the British automobile industry.

As it turned out, the future of the automobile was not to be with steam anyway. Because the steam engine was expensive and inefficient for supplying small amounts of power, inventive effort by the middle of the nineteenth century was being directed to the possibilities of the internal-combustion engine. The first practical machine of this type was a two-cycle engine patented in Paris in 1860 by a Belgian mechanic named Etienne Lenoir. It was a crude and noisy contraption, but it worked and it was a commercial success. A contemporary of Lenoir's, Beau de Rochas, filed a French patent description in 1862 explaining accurately the principle of the four-cycle engine, but there is no evidence that he ever built one. The four-cycle engine as an operational mechanism was introduced by a German, Nicholas Otto, in 1878. Meanwhile, George B. Brayton, an American engineer, designed a two-cycle engine of his own in 1872 and exhibited it at the Philadelphia Centennial Exposition in 1876. Brayton's engine compressed the fuel in a separate chamber outside the cylinder, whereas Lenoir's had no compression but depended solely on the expansion of the gases when the fuel was ignited.

These early efforts were clumsy affairs, intended mainly to provide power for small industrial plants. Coal gas was the principal fuel, with petroleum products coming gradually into use as that industry expanded. The possibility of using the internal-combustion engine for locomotion was appreciated from the start. Lenoir built a vehicle using his engine and ran it in Paris in the 1860's, but since this was an isolated experiment without continuing results, Lenoir has never been considered to be the originator of the automobile. This honor has also been claimed for the Viennese inventor Siegfried Markus, who began experimenting with motor carriages at about the same time. The evidence indicates, however, that Markus did not have an operable vehicle until the 1880's, and his experiments likewise failed to get into the mainstream of automotive history. He was handicapped by the disapproval of his neighbors and the Viennese police. He tried to make his test runs at night, but although darkness could conceal his vehicle from sight, he was totally unable to keep it out of hearing, and ultimately he had to discontinue his work.

In the United States the Brayton engine was tested on a street railway in Providence, Rhode Island, in 1873 with unsatisfactory results. But the model displayed at the Centennial Exposition attracted the attention of George B. Selden (1846–1932), a patent attorney and inventor of Rochester, New York. Selden believed that the Brayton engine could be adapted for use in a highway vehicle, and in 1879 he filed an application for a United States patent on a "road engine" combining a motor using a liquid hydrocarbon fuel, a mechanism for disengaging the engine from the driving wheels, and a steering devic. He did not at this time build a vehicle conforming to his specifications. None of these men—Lenoir, Markus, Selden—had any continuing influence on the evolution of the gasoline automobile, although Selden's patent would later create a major crisis in the American automobile industry. Nevertheless by 1880 the idea of a motor carriage driven by an internal-combustion engine was intriguing inventive minds.

The following decade saw still another source of power emerge—the electric motor. Technically the "horseless carriage" had become feasible, even though its ultimate form was still to be determined. A technical innovation, however, can run into a dead end if it arrives at the wrong time or in an unfavorable environment. More than a power plant was needed if the motor vehicle was to be accepted as a mode of transportation.

THE BICYCLE PRELUDE

A highway vehicle manifestly has to have an adequate highway system if it is to be of any use. Yet even in the industrial Western world good roads were limited in extent in the nineteenth century, not from any lack of ability to build them but simply because it was felt there was no need for extensive highway construction. Travel by road was of minor importance, because the railway was smoother, faster, and more economical than any existing method of highway transportation. Where a respectable highway system already existed, as in France, it was maintained; on the other hand, the United States as late as 1900 had only about two hundred miles of hard-surface roads outside the large cities.

Public interest in improving roads was first stimulated by the popularization of the bicycle. This became noticeable in the 1870's and rose to a high point after the introduction of the "safety" bicycle by J. K. Starley in Coventry, England, in 1885. Starley's invention was the modern low-wheeled bicycle with gearing and chain drive. It superseded the high-wheeled velocipede of the mid-nineteenth century whose use was limited to riders of considerable physical prowess. Because the driving wheel of the velocipede was turned directly by the pedals, it had to be of large diameter to give enough speed to keep the machine upright. The safety bicycle was of universal appeal; it could be ridden by women and children just as well as by men, and in the eighties and nineties it put people by the thousand on the roads of the Western world. This flood of bicyclists soon became conscious of the inadequacies of their highway systems and raised a clamor for something to be done. In the United States, for example, an organization known as the League of American Wheelmen was able to get action from state and local authorities to improve the condition of the roads. In 1893, in fact, the year the Duryea car made its appearance, pressure from the bicyclists induced Congress to appropriate $10,000 for a Bureau of Road Inquiry in the Department of Agriculture to study and provide information on improved methods of highway construction. This was the forerunner of the Bureau of Public Roads and of the federal highway program.

The influence of bicycling in reviving highway travel and preparing people's minds for the motor vehicle is lucidly expressed by Hiram Percy Maxim (1869–1936), one of the outstanding American automotive pioneers, in his charming autobiography, *Horseless Carriage Days:*

It has been the habit to give the gasoline engine all the credit for bringing the automobile—in my opinion this is the wrong explanation. We have had the steam engine for over a century. We could have built steam vehicles in 1880, or indeed in 1870. But we did not. We waited until 1895.

The reason why we did not build road vehicles before this, in my opinion, was because the bicycle had not yet come in numbers and had not directed men's minds to the possibilities of long-distance travel over the ordinary highway. We thought the railroad was good enough. The bicycle created a new demand which it was beyond the ability of the railroad to supply. Then it came about that the bicycle could not satisfy the demand which it had created. A mechanically-propelled vehicle was wanted instead of a foot-propelled one, and we know now that the automobile was the answer.

Maxim's appraisal can be accepted as generally valid, although in its entirety it is more accurate for America than for Europe, where the automobile did not supersede the bicycle so completely as it did in the United States.

There were other influences besides the stimulation of highway travel. From the bicycle manufacturers the early automobile industry inherited steel-tube framing that combined strength with lightness, the chain drive, ball and roller bearings, and differential gearing (developed for the multiwheeled variations produced at the peak of the bicycle craze). The vital role of the bicycle in preparing the way for the automobile is strikingly illustrated in the long roster of men and companies who moved from one industry to the other; prominent on the list are Morris in England, Opel in Germany, and Duryea, Pope, Winton, and Willys in the United States.

Beyond question, the most important contribution of the bicycle to the automobile was the pneumatic tire, invented by John B. Dunlop in Ireland in 1888 specifically for use on bicycles. (Reinvented, to be strictly accurate. It first appeared in the 1840's but was promptly forgotten because it could not be used to advantage on either the vehicles or the roads of that period.) The combination of the pneumatic tire and the hard-surface road was indispensable to the success of the motor vehicle. Without both, highway travel could never have competed with rail transport in comfort or speed.

EUROPEAN BEGINNINGS

The lineal ancestors of today's gasoline-powered automobile were the vehicles constructed in Germany in 1885 by Karl Benz and Gottlieb Daimler. Both men approached automobile manufacture after gaining experience as manufacturers of stationary internal-combustion engines; Daimler had been an engineer with Nicholas Otto's firm, Otto and Langen. Whether Daimler or Benz is entitled to priority is still an unsettled question. Daimler began with a motorcycle, Benz with a tricycle. Both used a one-cylinder engine. Daimler's was a high-speed motor and thus more distinctly the forerunner of the modern automobile engine, but Benz was using spark ignition where Daimler had the less efficient hot tube. The dispute between their partisans has no validity for us. The essential point is that from their work stemmed a continuing, uninterrupted development of the motor vehicle.

Within ten years after Daimler and Benz had successfully demonstrated their inventions, Armand Peugeot and the firm of Panhard and Levassor were making cars with Daimler engines in France, a syndicate was formed to do the same thing in Britain and was agitating for repeal of the red flag law, and in the United Sttes the piano manufacturer William Steinway was vainly trying to interest the American public in this German gadget. The most rapid progress was made initially in France where a good highway system encouraged motoring. There as early as 1891 Emile Constant Levassor designed the prototype of the modern automobile. The earlier "horseless carriage" was just that: a buggy (or sometimes a bicycle frame) with a motor attached wherever it happened to be convenient (under the driver's seat was a common location). Levassor's car was planned around the fact of mechanical propulsion. The engine was in front, where its weight helped to hold the vehicle on the road, leaving the rest of the chassis to support a body for the accommodation of passengers.

The decade of the 1890's saw an automobile industry in western Europe engaged in regular commercial production, with France in the lead, Germany second, and Britain energetically trying to overcome its self-imposed handicap. A variety of gasoline, electric, and steam vehicles were on the market, and road races and trials were attracting attention. Levassor won a Paris-Rouen race in 1894 and a year later performed the astounding feat of driving a Panhard the 1,200 kilometers from Paris to Bordeaux in forty-eight hours, maintaining an average speed of fifteen miles an hour. These cars were all individually constructed, and facilities for repair and maintenance were practically nonexistent. An automobile was therefore expensive to buy and operate. For the most part it was a plaything for wealthy sportsmen, although by the turn of the century the touring car and the limousine were beginning to gain acceptance at the upper levels of society as substitutes for the family carriage, and ladies were using electric automobiles for city travel.

THE AMERICAN INVENTORS

It is an oddity of automotive history that Americans should have had to reinvent the automobile for themselves, with the result that until the beginning of the twentieth century American development was about ten years behind European. The reasons are a historical mystery. There was ample mechanical skill available in the United States, and there was some knowledge of the early European experiments. It may be that American talent was slow to get interested in motor vehicles because of the discouraging prospect for highway travel in a land of vast distances and poor roads.

At any rate, if some earlier but unproductive experiments are disregarded, the automobile era in the United States dates from September 21, 1893, when a motor carriage with a one-cylinder gasoline engine chugged noisily along the streets of Springfield, Massachusetts. It was the creation of two brothers, Charles E. (1861–1939) and J. Frank Duryea (b. 1869), bicycle mechanics who had read a description of Benz's car in the *Scientific American* in 1889 and had gone to work to build one of their own. By coincidence powered flight was also achieved by two brothers who made a living by manufacturing and repairing bicycles. There is evidence here of the technological significance of the bicycle, but there the parallel ends. The Wrights had more a conclusive first than the Duryeas, and they did not plunge into an irreconcilable quarrel, as did the Duryeas, over which one was entitled to credit for the achievement.

A second, two-cylinder Duryea car with Frank driving won the highly publicized *Chicago Times-Herald* race on November 28, 1895, plowing through icy streets to complete the fifty-five-mile course at an average speed of five miles an hour (seven and one-half when time for repairs was deducted). Of the six entries only one other, a Benz, finished. This performance may be compared with the Paris-Bordeaux race of the same year. In 1896 the Duryeas gained further prestige by taking part in an automobile parade from London to Brighton, held to celebrate Britain's repeal of the red flag law. Shortly thereafter, however, the brothers parted and their subsequent roles in the history of the automobile were minor.

By this time others were coming into the competition. Elwood Haynes (1857–1925), a trained engineer, began working on a mechanical vehicle in 1891 because he was tired of the horse and buggy travel required by his job as superintendent of the Indiana Natural Gas and Oil Company. He enlisted the aid of two machinists, Edgar and Elmer Apperson of Kokomo, Indiana, and with them produced a one-cylinder car that made its first run on July 4, 1894. Haynes and the Appersons remained in partnership for the next ten years, eventually putting a car named the Haynes-Apperson on the market. Then they separated, and both Haynes and Apperson cars were made in Kokomo until the 1920's. The partners seem to have quarreled, among other things, over credit for the 1894 car. At any rate the Appersons later asserted that they, not Haynes, were its real designers, but they were unable to get this claim accepted. Haynes, for his part, tried with equal lack of success to argue that he was entitled to priority over the Duryeas, apparently on the dubious ground that he started working on his car first. He has a more convincing claim to have been the first American motorist to get a traffic ticket, having been ordered off the streets of Chicago by a bicycle-riding policeman in 1895.

Next came Hiram Percy Maxim, son of the inventor of the Maxim gun and a graduate of the Massachusetts Institute of Technology. Following the family bent, young Maxim went from college to the American Projectile Company in Lynn, Massachusetts. According to his own account, the idea of building a powered vehicle came to him late one night as he was pedaling a bicycle from Salem to Lynn, with his head somewhat up in the clouds after calling on an attractive young lady. His experience offers a striking revelation of the state of American automotive technology. He knew enough about the principle of the internal-combustion engine to be aware that it might provide the mechanism he wanted, but he had never actually seen one until after he started to work on his vehicle. Then he went to see an Otto engine working a pump. Even then he did not know whether gasoline could be used as a fuel, and he was completely unaware both of what had already been done in Europe and of the contemporary experiments of the Duryeas and Haynes.

So Maxim bought a secondhand Columbia tricycle for $30 and then took himself to a remote corner of the Projectile Company's lot with a half pint of gasoline and some empty cartridge cases to find out what happened when gasoline was ignited in a cylinder. He was lucky and got his information without damage to himself, but it took another three years of trial and error before he was able in 1895 to put an engine on his tricycle so that the combination functioned after a fashion. Maxim's work has a special significance because he attracted the attention of the Pope Manufacturing Company of Hartford, Connecticut, the country's largest producer of bicycles (Pope products carried the trade name Columbia, and so Maxim already had an association with the company). Maxim accepted an offer to go to Hartford as chief engineer for a motor carriage department established by Pope, and this was the first effort at large-scale commercial production of motor vehicles in the United States. Somewhat to his disappointment Maxim found himself concentrating on electric carriages because Colonel Albert A. Pope (1843–1909) at first insisted, "You can't get people to sit over an explosion." In two years the company built five hundred electric and forty gasoline carriages.

In the meantime other inventors were crowding into the American scene: 1896 saw the gasoline automobile arrive in Detroit. Charles Brady King drove a car down Woodward Avenue on March 6, and the first automotive venture of Henry Ford (1863–1947), the quadricycle, made its test run on Bagley Avenue. This was on June 4, after its builder had knocked down the wall of his landlord's barn to get his creation out on the street. The landlord arrived to protest and remained to push (the normal method of starting these pioneering experiments). The quadricycle was a relatively lightweight vehicle (500 pounds) and may therefore have foreshadowed in its design Ford's dream of a cheap car. It was sold for $200 to Charles Ainsley of Detroit, who later resold it; and so if Henry Ford was not, as many people have believed, the inventor of the automobile, he may well have contributed the first used car to appear on the American market. Two other famous names emerged on the automotive scene in September of 1896— Ransom Eli Olds (1864–1950) in Lansing, Michigan, and Alexander Winton (1860–1932) in Cleveland, Ohio. With them the gasoline automobile may be considered to have completed the stage of invention in the United States, since both Winton and Olds were able to go on promptly to production.

There was also Edward Joel Pennington (1858–1911), who

exemplified a direction the nascent automobile industry might have taken but fortunately did not. A glib promoter with some mechanical talent (he was the prototype of Get-Rich-Quick Wallingford, the fictional creation of American author George Randolph Chester), Pennington organized a company in Racine, Wisconsin, in 1895, purporting to manufacture motor carriages using the "Kane-Pennington Hot Air Engine." It was an engine that was supposed to cool itself by heat dissipation from the cylinder walls, and Pennington professed to have used it on a vehicle as early as 1890. No supporting evidence for this assertion has been found. His designs were published in technical journals and were plausible enough to give Henry Ford useful ideas during his experimenting days.

Pennington's performance never matched his claims. He was to enter four cars in the *Chicago Times-Herald* race, but they never appeared, allegedly because of mechanical difficulties. The same thing happened when Pennington went to Britain a year later to engage in promotional schemes. He was always going to display the superiority of his vehicles, but they invariably developed some undisclosed defect and were not available for the trial. Meanwhile Pennington joined forces with Harry J. Lawson, a British promoter who had at least acquired the British rights to the Daimler engine. The two men organized a concern in 1899 called the Anglo-American Rapid Vehicle Company with capital of $75 million, an alleged 200 motor-vehicle patents, and a proposal to merge the existing British and American automobile companies. Even if they had succeeded, their combined assets would have been far short of $75 million. When the scheme collapsed Pennington disappeared from the automobile business.

The origins of the gasoline-powered vehicle have necessarily attracted the greatest amount of historical attention because it was the type that came to dominate the automotive world. This outcome was far from obvious in the 1890's, and a good deal of inventive effort was expended on electric and steam cars. The first electric automobile to run on the streets of an American city appears to have been built by William Morrison of Des Moines,

Iowa, in 1891. Commercial production in the United States started with Henry G. Morris and Pedro Salom of Philadelphia, whose Electrobat appeared in 1894 and took part in the *Times-Herald* race a year later.

Because it was silent, clean, and easy to operate, the electric automobile enjoyed an early popularity. Colonel Pope's views on sitting over an explosion were widely shared. Pedro Salom, an electrical engineer, was even more vehement about the virtues of electricity and the evils of gasoline. He pointed out in the *Journal of the Franklin Institute* in 1896 that electric motors had no odor whereas:

All the gasoline motors we have seen belch forth from their exhaust pipe a continuous stream of partially unconsumed hydrocarbons in the form of a thick smoke with a highly noxious odor. Imagine thousands of such vehicles on the streets, each offering up its column of smell!

No one, however, has ever been able to provide an electric automobile with current other than through a battery, or to develop a battery of sufficient endurance to make long runs and high speeds possible.

The long history of experiments with steam power makes it impossible to say that the steam automobile was "invented." What was achieved in the 1890's was to design engines light enough for use in an automobile, as distinct from an omnibus or a steam roller, by using steam pressures of 600 pounds per square inch. A kerosene or gasoline burner was used to heat the boiler. The early steamers required about twenty minutes to work up a sufficient head of steam. The flash boiler, invented by Leon Serpollet in France in 1889 but not generally used until after 1900, removed this handicap by permitting steam to be raised in two minutes.

The first Americans to produce steam automobiles commercially were the twin brothers Francis E. (1849–1918) and Freelan O. Stanley (1849–1940), who went into business in Newton, Massachusetts, in 1897 after a few years of experimenting in their home town of Lewiston, Maine. They were also, for practical purposes, the last. By the time Francis died the market for steam automobiles had declined so much that his brother simply gave up. An engineer named Abner Doble subsequently acquired the Stanley designs and produced an improved steamer in the 1920's; but the Doble car, although technically of high quality, could not be made to sell for less than $8,500, and it was not a commercial success. The White brothers of Cleveland, Ohio, actually made better steam automobiles than the Stanleys. They went into production in 1901 and introduced the flash boiler for American cars. After ten years of successful manufacturing, however, the Whites gave up on steam and turned to gasoline-powered cars.

The steam automobile had and still has its partisans. Compared with the early gasoline cars, the steamer had definite advantages. It had more power, and it did not require a complicated transmission—there were a good many "experts" in those days who were convinced that the ordinary individual would never be able to learn how to shift gears. On the other hand, the makers of steam automobiles never could overcome fear of boiler explosions, although available records show that the fear was unfounded. Even if this ghost had been successfully exorcised, the steam automobile had handicaps which its enthusiasts overlook. A lightweight reciprocating steam engine operating on pressures of 600 pounds per square inch requires constant skilled maintenance, and so it would have been an unsatisfactory mechanism for a car intended for mass consumption. Moreover, keeping the boiler filled was simple enough in the Northeast, where soft water was readily available and where at the turn of the century there were towns and villages comfortably close together, each with its horse trough ready to serve the thirsty engine as readily as the thirsty animal. Conditions were different elsewhere. Any extensive use of steam automobiles in the Southwest, for example, would have necessitated service stations supplied with boiler water brought in from distant points, just as the railroads had to do for their steam locomotives.

These difficulties could have been surmounted if manufacturers had considered it worthwhile to make the attempt. The insuperable handicap for the steam-driven automobile was and is that an internal-combustion engine has greater thermal efficiency than a steam engine, so that the same amount of technical effort would inevitably produce better results with the gasoline car than the steamer. There is no evidence that the steam automobile was the victim of a conspiracy on the part of the manufacturer of gasoline automobiles, as has sometimes been alleged by its partisans. What happened to it was simply a manifestation of the survival of the fittest.

CHAPTER 2

The Horseless Carriage

By the late 1890's the automobile was emerging from the status of an experimental curiosity and was beginning to make a place for itself in American life—a minor place to be sure, but growing with phenomenal rapidity. In 1900 the Census Bureau lumped automobile manufacturing with "miscellaneous." Output for the year was 4,192 units, sold for an average price of just over $1,000 each, this total representing predominantly the work of innumerable small shops. In 1908, which is a landmark in the story of the American automobile as the year in which the Model T was born and General Motors was founded, production had risen to 65,000 and automobile registrations were approaching 400,000.

Production was not the whole story of the early horseless carriage days. In a variety of ways the social impact of the motorcar was beginning to be felt and still more to be foreshadowed. Nevertheless, production was the most pressing question because of a fact that became increasingly manifest: Americans wanted cars, so that the United States offered a practically limitless market for those who could offer the proper combination of quality and price.

THE FOUNDING OF THE AUTOMOBILE INDUSTRY

The total number of firms to engage in manufacturing automobiles in the United States can never be accurately determined. In the

early years especially, when regulations regarding motor-vehicle
registration were likely to be casual or nonexistent, there were
individuals or small concerns who turned out one or two experimental cars and then disappeared from view without leaving any
record. The most complete and authoritative list, compiled by the
Automobile Manufacturers Association and the Automobile Club
of Michigan, shows more than three thousand makes of cars and
trucks built by some fiften hundred identifiable manufacturers in
the United States from the time that Duryea car made its appearance to the present. The great majority of these went through their
brief life span before the First World War.

In those days automobile manufacturing was as classic an example of free competitive enterprise as could be found. All that was
needed to go into business was a modicum of mechanical ability and
a place to put the car together. No heavy investment in plant and
equipment was necessary because automobile production was almost exclusively an assembly operation, using parts and components bought from outside firms. This feature has remained characteristic of the automobile industry, although the role of the
independent supplier has gradually lessened in importance as automobile companies have become larger and more self-contained.
There was a time, indeed, when some producers, like the Cole
Motor Company of Indianapolis, proudly advertised the superiority of the "assembled" over the "manufactured" car, claiming
that the former incorporated the expert specialized talent of all the
separate parts manufacturers.

Financial requirements for entering the automobile industry
were also slight. Bank credit was seldom available because making
horseless carriages was such a speculative enterprise that no respectable banker would touch it. But very little cash was needed to get
the operation going. Many of the small firms financed themselves
by buying from suppliers on credit and selling to dealers for cash.
The marketing structure of the automobile business was also in the
preliminary stages of development. Cars were frequently sold
direct from the factory or else marketed through regional distribu-

tors who were free to create their own local sales agencies in their territories. There were also independent local dealers doing business directly with the manufacturer. The organization of marketing through elaborate networks of dealers came later, when there were producers with a sufficient volume of business to support them.

Nevertheless, the basic relationship that still prevails between manufacturer and distributors in the automobile industry was established at the outset. As a condition of his franchise the distributor or dealer agreed to accept the sight draft which came with the bill of lading on each shipment of new cars. In effect, much of the American automobile industry in its pioneering period was financed through its dealers and their banks. Since most dealers in those days had customers waiting in line and prepared to pay cash for their cars, this arrangement was not as one-sided in favor of the manufacturer as it might seem. Moreover, with hundreds of firms trying to put motor vehicles on the market, a dealer who felt aggrieved could change to a different line with considerably greater ease than was possible later.

This technique of buying on credit and selling for cash enabled the individual with limited finances to get started in automobile manufacturing and stay in it if he could produce and sell promptly enough to keep ahead of his creditors. It was by no means a foolproof method, as the high attrition rate in the automobile industry demonstrates, but it worked well enough and often enough to be an important factor in the growth of the industry. It accounts, for example, for the survival of the Ford Motor Company through the hazards of infancy.

But although getting into automobile production was easy enough, staying in it was another matter entirely. Competition was intense and rigorous, and with a novel commodity like the motor vehicle, deciding what the buying public would accept called for a combination of shrewd judgment and luck. The best prospects for survival among the initial entrants were generally those companies that grew from an established firm and therefore had some resources in plant, managerial and technical skill, and capital. The parent concern was most likely to be a vehicle manufacturer, either bicycles or carriages and wagons, or else to be making mechanical equipment of some kind. Thus Pope was the country's leading bicycle producer and Studebaker the largest manufacturer of horse-drawn vehicles in the world before they turned to automobiles; Ransom E. Olds made stationary gas engines; and the first White steamers were built in the White sewing machine factory. There were endless variations also. David Dunbar Buick (1855–1929) was a manufacturer of plumbing fixtures, and the once famous Pierce-Arrow emerged from a company that had started with bird cages. (The sequence was from wire cages to spokes for bicycle wheels, then to complete bicycles and motorcycles, and so to automobiles.)

The cars themselves were very much in the "horseless carriage" category, buggies with one- or two-cylinder engines. After the turn of the century the influence of European design brought the engine from under the driver's seat to the front of the car and added a *tonneau*, for the accommodation of passengers. The tonneau, or body, was made in carriage factories and showed its heritage even in the names given to body styles—brougham, stanhope, surrey, landaulet. In fact, the carriage tradition persisted so strongly that many automobile bodies came complete with whip sockets, which could well have been useful accessories in a day when any automobile trip might end with the cry, "Get a horse." Steering at first was by tiller rather than by wheel. There are several claimants for the distinction of introducing the steering wheel, but this is an irrelevant issue; the critical step was the invention of the steering knuckle in 1902, the little device that permits the front wheels to turn instead of the entire axle.

At the opening of the twentieth century the prospecive purchaser of a motor vehicle had a bewildering variety of choices available to him. He had to decide among electric, steam, and gasoline cars; if he picked gasoline he had an option between water- and air-cooled engines, and he could even have a two-cycle motor if he wished. There were various types of transmissions; Pope experimented with electric transmission, and one fairly prominent model, the Cartercar, had a friction drive. What was bewildering for the consumer was critical for the producer, since a small-scale manufacturer operating on a financial shoestring could not afford to make a mistake about what to offer. In a surprisingly short time, however, a discernible trend appeared—to the gasoline car with a multicylinder, four-cycle engine, ordinarily water-cooled. For those who combined the business and technical skill to judge this trend and adapt to it, there were glittering rewards; for the others at best a niche in the memories of the antique automobile enthusiasts.

PIONEERING PRODUCERS

These conditions can be observed in the companies that figured prominently in the founding of the American automobile industry. The sampling is of necessity incomplete because the total number of firms involved was so large, and it may be unrepresentative because information about the failures generally does not exist; but all the companies whose stories are related can be shown to have made an identifiable contribution to the development of the industry.

The year 1897 marks the effective start of the automobile industry in the United States, if production of a few vehicles of various types in previous years is discounted. In that year the Pope Manufacturing Company put its Columbia electrics and a few gasoline cars on the market; the Stanleys began to build steamers commercially; and Ransom E. Olds and Alexander Winton formed companies for the manufacture of gasoline automobiles. Only Pope at this time could rank as a major producer. Olds was handicapped by lack of capital and did not get into operation for another two years. Winton, a testy Scot who had been a successful bicycle manufacturer in Cleveland, built six omnibuses, each to carry six passengers, in 1897. They were intended for use on Cleveland's

Shore Drive, but the first trial trip frightened horses and brought so many threats of lawsuits that the promoters hurriedly abandoned the scheme and never even paid Winton. He then turned to passenger cars and was able to go into regular production and sale in 1898.

According to a plausible legend, Winton even helped to start a competitor. Winton No. 12 was bought by James W. Packard (1863–1928) of Warren, Ohio; and when Packard went to Cleveland to complain of defects in the car, Winton reputedly told him to go and make a better one himself if he was dissatisfied. Packard accepted the challenge. As a matter of fact, he had been experimenting on his own for some time, and in 1900 he began to make cars in Warren under the name of the Ohio Automobile Company. Given Packard's engineering talent (he was an engineering graduate of Lehigh University) and a solid base in the Packard Electric Company, this venture had good prospects from the start. Packard, for instance, introduced the H-slot gearshift employed almost universally until the introduction of the automatic transmission.

The company's rise to prominence, however, was fortuitous. In 1901 a group of Detroit capitalists headed by Henry B. Joy (1864–1936), son of the railroad magnate James F. Joy, was becoming interested in automobiles. Joy himself and Truman S. Newberry, who would run successfully against Henry Ford for the United States Senate in 1918, visited the 1901 automobile show in New York. After an unfortunate experience with a steam car, whose boiler gauge burst and showered them with hot water and broken glass, they were attracted to a Packard parked outside the exhibition building. While they were inspecting the car, a fire engine went by, whereupon the owner dashed out of an adjoining building, started his motor with one spin of the crank, and went off in pursuit. Joy and Newberry were greatly impressed and did not learn until later that for demonstration purposes the car was equipped with an imported French carburetor. The upshot was that Joy and his friends acquired control of Packard's company, changed its name to the Packard Motor Car Company, and moved it to Detroit in 1903. Packard himself stayed in Warren and gradually withdrew from active participation in the automobile business.

There is no indication whatsoever that Joy tried to force Packard out of his company, and it is beyond question that the change of location was fortunate. For a budding automobile manufacturer, there was greater promise in Detroit than in Warren, Ohio. The Michigan city was not yet Motoropolis, but it was visibly a major center of automotive activity. Certain features of this activity stand out as of primary importance. First in point of time was the arrival in Detroit of the Olds Motor Works in 1899, Ransom Olds having found a backer in a copper and lumber magnate named Samuel L. Smith who put $199,600 into the company in return for 95 per cent of its stock. Olds contributed the rest of the $200,000 of paid-up capital. They moved from Lansing because they believed that Detroit offered more in the way of skilled labor and accessibility of materials. Actually, the outstanding event of the company's stay in Detroit was that its factory burned down—a most historic conflagration. Only one thing was saved—a little buggy with a one-cylinder engine and a curved dash: Olds had designed this as a possible low-priced car. Since it was all that was left, the company concentrated all its effort on the curved-dash buggy. Engines were ordered from Leland and Faulconer, a firm of machine-tool manufacturers that had also been making motorboat engines, and transmissions from a machine shop owned by two brothers named Dodge, John (1864–1920) and Horace (1868–1920).

The result was spectacular. The little buggy became the "Merry Oldsmobile" of popular song, the first car in the world to be produced in really large quantity over a period of years: 600 were made in 1901, 2,500 in 1902, 4,000 in 1903, and 5,000 in 1904. At that point Olds broke with Smith. By then the company was back in Lansing, attracted by a fifty-two-acre site bought for it by the Lansing Businessmen's Association. Smith decided that the time had come to drop the buggy in favor of heavy touring cars. Olds disagreed and left the company, to be put right back into automobile manufacturing by a group of Lansing associates as the Reo (for R. E. Olds) Motor Car Company.

At first glance it appears that the Olds Motor Works threw away the opportunity that Henry Ford later grasped. Had Olds been allowed to continue, perhaps he would have progressed to full mass production; but it would have had to be with a different design. For all its charm the Merry Oldsmobile was not the car for the mass market. It was too light, too small, and lacking in power for an all-purpose family automobile.

Besides creating a famous car and a popular song, the Olds Motor Works in those years was a school for ambitious young men who would make their own way in the automotive world. One was Jonathan D. Maxwell (1864–1928), who had previously worked for the Appersons on the Haynes car. After three years with Olds, Maxwell left in 1903 to join Benjamin (1869–1945) and Frank (1875–1954) Briscoe in the production of a car named the Maxwell-Briscoe. The Briscoe brothers were sheet-metal manufacturers of Detroit who had turned successfully to making automobile radiators and unsuccessfully to backing David D. Buick. Oddly enough, the Maxwell-Briscoe combination was unable to raise funds in Detroit, but the Briscoes had Morgan connections in their sheet-metal business and were able to raise $100,000 to buy the Tarrytown, New York, factory of the defunct Mobile Company, a short-lived builder of steam automobiles.

A second Olds graduate was Robert C. Hupp (1861–1931). He went from Olds to Ford and then in 1908 raised $25,000 to start building his own car, the Hupmobile. It was a well-designed car and the enterprise prospered, although Hupp himself left in 1911. Still more distinguished were two men from the University of Michigan: Roy D. Chapin (1880–1936), who would rise to be one of the ablest executives in the automobile industry, and Howard E. Coffin (1873–1937), one of the greatest American automotive engineers. They left the Olds Motor Works in 1906 and after trying partnerships with two other automobile manufacturers, E. R. Thomas (1850–1936) and Hugh Chalmers (1873–1932), finally got their own company started in 1909 with the aid of $90,000 from J. L. Hudson, owner of the great Detroit department store. Chapin did the managing and selling and Coffin the engineering; in this instance, however, the Hudson car and the company that built it were named for the sponsor rather than, as was the usual custom, the designer.

While Ransom E. Olds was the leading American manufacturer, Henry Ford was struggling to get established. Although he was the son of a Dearborn farmer, he was not exactly the barefoot boy of popular legend, come to the city to astonish the world by mass production of a cheap car. Since his boyhood Ford had had a flair for machinery and he had spent close to twenty years as mechanic, machinist, and engineer before he built his first car, the "quadricycle" of 1896. Ford later claimed that he had actually built a car in 1892, but there is no evidence for this claim beyond Henry Ford's memory, notoriously unreliable where his own reputation or interests were concerned. The quadricycle has to be accepted as the first and for some time the only Ford car.

In 1896 Ford was chief engineer of the Edison Illuminating Company (now Detroit Edison), a respectable position but not one that enabled him to step directly into automobile manufacturing. It took him until 1899 to find support from a group of Detroit businessmen headed by a lumber dealer named William F. Murphy, organized first as the Detroit Automobile Company and later as the Henry Ford Company. Neither succeeded. Ford drove in automobile races as a means of advertising, but the Murphy syndicate complained that he was so absorbed in building racers that he ignored the desirability of having something to sell. He was dropped in 1902, and Murphy called in Henry M. Leland (1843–1932), the sixty-year-old head of Leland and Faulconer, to straighten things out. Leland, a bearded patriarch and a precisionist with a lifetime of experience in machine tools, got the company into production and reorganized it under a new name—Cadillac. So Ford and Cadillac have a common ancestry.

Ford himself was not long unemployed. In 1903 he founded the

Ford Motor Company with another group of partners. Alexander Y. Malcomson, a Detroit coal dealer, supplied the $28,000 that represented the company's liquid capital. The Dodge brothers became stockholders in return for providing chassis, engines, and transmissions for the first Ford cars; and Malcomson's bookkeeper, James S. Couzens (1872–1936), put in $2,500 and joined the Ford Motor Company as its business manager. So far Ford's experience resembled closely that of most other automotive pioneers. The departure from the pattern came when Ford quarreled with Malcomson in 1905, just as Olds had quarreled with Smith, and as Henry Ford would quarrel with almost every outstanding individual who worked with or for him. The significant fact is that on this occasion Ford won and emerged in complete control of his company, free to pursue his own policies. It was an outcome with momentous consequences for the future of the automobile in America.

Reference has been made to David D. Buick as an automotive pioneer. He was a Detroiter who turned from plumbing supplies to automobiles in 1899, and in three years lost all his money. His engineering was good enough—the Buick valve-in-head engine was a notable contribution to automotive design—but he could not get into production. Then after several backers, including the Briscoes, had become discouraged, the Buick Motor Car Company in 1904 came under the control of William Crapo Durant (1860–1947), a carriage manufacturer of Flint, Michigan.

"Billy" Durant came from a wealthy family, but he started making his own living when he was sixteen, and he had risen to be head of the Durant-Dort Carriage Company, the largest of a group of companies that made Flint the "carriage capital" of the country. He proved to be what the ailing Buick concern needed. He moved it to Flint, and by 1908 he had made it one of the Big Four of the automobile industry—the others being Ford, Reo, and Maxwell-Briscoe. At that time, their eminence rested on the fact that each had attained an annual production in excess of 8,000.

The rise of Detroit should not obscure the fact that automobile

production was still widely dispersed. New England had the Pope
and Stanley companies as well as a host of smaller competitors. The
five Mack brothers of New York City built their first truck in 1900,
and Syracuse, New York, in 1902 became the home of the Franklin,
the best-known American car to use an air-cooled engine. There
were important producers in Buffalo, Pittsburgh, Cleveland, and St.
Louis, and until about 1905 Indianapolis had more automobile
manufacturers than Detroit. Two can be singled out for special
mention. The Marmon Motor Car Company, started by a firm that
had previously made flour-milling machinery, eventually produced
the nearest American approximation to the Rolls-Royce; and its
founder, Howard C. Marmon (1876–1943), was the first American
to be chosen as honorary member of the British Society of Automotive Engineers. The Overland was an Indianapolis product (except
for the first model which was built in Terre Haute in 1902) until
John North Willys (1873–1933), a bicycle and automobile dealer,
took it over during the panic of 1907 when the company was about
to collapse under an indebtedness of $80,000. Willys, faced with
the prospect of being unable to fill his customers' orders for cars,
decided that the remedy was to take charge of the manufacturing
operations himself. He satisfied the creditors and then, in search of
better production, moved Overland into the Pope Manufacturing
Company's plant in Toledo. Pope, as we shall see, had been the
victim of bad judgment and Willys got the factory for $285,000.

In South Bend, Indiana, the Studebaker Brothers Manufacturing
Company began to experiment with electric automobiles in 1898
but did not fully commit itself to motorcar manufacturing until
1904. In that year Studebaker, besides making some cars in its own
plant, arranged to buy motors and chassis from the Garford
Manufacturing Company of Elyria, Ohio, added the bodies in
South Bend, and marketed the product through its established
network of dealers in carriages and wagons. Studebaker therefore
varied from the customary pattern in that its principal asset in
entering the automobile business was not its technical capabilities
but its organization for distributing and selling wheeled vehicles.

Before long the Garford capacity proved inadequate, and in 1908 Studebaker made a similar arrangement with the newly formed Everitt-Metzger-Flanders Company of Detroit, builders of the EMF car.

This company, an amalgamation of several small Detroit automobile concerns, was the creation of three pioneer figures of the automobile industry, none of whom quite achieved greatness: B. F. Everitt, whose Wayne Automobile Company was one of the nuclei of EMF; William E. Metzger, who became Detroit's first automobile dealer in 1898 and later was sales manager for Cadillac; and Walter E. Flanders (1868–1923), who came to EMF from a brief period of organizing production for the Ford Motor Company. The Studebaker-EMF partnership proved unsatisfactory, with each party accusing the other of failing to live up to its obligations. The result was that in 1910 Studebaker bought out the EMF partners and consolidated its automobile activities under its own name, with factories in South Bend and Detroit. Thus Studebaker in part also contributed to the concentration of major automobile manufacturers in Detroit.

Finally, Thomas B. Jeffery (1845–1910), who had been Pope's principal competitor as a bicycle manufacturer, began to make cars in 1901 at Kenosha, Wisconsin, with the same trade name he had used for his bicycles: Rambler. Unlike his New England rival, Jeffery had enough sense to stay out of the bicycle business once he had left. His company has gone through several reincarnations, but it has survived.

This picture of the geographical distribution of the automobile industry shows a marked Middle Western orientation almost from the beginning. For this a variety of reasons can be offered. The claim has been made that Middle Western bankers were more sympathetic to the fledgling automobile industry than the tradition-bound Easterners, but the evidence on this point is unconvincing. The self-financing technique so generally employed has been described; until about 1905 bank credit, Eastern or Middle Western, was available only to companies already well established in another field, such as Pope or Studebaker. The Middle West's chief initial advantage over its principal competitor, New England, was that the hardwood forests of Michigan and Indiana had made the region the center of carriage and wagon manufacturing, from which the transition to motor vehicles was natural. There was little to choose between the two areas in machine-shop facilities and supply of skilled labor; but when in the course of time automobile manufacturing became large-scale enterprise, the odds swung inexorably in favor of the plants that were close to the major centers of industrial production.

THE RESPONSE TO THE HORSELESS CARRIAGE

All this energetic production of motor vehicles was based on a strong public demand for them. From the outset the American people took enthusiastically to the horseless carriage. There were exceptions. There was bitter hostility from horse lovers and opposition from those who are always suspicious of something new. The feeling that the automobile was somehow undesirable expressed itself all the way from petty legal harassment of motorists to Woodrow Wilson's pronouncement in 1906, when he was president of Princeton, that possession of a motorcar was such an ostentatious display of wealth that it would stimulate socialism by inciting envy of the rich.

Wilson was wrong. The motorcar did incite the common man in the United States, but what it incited was a desire to own an automobile, not to change the social system. This response was not fully manifest in 1906, but the indications were clear that the horseless carriage was exerting a powerful attraction on people at all levels of American life.

The first automobile magazines, *Horseless Age* and *Motocycle*, began publication in New York and Chicago respectively in 1895 with enough support for the former to stay in business more than twenty years. The more appropriately named *Motor Age* followed in 1899. The American Automobile Association was organized in

Chicago in 1902 as a federation of local automobile clubs, the form
it has retained ever since. Its founding in that year implies that
before 1902 there already existed local automobile clubs with
sufficient membership and vigor to warrant promoting a national
association. The Society of Automobile Engineers, later changed to
Society of Automotive Engineers, followed in 1905, demonstrating
that in just ten years the horseless carriage had become an important factor in American technology. These events were symptoms
of the emergence of the motor vehicle in America to a position
beyond that of a curiosity or plaything. A Duryea "motor wagon"
was featured in a Barnum and Bailey circus parade on April 2, 1896,
but the concept of the automobile as a freak was short-lived.

There was a longer period in which much of the effort of
designers and builders was directed toward racing. There was valid
reason for this because racing was good advertising and also
provided a means of testing designers' ideas. Both Alexander Winton and Henry Ford drove in automobile races, and the Ford Motor
Company received much favorable publicity in its beginning years
from the exploits of racing driver Barney Oldfield and the Ford
999.

The first track used for automobile racing was Narragansett Park
in Cranston, Rhode Island (not the present horse-racing track of
the same name). There on September 7, 1896, two electric automobiles and three Duryeas rolled through five one-mile heats with the
same entrant (an electric) winning each until the bored spectators
began to call, possibly for the first time in America, "Get a horse!"
The maximum speed attained was 26.8 miles an hour. Subsequently
automobile racing provided better entertainment. In the course of
time it provided not much else. Both testing and advertising came to
be done in other ways, although as late as 1911 the Indianapolis
Speedway was built for the ostensible purpose of providing a test
track for American automobiles.

Of greater importance in getting the motor vehicle accepted
were demonstrations of ability to cover long distances. In 1897
Alexander Winton drove one of his cars from Cleveland to New

York in 78 hours 43 minutes actual running time. The whole trip, including stops for repairs, took from July 28 to August 7 and covered 800 miles via Rochester, Syracuse, Utica, and Albany. Four years later Roy D. Chapin drove a curved-dash Oldsmobile 820 miles in seven days from Detroit to the automobile show in New York, and the Apperson brothers drove one of their cars the 1,050 miles from Kokomo, Indiana, to New York. In 1903 no fewer than three trips from San Francisco to New York were made, each requiring about two months. The first was undertaken by Dr. H. Nelson Jackson of Burlington, Vermont, and his chauffeur, Sewall K. Crocker, to settle a $50 bet. On his return to his home Jackson was fined for exceeding a six-mile-an-hour speed limit. The climax of this kind of road test was a New York-to-Paris race in 1908, westward across the United States, thence by sea to Vladivostok, and so to Paris. The original intention of going via Alaska and the Bering Strait was abandoned; just getting across the United States was difficult enough. The race began on February 12, 1908, with American, French, Italian, and German cars and drivers participating and was won by an American "Thomas Flyer" which arrived in Paris on July 30, to the accompaniment of the claims and counter-claims over interpretation of the rules that seem to plague most sporting events aimed at promoting international goodwill.

These spectacular feats attracted attention to the potentialities of the motor vehicle but otherwise had little bearing on what use an ordinary individual might make of an automobile. More useful for this purpose were the Glidden Tours, begun in 1904 by Charles Jasper Glidden (1857–1927), who made a fortune in the telephone business and then retired to pursue his interests in automobiles and aviation. The tours were not races; they were intended to demonstrate the reliability of the automobile as a means of travel. Entries were expected to be stock cars operated by their owners, ample time was allowed to cover the designated route, and the Glidden Trophy was awarded to the entrant with the best all-round touring record. However, the Trophy came to carry so much prestige that automobile firms took to entering specially built cars, so that the tours lost their real purpose and were finally discontinued in 1914.

The endurance runs and Glidden Tours both served to reveal the woeful inadequacy of the American highway system. On his Cleveland–New York run Winton described the roads as "outrageous," and in 1901 Chapin, following his predecessor's route through upstate New York, took to the towpath of the Erie Canal for 150 miles because it was better than the highways. Roads were not only poor in quality but inadequately marked. Guide books began to appear in 1901, not as efficient perhaps as the tourist aids now available but somewhat more colorful: "Bear left at the town hall and proceed 0.8 miles to covered bridge. Turn sharp right—." A Good Roads Association was formed, with understandably strong support from the automobile industry, but some time would elapse before tangible results appeared.

There were also less glamorous but equally significant events in the development of the automobile. Trucks came into use in the late 1890's, in small numbers and chiefly for light local deliveries, but nonetheless recognizing the commercial potential of the motor vehicle. In 1899 the Post Office Department began to experiment with trucks for delivering mail, a step that might be construed to give official sanction to this new device.

In those horseless carriage days no one could have foretold just what the future of the automobile would be. Some enthusiasts were carried away. The editor of *Horseless Age*, writing in 1896 of the perils of runaway horses, said "The motor vehicle will not shy or run away. These frightful accidents can be prevented. The motor vehicle will do it." He was no farther amiss than his counterpart of *The Automobile*, who predicted in 1909 that the general use of automobiles would relieve traffic congestion. Yet if the enthusiasts were wrong in specifics, they were right in their vision that the automobile would change American life.

CHAPTER 3

Growing Pains

Between 1900 and 1910 motor-vehicle production in the United States rose from 4,000 to 187,000 and registrations from 8,000 to 469,000. The automobile industry was moving up to become big business, with ancillary enterprises such as sales, service, and repair facilities growing from it and a pronounced influence on related industries such as petroleum and rubber. As this process of growth continued, the organization of the industry naturally changed, including some ambitious efforts at consolidation and combination. Although the initial attempts misfired, they left their mark on the history of the automobile.

THE SELDEN PATENT

At this point we have to go back to George B. Selden and his patent application in 1879. If Selden had operated under slightly more favorable conditions, he would now be regarded, beyond doubt or challenge, as the inventor of the gasoline automobile. He showed excellent engineering insight when he realized that the clumsy Brayton engine, which weighed almost half a ton per horsepower, could be refined for use in a highway vehicle, and he and a Rochester machinist, William Gomm, performed a considerable mechanical feat in designing and building a three-cylinder Brayton-type engine with a ratio of 185 pounds per horsepower. According

to William Greenleaf, whose *Monopoly on Wheels* is the most
thorough study of Selden's career, the engine in its tests never ran
for more than five minutes or on more than one cylinder. It was
enough, nevertheless, to justify Selden in applying for a patent,
claiming novelty in the combination of a liquid hydrocarbon engine
with the other elements of his vehicle—clutch, steering gear, and so
on. Normally he would have received his patent in 1881, two years
after filing his application, and it would have expired in 1898, just
when it might have begun to have commercial value. As the law
then stood, however, an inventor could delay issue of his patent
without sacrificing his claims to priority by filing amendments to
his application, provided he did not let more than two years elapse
without acting. Selden, a competent and experienced patent law-
yer, contrived by this means to keep his application pending for
sixteen years, finally getting United States Patent No. 549,160 on
November 5, 1895.

What did he intend? The conventional interpretation is that
Selden deliberately held up the issue of his patent until such time as
there was prospect of an automobile industry coming into existence
to pay tribute to him. Greenleaf characterizes Selden as "a consum-
mate master of systematic and intentional delay." Supporting this
thesis is the fact that Selden kept in close touch with automotive
development in both Europe and the United States and in amending
his patent was careful to broaden its language so as to have it cover
the advances that were taking place. Specifically, he changed his
wording so as to include compression-type internal-combustion
engines, which would presumably extend his patent to include
highway vehicles using Otto or Daimler engines.

Yet this explanation of Selden's performance is only partially
satisfactory. If he was acting with such Machiavellian calculation,
he showed remarkably poor ability in exploiting his patent when he
finally got it. His long delay could equally well have been due to a
desire to hold up the issue of his patent until he had a marketable
vehicle. It was his misfortune that he was ahead of his time and
could not get financial support. He almost had a promise of $5,000.

but when he remarked that some day there would be more motor vehicles than horses on the streets of Rochester, the prospective investor was frightened away. He can be justified for changing his patent specifications regarding the engine. He had never claimed that he invented the internal-combustion engine, nor had he stipulated that his vehicle must use the constant-pressure engine that he himself had worked on. He sincerely believed that he was entitled to priority for the *combination* of mechanical features that would create a highway vehicle powered by an internal-combustion engine; from this point of view, the particular kind of engine employed was immaterial so long as it used liquid hydrocarbon fuel. If during the 1880's he had built even the clumsy car that he and his sons later constructed as an exhibit in the patent suit, his claims would have been extremely difficult to refute. History has been unkind to George B. Selden.

As it was, he got his patent and then did nothing with it. Lack of funds is offered as the explanation; another possibility is that until 1900 there was no one really worth suing, but there is an exasperating obscurity about what Selden did or thought. All we can say for certain is that in 1899 he sold his patent, for $10,000 and one-fifth of any royalties collected, to a syndicate composed of William C. Whitney, Thomas F. Ryan, and other prominent Wall Street figures of that day. Their immediate objective was to promote a scheme for operating fleets of electric cabs in the principal American cities. The origin of the plan was a company organized in New York City by Isaac L. Rice, founder of the Electric Storage Battery Company and the Electric Boat Company and originator of the Rice gambit in chess. After some complex financial and corporate maneuvering, Rice's company and the motor carriage department of the Pope Manufacturing Company became the Electric Vehicle Company.

What the promoters of a project based on the electric automobile wanted with a patent for a gasoline automobile was never spelled out. However, they were shrewd businessmen with a fondness for monopoly, and it was an understandable precaution for them to secure a foothold in the gasoline car field at a time when the course of automotive development was unpredictable.

As it turned out, the electric cabs were a monumental failure. About two thousand were built and put into service, but they were clumsy, expensive vehicles to operate, with batteries that weighed a ton and had to be replaced after each trip. Before long the Electric Vehicle Company, dubbed by the press "the Lead Cab Trust," was in serious trouble and had to try to make what it could of whatever assets it had, including the Selden patent.

Legal proceedings charging infringement of the patent were begun in 1900 against the Winton Motor Carriage Company, then the biggest of the gasoline automobile manufacturers, and others. Before any decision was reached, however, the attractions of a negotiated settlement and the needs of the participants led to an agreement in 1903 placing control of the patent in the hands of an Association of Licensed Automobile Manufacturers (ALAM). An executive committee of five, with the Electric Vehicle Company as a permanent member, allocated licenses. The licensees paid a royalty of 1¼ per cent on the list price of each car manufactured, and the royalties were to be divided two-fifths to the Electric Vehicle Company, one-fifth to Selden, and two-fifths to the ALAM, to be used for the benefit of the industry.

For the participating manufacturers this was a very satisfactory arrangement. It is doubtful whether any of them really accepted the validity of Selden's patent, but none of them felt strong enough to face a prolonged and costly lawsuit with equanimity, and they saw in the control of the patent by the ALAM a means of stabilizing their industry, especially by eliminating what they termed the "fly-by-nights"—the people who went into the business, built a few cars, and then for one reason or another disappeared, leaving "orphan" vehicles in the hands of the public. The Electric Vehicle Company accepted the arrangement because it promised revenues instead of a long and uncertain court battle. Selden remained the forgotten man. He is reported to have been obligated to pay part of his share of the royalties to George H. Day, president of the Electric Vehicle Company. The evidence on this point is hazy, but it is reasonably well established that his earnings from his patent were somewhere between $200,000 and $500,000, and probably nearer the lower than the higher figure.

At this juncture the Ford Motor Company came into existence. Henry Ford did not believe in patents, but he inquired among friends in Detroit about the possibility of getting a license from the ALAM and was told that his application would be refused because he had still to demonstrate that he could build cars capable of meeting the association's standards. What newcomers in the automobile industry were supposed to do is puzzling. They could not get a license until they had established themselves as responsible manufacturers; on the other hand, if the Selden patent was valid, no one could legally manufacture motor vehicles without a license. The peak of absurdity was reached in 1908 when George B. Selden himself finally found the means to start making cars in Rochester and, for precisely the same reason that was given to Henry Ford, was denied a license to manufacture under his own patent. As it happened, a year later he was able to become legitimatized by acquiring a defunct company that had a license, but the incident provided an illuminating commentary on the situation created by Selden's claims.

At any rate, Henry Ford and his business manager, James S. Couzens, decided to fight the patent, partly on the strength of a promise of support from John Wanamaker, who at that time included Ford cars in his merchandise. They were not alone. Other prominent producers such as Ransom E. Olds and the Briscoes refused to recognize the Selden patent and formed their own organization, the American Motor Car Manufacturers Association, which at the start had more members than the ALAM. The French firm of Panhard also challenged the patent.

The resulting lawsuit dragged through the courts for eight years. Batteries of experts on both sides delved into the history of the automotive art, and two vehicles were built to Selden's original specifications of 1879 in order to prove that his idea was workable.

It was—just barely. The battle raged in the advertising columns as well as the courtroom. ALAM members warned prospective purchasers, "Don't buy a lawsuit with your car," and Ford and his allies countered by posting a bond with each car sold guaranteeing the buyer against liability. Ford won both the legal and the public relations battles. The district court ruled against him in 1909, causing an abrupt dissolution of the AMCMA, but two years later the Circuit Court of Appeals held that the Selden patent was valid but not infringed, on the grounds that Selden's claim covered only the Brayton-type two-cycle engine.

Although by 1911 Ford had become the largest single American automobile manufacturer and the Electric Vehicle Company had disappeared in bankruptcy during the panic of 1907, in the public eye the Selden patent case pitted Henry Ford as the champion of the "little man" against the monopoly. The ALAM was never an effective monopoly: its members competed among themselves; and if they expected to restrict competition by excluding newcomers from the automobile industry, they were conspicuously unsuccessful. Even if the association had won its case, it would have been little better off since the patent was going to expire in 1912 anyway. There might have been back royalties due from the Ford Motor Company, but Ford could have absorbed these by 1911 without undue difficulty and still been very much the gainer because of the advertising the company had received. The legend of Henry Ford, marked by his emergence as an American folk hero, began with the Selden patent case.

CROSS-LICENSING AND STANDARDIZATION

There were other important consequences of the patent controversy as well. The automobile industry concluded that patent litigation offered no advantages to offset its cost, and in 1915 adopted an agreement for a mutual cross-licensing of patents. All patents, except those embodying a major technical change, were to be made freely available to the participating companies one year after issuance. Supervision of the system was in the hands of the National Automobile Chamber of Commerce, successor to the ALAM (which became defunct at the end of the Selden suit) and predecessor of the Automobile Manufacturers Association. During the first ten years of the agreement only one patent was claimed to be revolutionary and this claim was rejected.

There were some exceptions. The cross-licensing system did not apply to parts manufacturers or to specialized vehicles such as motorcycles and fire engines. Packard stayed out of the agreement because it wished to keep control of some of its engine patents, and the Ford Motor Company refused to participate because Henry Ford disapproved of both associations and patents. Nevertheless the system worked. Ford took out patents merely as protection and permitted free use by others, in return considering himself eligible to help himself to the patent pool. The agreement was renewed at intervals until 1955, when the reduction in the number of automobile firms to five made its continuation needless.

The other major consequence of the Selden patent was the promotion of technical standardization in automobile manufacturing. In the agreement creating the ALAM it was stipulated that two-fifths of the income from royalties was to go to the association for the benefit of the industry. The money was used for precisely this purpose. The ALAM established a technical section in Hartford whose principal achievement was to initiate a program for standardization of parts and materials. With several hundred firms engaged in making motor vehicles, it was manifestly desirable for manufacturers, parts suppliers, and automobile owners alike that parts should be as uniform as possible so that, for example, any sparkplug would fit any engine, and that such elementary components as nuts and bolts should conform to generally accepted specifications.

When the ALAM dissolved, its technical section was taken over by the Society of Automotive Engineers, which had been an advocate of standardization since its founding in 1905. The subsequent development of the SAE program revealed a sharp divergence between the large and the small automobile manufacturers. The latter wanted maximum standardization of everything that went into a car; some of their spokesmen even suggested the adoption of standard designs. The small producers were assemblers. Industrywide standardization of parts would mean economies in production for them, and it was much to their advantage not to be dependent for a given part on a single supplier. Besides lessening the risk that parts might not be available when they were needed, standardization offered firms placing comparatively small orders the benefit of being able to shop among competitors.

The big companies, on the other hand, could achieve the necessary efficiency in production by internal standardization, which gave them greater flexibility in controlling their own operations that conforming to industrywide specifications would have permitted. They were less dependent on supplier firms because they had their own parts-making subsidiaries, and when they bought in the open market they bought as large-scale purchasers who could negotiate with the suppliers for price concessions. Consequently they were less interested than their small competitors in intercompany standardization, although they accepted it in such obvious essentials as screw threads and poppet valves.

The result was that during its early years the SAE standardization program was dominated by the small companies. The driving force was Howard E. Coffin, one of the founders and an early president of the SAE. The large firms by and large were indifferent. Subsequently, however, the possibilities of interindustry standardization began to attract the big companies. As large-scale producers they stood to benefit by steps that would encourage the wide use of motor vehicles, such as standard specifications for tires and petroleum products; and as heavy buyers of commodities like steel, they were interested in the adoption of standard grades, which would make for more efficient and economical purchasing.

Eventually, as might have been expected, the standardization program conformed to the pattern preferred by the big companies.

The early 1920's saw a rapid shrinkage in the number of minor producers, with a consequent reduction in pressure for detailed intraindustry standards. By 1925 the policies of the large firms were clearly dominant. In spite of this internal conflict in the automobile industry, the standardization program was a most significant achievement. SAE concepts of standardization were carried by automotive engineers into the aircraft industry, and the society contributed to the creation of the American Standards Association. The steel, rubber, petroleum, and other industries accepted SAE specifications, sometimes reluctantly. For the development and use of the automobile itself, standardization was of paramount importance. Without it, maintenance and servicing would be considerably more difficult and expensive. Very few motorists have been aware that the program exists; yet anyone who drives his car into a gas station is likely to make use of SAE standards.

THE COMING OF BIG BUSINESS

The promotion of the Electric Vehicle Company was the first serious attempt at large-scale organization in the automobile industry. It was badly conceived, first concentrating on the wrong kind of motor vehicle and then making a clumsy effort at patent monopoly just when public opinion was acutely trust-conscious. It was also premature. The automobile was not yet a large enough factor in the American economy to support an overcapitalized experiment in high finance on the late nineteenth-century pattern. The Electric Vehicle failure was matched by the Pope Manufacturing Company, which started from a far more substantial foundation. After selling their motor carriage department, the Popes turned to organizing a bicycle trust, the American Bicycle Company, but this venture failed and they returned to automobiles, making cars that were well known in their day, the Pope-Hartford and Pope-Toledo. Yet the company had made a basic blunder when it fell for the allure of the Electric Vehicle scheme and gave up its own promising start in motor-vehicle manufacturing. Pope could not survive the 1907 depression, and with its fall the automotive center of gravity shifted conclusively to the Middle West.

In that region big business organization in the automobile industry developed at the hands of men who had a clear, if sometimes overenthusiastic, vision of the future of the motor vehicle in the United States. The Ford Motor Company presents a unique pattern of a monolithic structure built on mass production of a single model, and it will be considered later in connection with the rise of mass production. The other large-scale organizations were combinations, typified by General Motors.

The founder of General Motors was William C. (Billy) Durant, the Flint carriage maker and salesman extraordinary who took over the ailing Buick Motor Car Company in 1904 and made it one of the leading producers. Durant had a boundless faith in the market potential of the automobile, and he saw brilliant prospects for a big company producing a variety of cars. In this way, if one model failed to sell in a given year, the others would pull the company through, whereas for a small manufacturer with only one make, a single bad year was likely to mean ruin. The large combine, as Durant saw it, would also have its own parts manufacturers and thus be free from dependence on supplier firms.

His first effort, made in 1907 in conjunction with Benjamin Briscoe, aimed at uniting the four major producers: Buick, Maxwell-Briscoe, Reo, and Ford. Negotiations seemed well on their way to fruition, with a price of $3 million agreed on for both the Ford and Reo firms, when Henry Ford wrecked the project by requiring payment in cash. When R. E. Olds heard of Ford's demand, he insisted on getting cash too, and $6 million was more than the two promoters could scrape together. The deal was abandoned—certainly a fateful moment in the history of the American automobile—and Durant and Briscoe then went their separate ways.

Durant's next move was to incorporate the General Motors Company in September, 1908. Buick was the base and to it were added Cadillac, Oldsmobile, Oakland (eventually Pontiac), and a miscellaneous assortment of other concerns acquired in an aggressive campaign without much attention being paid to the actual value or earning power of the property. There was apparently a second attempt to buy Ford. By this time Henry Ford had raised his price to $8 million, still in cash and still beyond Durant's resources. Whether Ford would actually have sold his company for any price just when the Model T was being put on the market is open to question. It is difficult to believe that he really was serious about this second negotiation with Durant.

Durant's whirlwind empire-building caught up with him in just two years. By 1910 General Motors was in trouble. Its rapid expansion had exhausted the resources of cash and credit with which Durant had started. Most of the purchases had been financed by issuing securities, and the accumulation of unprofitable subsidiaries at exaggerated prices had saddled the corporation with a burden of debt considerably beyond its earning capacity. General Motors was saved from dissolution only by the intervention of a bankers' syndicate headed by James J. Storrow of Lee, Higginson and Company. This syndicate has been harshly criticized for the severity of the terms it imposed. It advanced $15 million at 6 per cent but took $2½ million of this amount as commission along with $6 million worth of General Motors stock. Durant, needless to say, was removed from control of the company, although he retained a seat on the board of directors.

Yet there is a case for the Storrow syndicate. The General Motors situation was so bad that the bankers initially thought of dissolving the company and salvaging the sound parts, Buick and Cadillac, independently. General Motors was kept alive at this juncture largely by the urging of Henry M. Leland and a pledge of Cadillac's resources. Even then the trust debentures could be sold only by distributing the $6 million in General Motors stock as a bonus to purchasers. The Storrow regime, moreover, effected a healthy reorganization; among other things it brought Charles W. Nash (1864–1948) and Walter P. Chrysler (1875–1940) into the top echelon of management.

Both these men of course would make their mark on the American automobile industry, and both personified the traditional American success story. Nash rose literally from rags to riches. Orphaned in early childhood, he was bound out to an Illinois farmer from whom he ran away at the age of twelve. He spent his adolescence in poverty as a migrant farm laborer, until eventually he found a job as a trimmer in the Durant-Dort carriage factory. He rose to be general manager, and just before the 1910 crisis he moved over to become head of Buick, largely because Buick owed the carriage company several million dollars for automobile bodies and Nash asked Durant for a chance to set things right. He was recommended to Storrow by Durant, with the result that in 1912 the onetime penniless orphan became president of General Motors.

Walter Chrysler did not start quite so far down the economic ladder. He was a Kansas farm boy with a passion for machinery and the good fortune to grow up in Ellis, Kansas, where the Union Pacific had railroad shops. Chrysler rose to be master mechanic on several Middle Western railroads and eventually to be superintendent of the American Locomotive Works in Pittsburgh, where he became acquainted with Storrow. By this time his enthusiasm had switched from locomotives to automobiles, beginning with the purchase of a Locomobile at the Chicago Automobile Show in 1905. He paid $5,000: his entire savings of $700 plus $4,300 that Chrysler borrowed from a banker friend. He reports in his autobiography that his wife had nothing to say when he took his treasure home and told her what he had done, but he thought the kitchen door banged shut a little harder than usual. At any rate, when Storrow asked him to join Buick to provide the technical skill that Nash lacked, he accepted the offer even though it meant a reduction in salary from $12,000 to $6,000 a year. Then, when Nash moved up to be president of General Motors, Chrysler replaced him as president of the Buick Motor Car Company.

So General Motors survived and indeed flourished. What might have happened is illustrated by the experience of Durant's former associate Benjamin Briscoe, who tried at this time to organize a rival corporation, the United States Motor Corporation. Founded in 1910, it was based on one prosperous company, Maxwell-Briscoe, and its other acquisitions were a collection of lame ducks, including the Columbia Motor Car Company, formed from the wreckage of the Electric Vehicle Company. In 1912 United States Motor went bankrupt. Alfred Reeves, who was an official of the company before serving for forty years as manager of the National Automobile Chamber of Commerce and the Automobile Manufacturers Association, explained what happened thus: "Ben just plain ran out of money." There was no syndicate to rescue United States Motor. Instead, Walter Flanders, formerly of Ford and Everitt-Metzger-Flanders (EMF), was called in to salvage what there was of value. He reorganized the company as the Maxwell Motor Car Company, which would in time be the parent of the Chrysler Corporation.

The record of attempts at large-scale organization before the First World War is therefore unimpressive. Yet Durant and Briscoe were right in their basic assumptions. They were not mere speculative promoters; their principal error was an excess of optimism about the speed with which the automobile industry would grow. They also gave inadequate attention to production and technology, as compared with promotion and finance. Durant made some wild guesses about what might be useful for his company, but he can readily be excused on the ground that no one then could be certain of the technical development of the automobile. The fact remains that Durant and Briscoe first envisaged the organizational pattern that the automobile industry would finally adopt. Like so many pioneers, both were destined to see their dreams realized by others.

TECHNICAL PROGRESS

While the automobile industry was wrestling with the organizational problems of growth, its product was also undergoing changes. By the time Durant and Briscoe made their bids for leadership, the day of the horseless carriage was definitely over. By 1910 most American passenger automobiles were powered by four-cylinder engines, although in the higher-priced lines (including one Ford model offered in 1906) there was an increasing trend to sixes. The first passenger car to go into production with a V-8 engine was put on the market in 1907 by Edward R. Hewitt, son of Abram S. Hewitt and grandson of another inventor in the field of transportation, Peter Cooper. The Hewitt car failed to sell. There was nothing wrong with the engine technically; it was just too expensive to find an adequate market. Yet within ten years sufficient progress was made so that a number of manufacturers, led by Cadillac in 1914, were able to offer eight-cylinder engines successfully, and in 1915 Packard went up to twelve.

The touring car continued to be the most popular type, since the cost of the closed car body was too high for general use. There was during this period a beginning of metal body construction on a limited scale. More important was the employment of alloy steels and aluminum in engines and chassis in order to save weight. A minor but significant change in styling that occurred about 1910 was shifting the steering wheel from the right to the left side of the car. This change represented an abandonment of the practice of imitating European usage for the sake of prestige and an adaptation to the conditions of American driving.

None of these steps did more than keep American automotive design up with European. From other developments, however, came indications that Europe's leadership in the automotive field was terminating. Excluding for the present the events connected with the introduction of mass production, several distinctive American contributions to the automobile can be identified about 1910. In 1908 Otto Zachow and William Besserdich produced a four-wheel-drive car in Clintonville, Wisconsin, the long-range precursor of the jeep. Of more immediate impact was the introduction in the same year of Charles Y. Knight's sleeve-valve engine. As the name implies, the engine had valve ports operated by a sleeve outside the cylinder. The Knight engine was more expensive to build and maintain than the poppet-valve motor, but it was smoother and quieter, especially in a day when low-grade gasoline left carbon deposits on cylinder walls and valve seats. The "silent Knight" survived until further progress in engine design and fuels destroyed its advantage over the simpler poppet-valve engine.

The outstanding American technical contribution of this period, apart from production methods, was the electric starter. The desirability of some kind of mechanical starting system for the gasoline automobile was obvious from the beginning. Hand cranking an automobile engine was a backbreaking, frustrating, and risky job, as many readers of this book will undoubtedly remember. Consequently, there was constant experimenting with a starting device, but without success until the combined talents of Henry M. Leland and Charles F. Kettering (1876–1958) were applied to the problem.

Leland came into the picture because a friend and business associate, Byron Carter, had died as the result of a starting accident. Carter, builder of the Cartercar (remembered for its friction drive), went to the assistance of a lady whose car had stalled; he suffered a broken jaw when the crank handle kicked back, and gangrene subsequently caused his death. Leland thereupon determined to keep such tragedies from happening again and turned the energies of the Cadillac engineering department to the starting problem. There it was determined that an electrical system was the answer. The major difficulty was to provide an electric motor small enough to put in a car and at the same time powerful enough to turn the engine over.

Charles F. Kettering, electrical engineering graduate of Ohio State University and free-wheeling genius, offered the solution as the first of his several vital contributions to the development of the motor vehicle. After leaving college he went to work for the National Cash Register Company, where one of his assignments was to design a motor for an electric cash register. He did this by recognizing that this motor need not be built to carry a constant load but only to deliver occasional bursts of power. Kettering left National Cash Register to join Edward A. Deeds in organizing the Dayton Engineering Laboratories Company (Delco) to design and manufacture automobile ignition systems. This operation brought him into contact with Cadillac, and when his aid was invoked on the starting problem, he saw that the motor that was required involved the same principle as his electric cash register. It was possible to install electric starters on Cadillac cars in 1912, although the final step in making the technique complete came a year later when Vincent Bendix (1883–1945) contributed the starter drive that still bears his name.

The electric starter was more than just a convenience or a safety measure. It was a major factor in promoting widespread use of the gasoline automobile, particularly because it made the operation of gasoline cars more attractive to women. In fact, the electric starter may be regarded as the decisive factor in the triumph of the gasoline over the steam automobile. Once the starting problem was solved, the internal-combustion engine appealed more to the ordinary motorist than the steam engine with its high pressures and need for constant skilled care of boiler tubes.

ANCILLARY INDUSTRIES

As more and more motor vehicles poured onto American highways, their effect on the American economy became increasingly pronounced. In the first ten years of the twentieth century, automobile manufacturing climbed from 150th to 21st in value of products among American industries, and in this phenomenal climb it had a marked influence on the growth and direction of other industries. It was becoming a major consumer of steel. In addition, automotive demand was not only becoming the largest single outlet for machine tools but was affecting the character of the product. For example, the need to process alloy steels in automobile manufacture called for elaborate development of grinding machines.

The effects were naturally greatest in the industries that contributed most directly to the motor vehicle, specifically those that provided it with fuel and tires. The petroleum industry was literally revolutionized. Before 1900 only about one-tenth of the

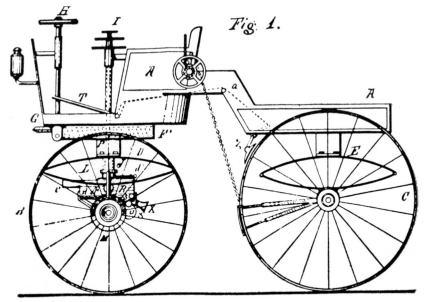

Fig. 1.

THE SELDEN PATENT

"The object of my invention is the production of a safe, simple, and cheap road-locomotive light in weight, easy to control, and possessed of sufficient power to overcome any ordinary inclination. . . ."

EARLY ELECTRIC CAB

Produced by the Electric Vehicle Co. in Hartford, Conn., these electric hansoms were often seen on the streets of big cities in the early years of the twentieth century.

COLUMBIA CARRIER

The Columbia Carrier of 1897, designed by Hiram P. Maxim for the Pope Manufacturing Co., was a gasoline-powered delivery vehicle employing a three-wheeled chassis.

THE DURYEA CAR

This is the original "Motor Wagon" of 1893 after restoration in 1958. It is on display at the Smithsonian Institution.

THE STANLEY STEAMER

This picture shows the Stanley brothers in their first steam car, 1897.

THE MERRY OLDSMOBILE

A TRANSCONTINENTAL RACE

Two curved-dash Oldsmobiles prepare to start from New York City in 1905 for a transcontinental race to celebrate the Lewis and Clark Exposition in Portland, Ore. "Old Scout," which is still in running condition, won, making the trip to Portland in 44 days.

EARLY CRANKSHAFT FACTORY

This picture, taken in 1911, shows crankshafts being ground in the plant of the Norton Company, Worcester, Mass. These automatic grinders could turn out a crankshaft in fifteen minutes, compared with five hours by the earlier method of turning, filing, and polishing.

EARLY STUDEBAKER

This car was produced in 1909–10.

TIN LIZZIE

THE FIRST CHEVROLET

In 1912 Louis Chevrolet (standing at left, without hat), after two years of development work on the car, poses beside the first Chevrolet, a massive six-cylinder model. At the wheel is W. C. Durant's son Cliff.

THE FIRST MOVING ASSEMBLY LINE

A pivotal point in the history of mass production was the setting up of this moving assembly line at the Ford plant in 1914.

Somewhere West of Laramie

SOMEWHERE west of Laramie there's a broncho-busting, steer-roping girl who knows what I'm talking about. She can tell what a sassy pony, that's a cross between greased lightning and the place where it hits, can do with eleven hundred pounds of steel and action when he's going high, wide and handsome.

The truth is—the Playboy was built for her.

Built for the lass whose face is brown with the sun when the day is done of revel and romp and race.

She loves the cross of the wild and the tame.

There's a savor of links about that car—of laughter and lilt and light—a hint of old loves—and saddle and quirt. It's a brawny thing—yet a graceful thing for the sweep o' the Avenue.

Step into the Playboy when the hour grows dull with things gone dead and stale.

Then start for the land of real living with the spirit of the lass who rides, lean and rangy, into the red horizon of a Wyoming twilight.

ROMANCE IN AUTOMOTIVE ADVERTISING

This advertisement, which first appeared in 1926, marked a change of emphasis in automobile advertising from the car itself to the pleasures of automobile travel. The "Playboy" referred to was a Jordan model, not related to the car which appeared briefly in the late 1940's.

petroleum refined was converted into gasoline. Gasoline, in fact, was frequently regarded as an undesirable waste product and thrown away. It was known to have high illuminating qualities, but its volatility made it dangerous. As a fuel for internal-combustion engines, however, gasoline was clearly to be preferred.

The advent of the gasoline automobile was materially aided by a spectacular increase in the supply of crude oil through the opening of new fields, beginning with the Spindletop field in East Texas in 1901. The presence of oil there was dramatically demonstrated on January 10 of that year when the first gusher in the United States shot 160 feet into the air, carrying with it the drilling rig and the derrick. Other new fields followed in quick succession, with the result that by 1914 crude-oil production rose from the 60 million barrels of 1900 to about 250 million. Without the motorcar the petroleum industry would have been in trouble, since the kerosene lamp was retreating before gas and electric illumination; but this great increase in the supply of petroleum occurred fortuitously just as the automobile began to create a seemingly limitless demand for gasoline.

Remarkable as the expansion of the oil industry was, it still had trouble keeping pace with the increasing numbers of motor vehicles. By 1910 there was serious concern that the future development of the automobile would be jeopardized by lack of fuel, and in the next three years it was demonstrated that this was not mere alarmism when the price of gasoline in the United States rose from 9½ to 17 cents a gallon. The heart of the difficulty was that existing techniques of refining yielded less than 20 per cent of gasoline from crude. If this proportion could be significantly raised, the problem would be solved.

Important as this matter was to the automobile industry it was still more so to the petroleum industry, already largely dependent on automotive demand for its markets. The Standard Oil Company addressed itself to the problem as early as 1909. Four years and $1 million later the Standard Oil Company (Indiana) patented and simultaneously put into production the Burton cracking process, named for William M. Burton, who supervised the research and development, although much of the actual work was done by his lieutenant, Robert E. Humphreys. The Burton process doubled the yield of gasoline from a given quantity of crude and took care of the automotive fuel supply until the 1920's, when new and improved techniques were being developed. In all this process of change, one overmastering factor remained constant: the energies of the petroleum industry were focused on satisfying the demands of the automobile.

With rubber the story was similar. The manufacture of rubber goods had reached respectable proportions in the nineteenth century, especially after Charles Goodyear introduced vulcanizing in 1839; but the character of the industry changed completely with the appearance of the automobile. Rubber manufacturing in the United States migrated from the eastern seaboard to Akron, Ohio, and concentrated on turning out automobile tires. The career of one man dramatically illustrates what happened. Paul W. Litchfield, who went to the Goodyear Tire and Rubber Company when it was founded in 1900 and rose to be its head, calculated that in his various official capacities with the company, he had been responsible for ordering the purchase of one-eighth of all the natural rubber produced in the world from the time it was discovered by the white man until Litchfield's retirement.

In view of the marked bicycle strain in its ancestry, it was natural for the automobile in its early days to take over from the bicycle the clincher tire in which the bead locked on the rim. By 1905, however, both Firestone and Goodyear (there was no connection with Charles Goodyear—the name was simply picked for sales appeal) had abandoned the clincher for the straight-sided tire. There were two reasons. One was that the manufacture of clincher tires threatened patent complications; the other, and more compelling, was that as cars became bigger, the physical effort needed to get a clincher tire on or off the wheel was too much for the ordinary motorist. The straight-sided tire was difficult enough, in spite of demountable rims and other ingenious devices intended to facilitate the tire changing and repairing which were integral features of travel by automobile. In those days, a familiar sight on the highways of America was sweating motorists laboriously and profanely removing tires, patching them, pumping them manually to their sixty pounds pressure, and wrestling them on the wheels again.

The need to satisfy the motoring public led the rubber industry into a constant search for better methods of making tires, with results which reflected back on the design and use of motor vehicles. In 1907, for example, an automotive editor argued that passenger cars would have to be limited in size because no pneumatic tires could carry a load of more than 3,000 pounds. Larger vehicles, such as trucks, had to depend on solid rubber tires, which put definite limits on their utility. The development of stronger tire fabrics changed these limitations until in 1915 it was possible to introduce pneumatic tires for trucks.

Along with these major industries were the service operations that grew up around the automobile: the garages, the service stations, the repair shops, the automobile supply houses. In this era before the First World War gasoline pumps were not as plentiful as in later years, and in wide stretches of the West and the South automobile travel still required the traveler to be equipped as for a safari. Nevertheless, over a growing area motorists no longer had to gamble on the next general store carrying gasoline or trust the ingenuity of the village blacksmith if the car broke down. Highway conditions were still unsatisfactory but action was being taken to improve them. The Lincoln Highway Association was founded in 1913 for the purpose of promoting a high-quality, coast-to-coast highway across the United States. The idea originated with Carl Graham Fisher, founder of the Electric Auto-Lite Company of Indianapolis, and it was supported by other distinguished automotive figures, notably Henry B. Joy and Roy D. Chapin. Segments of the route were eventually marked, but the financial magnitude of the operation and difficulties of dealing with state and local authorities led the association to terminate its work when the federal Road

Aid Act of 1916 offered a prospect of attaining an effective national highway system.

This law provided for federal aid to the states to improve their road systems. Technically it was based on Congress's constitutional power "to establish post offices and post roads," but the declared intent of the law was to promote farm-to-market communication. Rural congressmen were not yet ready to cherish the motor vehicle for its own sake, although the impact of the Model T can be discerned in the enactment of this law. If the automobile was to justify its existence, it was expected to do so by demonstrating that it could help the farmer.

CHAPTER 4

The Assembly-line Revolution

One of the great paradoxes of American life is that mass production, the greatest distinctively American contribution to present-day industrial civilization, is a concept widely misunderstood even in the country of its creation. To its critics (generally speaking, those who don't have it) mass production has meant the manufacture in quantity of cheap articles, inferior in quality to the product of handicraft methods and acceptable only because they are lower in price. Too often the apologists for mass production have meekly accepted this definition and tried to defend the technique accordingly. Yet this interpretation of mass production is almost wholly erroneous. The purpose of mass production is to combine increased output with decreased unit cost. It achieves this purpose by using manufacturing methods that have an exactness of co-ordination and synchronization and standards of accuracy and interchangeability far beyond the capacity of the most skilled craftsman. The alleged sacrifice of quality to quantity is a myth.

In his autobiography, *Adventures of a White Collar Man*, Alfred P. Sloan, Jr. (b. 1875) tells how, early in his career as president of the Hyatt Roller Bearing Company, he had to go to Detroit to investigate complaints about the accuracy of bearings purchased from Hyatt by the Cadillac Motor Car Company. Henry M. Leland, the perfectionist, showed Sloan by micrometer measurement that the rejected bearings did not meet the exact specifications

53

demanded of them and waved aside Sloan's excuses with, "Young man, Cadillacs are made to run, not just to sell. You must grind your bearings. Even though you make thousands, the first and last should be precisely alike." Sloan credits this encounter with impressing on him that mass production demanded the utmost in accuracy and precision. But grinding thousands of bearings exactly alike can be done far better by automatic grinding machines than by any manual process; indeed it cannot be done manually at all with the same degree of accuracy or within any reasonable limit of time and cost.

True mass production requires not only mechanization, but a systematic combination of precision, standardization, interchangeability, synchronization, and continuity. Its origins go back at least five hundred years into history. Johann Gutenberg's movable type was one of the earliest identifiable applications of the idea of interchangeable parts. During this same period Venetian war galleys were fitted out by installing components and stores while the hulls were being towed through the Arsenal. At the end of the line the galleys were fully equipped for sea, and as many as ten could be thus processed in a single day. The concept of true mass production, however, first emerged with the coming of industrialism in the eighteenth century. Early in that century a Swedish engineer and manufacturer, Christopher Polhem, attempted with some success to make iron products by mechanized processes that did not require skilled craftsmen, but he could not make his ideas fully effective because he was just ahead of the development of efficient metal-working tools. Toward the end of the eighteenth century a superintendent in the French royal arsenals, whom we know only as Blanc, fully anticipated the work of Eli Whitney and others in making muskets by machine manufacture of interchangeable parts. During the French Revolution, however, pressure from the gunsmiths compelled the government to terminate Blanc's experiments.

Great Britain became familiar with the mechanization of production during the late eighteenth and early nineteenth centuries. It also witnessed one interesting experiment embodying some of the principles of mass production. This was a factory engaged in making pulley blocks for the Royal Navy during the Napoleonic wars. It was established by three colorful individuals: Marc Isambard Brunel, French emigré engineer and father of the still greater Isambard Kingdom Brunel; Samuel Bentham, inspector for the Royal Navy and brother of the eccentric Utilitarian philosopher Jeremy Bentham; and Henry Maudslay, mechanical engineer and one of the outstanding pioneers in the development of machine tools. The factory used forty-four machines designed and built by Maudslay, arranged in a planned sequence so as to eliminate handwork. Ten unskilled workers were employed, and the plant was capable of turning out 130,000 blocks a year. With the end of the Napoleonic wars, however, the mass market for pulley blocks disappeared, and the operation was discontinued.

So the evolution of mass production was left in American hands. The fast-growing United States offered conditions in which it was profitable to employ techniques that achieved quantity production with a minimum of labor, particularly if the high cost of skilled craftsmen could be dispensed with, and there were no strong vested interests to resist innovation. Eli Whitney is generally regarded as the father of machine production of interchangeable parts in the manufacture of firearms, although recent scholarship indicates that he probably knew about Blanc's work and that his methods were certainly known and used in the Springfield and Harpers Ferry arsenals before Whitney succeeded in putting them into operation. The important feature, however, is not who did it first but the fact that in the United States the initial achievements of men like Whitney and Simeon North in the manufacture of firearms were continued by Samuel Colt and others. The same technique was applied to making clocks and watches by Eli Terry and Chauncey Jerome, and it spread to other industries until by 1850 machine fabrication of standardized parts was generally referred to as the "American system of manufacturing."

Continuous-flow operation was given its first practical commercial application by Oliver Evans, who built a grist mill near Philadelphia in 1787 in which the grain was passed mechanically through each stage of the milling process. His technique became accepted practice in American flour-milling. In the latter half of the nineteenth century American meat-packing establishments used conveyors to carry carcasses through the plant in what might be termed a disassembly line, and in 1890 the Westinghouse Company had an endless-chain arrangement for carrying sand into its foundry and bringing the castings out.

By the turn of the century, therefore, the ingredients of mass production already existed in American industry but had not yet been integrated into a coherent system. For that, there was needed a commodity of some mechanical complexity whose manufacture required the assembly of a large number of components and for which there was a prospective mass market if low-cost production were achieved. These conditions were met by the automobile. There was one other prerequisite, quite indispensable: there had to be men with the vision to see what was possible and the ability to do it.

PRELIMINARY STEPS

The dream of the low-priced car followed the introduction of the automobile into the United States in astonishingly short order, and equally astonishingly it appeared nowhere else until after it had become an American reality. What there was in the American scene to stimulate development in this direction can be at least partially identified: a higher standard of living that made widespread purchases of motor vehicles a practical possibility; and a greater propensity among American businessmen than among European to think in terms of a mass market rather than the luxury trade. Business in the United States had become accustomed to a domestic market of continental proportions, with disposable income distributed through more levels of society than was the case in Europe. At any rate, if we date the beginning of the commercial production of automobiles in the United States with Pope and Winton in 1897, fewer than four years elapsed before the first major bid for the low-priced market was made by Ransom E. Olds.

We have already touched on the rise and fall of the curved-dash Oldsmobile. To achieve his peak output of four to five thousand cars a year, Olds organized production according to the most efficient techniques then available. The flow of materials was carefully controlled to eliminate delays, and the cars were assembled by work gangs whose members each had specific functions to perform. Perhaps Olds would have arrived at the assembly line if he had been able to continue with his buggy. Yet he seems to have realized that this lightweight car was a dead end, because he dropped the idea and turned to heavier vehicles when he left the Olds Motor Works and founded Reo.

Nevertheless he had numerous imitators. The first decade of the twentieth century saw a variety of lightweight, low-priced, buggy-type cars offered to the American public. Next to the Oldsmobile, the best known was probably the Brush Runabout. It used wooden construction extensively, had a one-cylinder 10-horsepower engine, and sold for $500. Its designer, Alanson P. Brush, had previously designed the first Cadillac. The company that made the Brush was headed by Frank Briscoe, brother of the organizer of Maxwell-Briscoe. It became part of the United States Motor combine and disappeared when that venture collapsed.

Whether the Brush would have survived longer by itself is dubious. These experiments with light buggies all had the same basic defect: a car designed with cheap construction as the prime consideration came out a cheap car. It simply would not stand up to the stresses of day-to-day use on rough roads. Popular as it was for a while, the Brush was still described, somewhat unjustly, as "wooden body, wooden axles, wooden wheels, wooden run."

The road to the mass-produced car lay through superior rather than inferior manufacturing techniques. That the American automobile industry possessed the requisite standards of precision and accuracy was dramatically demonstrated in 1908 by the Cadillac Motor Car Company. Three Cadillacs were dismantled at Brooklands, the test track of the British Royal Automobile Club. The parts were heaped in a pile, ninety of them removed and replaced from the stocks of the Cadillac agency in London, and the pile scrambled. Cadillac mechanics reassembled the three cars, which then made perfect scores in a 500-mile test run. The achievement made a profound impression on British observers and made Cadillac the first American car to be awarded the Royal Automobile Club's Sir Thomas Dewar trophy. The Cadillac was not a mass-produced car and it was not aimed at the mass market, but the fact that interchangeability of this order of accuracy could be achieved in American automobile manufacturing was the most important single item in making mass production possible.

HENRY FORD AND THE MODEL T

For all the millions of words that have been written about Henry Ford and the Model T, much of the story of the innovation of full-fledged mass production by the Ford Motor Company remains fragmentary. Ford himself still defies interpretation: mechanical genius (probably) but woefully ignorant in most other matters; visionary, sometimes shrewdly so and sometimes incredibly naive; and completely imbued with the attitudes and prejudices of nineteenth-century rural America. It is impossible to say when he first had the idea of a "car for the great multitude," or more specifically, as he sometimes said, a car to help the farmer. His own reminiscences have to be disregarded. Except where machinery was concerned, Henry Ford's thought processes were seldom logical, and he had the human propensity for remembering things the way he wanted them to be.

The first models offered by the Ford Motor Company after its establishment in 1903 were definitely not aimed at the low-priced market. They were competitive in the medium-price range ($1,000–$1,500) with cars like Buick and Maxwell-Briscoe. At the same time Ford's quarrel with Malcomson, insofar as it involved a policy issue and not simply Henry Ford's distaste for any rival in the control of his company, appears to have stemmed from Ford's desire to experiment with a low-priced car. It is clear that Ford had definitely set his sights on the mass market and knew what must be done to reach it. In 1903 he told one of his partners, John W. Anderson, "The way to make automobiles is to make one automobile like another automobile, to make them all alike, to make them come from the factory just alike—just like one pin is like another pin when it comes from a pin factory."

Henry Ford succeeded where others failed, principally because, instead of starting out to produce a car as cheaply as possible, he concentrated first on designing a car that would be suitable for the mass market and then turned his attention to the problem of cutting manufacturing costs. There is nothing to suggest that he himself was consciously aware of the significance of this two-step progression; if he grasped it he did so intuitively. Low price was only one of the characteristics required in an automobile intended for use by the general public. It also had to be durable, easy to operate so that it could be driven by any ordinary individual, economical to maintain, and simple to repair—preferably simple enough for the owner to do most of the maintenance and repairs himself. After some experimentation these qualities were achieved in 1907 with the Model T—the "flivver," or "Tin Lizzie,"—the most famous motor vehicle ever built. First offered to the public in 1908, it had a rugged body, mounted high to enable it to negotiate country roads. Its 20-horsepower four-cylinder engine was a marvel of mechanical simplicity, as was its planetary transmission, which had two speeds forward and one in reverse and required only the pressing or releasing of foot-pedals to operate. Some of the strength in its construction was achieved by using alloy steels, an innovation in American practice although European automobile builders had been using them for some time. Ford, in fact, was responsible for introducing the manufacture of vanadium steel to the United States, since the market for it had previously been so small that American steel firms did not consider it worth producing.

The basic concept of the "car for the great multitude" and the qualities it ought to have was definitely Henry Ford's. In the design of the car itself he contributed a good deal but has to share credit with others, conspicuously C. H. (for Childe Harold) Wills (1878–1940), who was the proponent of alloy steels, and Joseph Galamb, who worked out many of the mechanical features of the Model T. Only Ford himself, however, could have taken the next step along the way: namely, the decision in 1909 that the Ford Motor Company should give up all its other models and concentrate exclusively on the production of the Model T.

The car was there; so was the market. The problem was to bring the two together. The company's calculations—undoubtedly those of its brilliant business manager, James S. Couzens, later United States senator from Michigan—were that to tap the mass market, the selling price of the car should not exceed $600. The Model T, however, could not be produced by existing methods to sell for less than $850. An impressive array of talent was directed to finding a solution: Ford himself and Wills; P. E. Martin, in charge of production (Ford executives were never dignified with titles or even clear definition of their responsibilities); the two "Great Danes," Charles E. Sorensen (b. 1881)—cast-iron Charlie—who would perform the remarkable feat of retaining Henry Ford's confidence and goodwill for forty years and William S. Knudsen (1879–1948), future president of General Motors; Clarence Avery, one-time manual training teacher of Edsel Ford (1893–1943) at the Detroit University School, who probably made the initial suggestion of the moving assembly line; and Walter E. Flanders, machine-tool expert and production engineer. Among them they achieved their goal. After prolonged experimentation with the improvement of existing production techniques, they decided early in 1913 to try a conveyor-belt system for assembling magnetos. The results were highly encouraging, and in the same year the idea was tested for chassis assembly by pulling some chassis through the plant with rope and windlass. Even this crude technique cut the time of chassis assembly in half from the twelve hours and twenty-eight minutes which was the best that was achieved by stationary assembly.

When full assembly-line production was attained early in 1914, the time for chassis assembly was reduced to an hour and a half.

This brief account cannot give a clear picture of the detailed experimentation that had to be done to determine the optimum speed for the various assembly lines, the correct height at which work should be placed, the positioning of the workmen, and countless other items that required accurate co-ordination and synchronization. While this work was going on in Detroit, the Ford Motor Company was also introducing a system of branch assembly plants, largely Knudsen's responsibility and an important device for cutting costs, since it was much cheaper to ship frames and parts from Detroit than finished cars. Nor should the contribution of James S. Couzens be overlooked. The ultimate success of the assembly-line experiment depended on selling Ford cars in quantities beyond anything previously achieved in the automobile industry. Couzens not only managed capably the business affairs of the Ford Motor Company, an area in which Henry Ford had neither interest nor ability, but he also put together a body of carefully selected dealers, numbering more than seven thousand in 1913, who went out and peddled the Model T's with evangelical zeal. The results of all these developments are shown in the accompanying table.

TABLE 1

MARKETING OF MODEL T FORDS, 1908–16

Calendar Year	Retail Price (Touring Car)	Total Model T Sales
1908....	$850	5,986
1909....	950	12,292
1910....	780	19,293
1911....	690	40,402
1912....	600	78,611
1913....	550	182,809
1914....	490	260,720
1915....	440	355,276
1916....	360	577,036

The spectacular nature of this achievement naturally gave rise to conflicting claims for credit. These need not concern us. However credit may be allocated, there can be no question of where responsibility must be placed. It was Henry Ford's and his alone. No one else could have made the critical decision to commit his company to a technique of production that involved such great risk. In order to achieve the price level Ford desired, it was necessary to make a large number of units at a low cost per unit, and this process demanded a heavy initial investment in specialized equipment and tools. To justify this investment there had to be a market capable of absorbing all these units. As it turned out there was, but Ford could have been catastrophically wrong. He had a good many contemporaries who expected him to fail. Considering that in 1908, when the Model T first appeared, the total output of motor vehicles in the United States was 65,000, it would have taken a vivid imagination to predict that in less than ten years one company would be able to sell more than half a million cars in a single year.

The Ford Ascendancy

The achievement of full-scale mass production was enough in itself to give Henry Ford his place in history. His assembly-line technique was crude by present-day standards, but to an astonished world it was a miracle of production to have Model T Fords, all identical in engine and chassis, pour off the assembly line at the rate of one every three minutes. By 1920 every other motor vehicle in the world was a Model T Ford, and the Ford Motor Company simply had no competition in its price class.

But that was not all. Simultaneously with the appearance of the complete assembly line came the announcement of a basic wage rate at the Ford Motor Company of five dollars a day, approximately twice the going rate in Detroit at the time. This announcement likewise drew worldwide attention to Ford, besides giving consternation to a good many business leaders. Job seekers converged on Detroit by the thousand; in fact, shortly after the new policy was put in effect, fire hoses had to be used to disperse the mob of applicants around the Highland Park plant. There was some fine print in the contract. Ford employees had to work for six months to become eligible for the five-dollar rate and even after that had to be "worthy" of it.

The precise origin of the five-dollar day is as much a mystery as that of the moving assembly line. Part of the motive behind it was a desire to reduce the high turnover in the company's labor force, and for this purpose James S. Couzens was interested in raising wages. Again, however, the final decision had to be made by Henry Ford. The five-dollar figure—simple and dramatic—came from the flair for publicity that he possessed to an unusual degree. Beyond this, and more important as a contributing factor, was Ford's own philosophy of business. He believed that the gains made by improving techniques of production should be passed on to society as a whole in three ways: to stockholders in the conventional form of dividends, to consumers in the form of lower prices, and to labor in the form of higher wages.

In Ford's mind this was undoubtedly an intuitive concept rather than a logical body of thought—the rationalizing was done for him later by others—but it was still as revolutionary in its implications for the economic structure of capitalism as the assembly line was for its technological development. He was the first man not only to preach but to practice the doctrine that the buying public had a legitimate interest in the operations of a big business organization, and he grasped a vital aspect of the relationship of mass consumption to mass production: namely, that labor is something more than a commodity to be procured at the lowest possible cost. The worker is also a consumer. For this reason a distinguished French observer of American society, R. L. Bruckberger, insists in *The Image of America* that for the twentieth century Ford's revolution is far more important then Lenin's.

Henry Ford being Henry Ford, the implementation of his ideas was colored by his own personal quirks. In 1915 he not only continued to reduce the price of his cars but gave his customers a rebate of $50 on each car purchased. The inflationary pressures of the First World War prevented continuation of this policy. His attitude to his workers was strictly paternalistic. To be worthy of the five-dollar wage rate his workers were expected to live according to his own rather puritanical standards, and to see that they did so, he organized a Sociological Department, headed by an Episcopal clergyman, Samuel N. Marquis. To what extent Ford workers resented having their private lives investigated by this agency is uncertain; it may be that if they felt resentment they were afraid to show it. On the other hand, the Sociological Department was in some respects the spokesman for the workers. It heard their grievances and tried to find remedies. Since the Detroit Manufacturers Association had just succeeded in making Detroit a non-union town, there was no other agency to which workers could turn, and to this extent Ford's Sociological Department represented a forward step in labor relations.

The third of the beneficiaries of mass production, the stockholders, held a low priority in Henry Ford's scale of values. He felt that they contributed nothing to increasing the efficiency of production and so had no real claim on profits after they had recovered their original investment and a reasonable return on it. In 1914 his low opinion of stockholders (other than himself) was accentuated by the fact that the Dodge brothers had very successfully put their own car on the market, financed, as Ford saw it, by Ford Motor Company profits. So Ford simply stopped paying dividends, whereupon the Dodges still further incensed him by suing and eventually in 1919 compelling him to pay $19 million in back dividends. Ford's rejoinder was to buy out all his remaining stockholders at a cost of $100 million. Couzens made the best deal. He too had joined the ranks of the Ford alumni by 1919, but he knew Henry Ford and the condition of the company better than any other man, and so he held out for a thousand dollars a share more than the other stockholders accepted. He sold his holdings for $29 million, a spectacular return on the $2,500 he had put into the Ford Motor Company in 1903. The Dodges came out with $25 million between them on an original investment of $20,000.

THE COMPETITORS

Ford's brilliant success naturally stimulated others to adopt his methods, or at least to try. One of the most ambitious of these attempts even tried to utilize the glamour of the Ford name. Hugh Chalmers, builder of the Chalmers car, raised $100,000 in 1914 to start a company for the purpose of manufacturing a car called the Saxon, which was to compete with the Model T, and the head of this company was an advertising man named Harry Ford. But advertising was no substitute for production, and the Saxon was never able to match the Model T in price. Harry Ford died of influenza in 1918, and after that the venture quietly collapsed.

A greater potential threat came from William C. Durant. Always irrepressible, Billy promptly rebounded from his General Motors debacle. In 1911 he joined forces with Louis Chevrolet (1878–1941), a Swiss-born mechanic and racing driver who had worked for Buick, to produce a popular-priced car. This first Chevrolet challenge to Ford reached its peak in 1915 with the Chevrolet 490, so named because it was supposed to sell for $490, although in fact it could not be produced at that price level. Perhaps if Durant had concentrated his unquestioned talents on the Chevrolet, he might have done for it what William S. Knudsen was to achieve ten years later, but it is doubtful. The popularity of the Model T was rising rapidly in 1915—its sales passed the first million mark in that year—whereas a decade later it was definitely on the decline.

As it was, the initial success of the Chevrolet diverted Durant to the more absorbing prospect of recovering control of General Motors. He began by offering to exchange Chevrolet for General Motors stock, which currently was not paying dividends. He also found allies in the Du Pont family, who saw in General Motors a potentially good investment for their own company's large war-time earnings. The result was that when the bankers' trust expired in 1916, Durant triumphantly returned to power, in the anomalous situation that General Motors was controlled by the Chevrolet

Motor Car Company—surely a striking example of the tail wagging the dog.

When his old boss returned, Charles W. Nash, far too conservative and cautious to work with Durant, left. With Storrow's support he bought the Thomas B. Jeffery Company of Kenosha, Wisconsin (Rambler), and reconstituted it as the Nash Motor Car Company. He was not, however, interested in competing with Ford. Neither, for that matter, was Durant. He did not give up the idea; it was just that with all of General Motors under his management, the promotion of Chevrolet became a secondary consideration.

For the time being therefore Tin Lizzie had the low-priced field (below $600) almost to herself, but this was not the whole story. Between 1914 and 1917 the output of motor vehicles in the United States more than trebled, from 573,000 to almost 1,900,000. Ford's success was a stimulus to the entire automobile industry by popularizing the idea that ownership of a car, instead of being a luxury, was something that any American family might reasonably aspire to. Next to Ford himself, the principal beneficiaries of this expansion were naturally the cars in the medium-price range (up to about $1,500), a category that then included Willys-Overland, Dodge, Maxwell, Buick, Studebaker, Reo, and Chevrolet. To offset their higher cost they could offer the buying public something the Model T could never match and which would become an increasingly important consideration in the motor-vehicle market—status. Even in those days the automobile was enough of a status symbol so that people who could buy something more elegant than a "flivver" did so. In fact, during most of the lifetime of the Model T, for most purchasers it was the family's first car. After cutting their automotive teeth on Henry Ford's creation, people were likely to seek a higher level for subsequent purchases. Some of these companies, moreover, were already beginning to appeal to families with modest incomes by offering time-payment plans.

It would be several years before this activity posed a challenge to Tin Lizzie. At the end of the First World War, Ford had half the market for automobiles in the United States. General Motors, despite having two of the strongest sellers in Buick and Chevrolet, had a fifth of the sales, and the remainder was divided among the mass of other producers. These proportions could be, and soon were, changed and they did not affect the total picture. In 1918 the number of motor-vehicle registrations in the United States passed the five million mark and doubled that figure in the ensuing four years. Fundamentally, this was the direct result of the introduction of the assembly-line technique. A longer-range consequence that would presently emerge was the domination of the industry by a few large firms. The small-scale manufacturer found himself in an impossible quandary; he could neither compete in price with the mass-produced car nor could he afford to adopt the assembly-line technique for a limited output. In the course of time, therefore, the smaller firms found it increasingly difficult to preserve a share of the market for passenger cars.

The effects of the assembly line were worldwide. Ford, with subsidiaries in every important country, made the Model T a familiar sight around the globe, even though the car was heavy and high-powered by European standards. Where motor-vehicle taxes were based on horsepower, the Ford, like most American cars, was at a disadvantage, but its durability and ease of operation still made it a popular car. There was no overseas competition in production techniques. The assembly line did not appear in European automobile manufacturing until some years after the First World War.

The absence of direct competition for Ford at this early stage of mass production was of minor consequence. What mattered was the demonstration that a fairly complicated mechanical contrivance like an automobile could be manufactured in quantity and marketed at a price within the reach of even the low-income groups in American society. Ford's example was certain to be followed, not only for motor vehicles but for other commodities in the category of "durable consumer goods," such as refrigerators, washing machines, and similar household appliances. It was appropriate that the first widely known electric refrigerator, the Frigidaire, should have been a General Motors product. The mass-production technique was also extended to farm machinery. This indeed seemed such a logical field in which automobile manufacturers might apply their skills and methods that most of the larger firms experimented with it, but only Ford had any success, and that was limited to tractor manufacturing.

Principally, however, the assembly line meant an unending stream of motor vehicles pouring into American life, a technological cornucopia from which would come not only cars but new industries, new economic forces, and sweeping changes in the structure of American society. In 1917 the process was still in its preliminary stages; it was not even clear what was going to happen within the automobile industry itself.

CHAPTER 5

War and Readjustment

When the First World War broke out in 1914 the automobile and
the automobile industry had achieved sufficient stature to play
major roles in the conflict. Although this was not a motorized war
on anything like the scale of the Second World War, motor
vehicles were an increasingly important factor in the conduct of
military operations. Armored cars were employed, although the
static warfare of the western front severely limited their usefulness;
to remedy this condition the tank was introduced and demonstrated
what mechanized war could become. Still more important was the
use of ordinary cars and trucks for the movement of troops and
supplies. This potential of the motor vehicle was dramatically
illustrated at the very beginning of the war when the taxicabs of
Paris rushed troops from the city to strike at the flank of Von
Kluck's columns. There was less glamour but more underlying
significance two years later in the unending line of *camions* rolling
along the *Voie Sacrée* to beleaguered Verdun, carrying the supplies
and reinforcements that kept the defense alive.

Of equal or possibly greater importance was the capacity to
produce offered by the automobile industries of the belligerent
countries. In each of them the automobile manufacturers supplied
the armies not only with vehicles but with a multitude of other
items of military equipment. Had this productive capacity not
existed, the needs of the military machines would naturally have

been supplied in some other way. In this case the war would have had a somewhat different character, perhaps not decisively so, although the Germans, with superior rail communications but a critical lack of oil and rubber, would have been better off if the Allies had been unable to use motor transport as freely as they did.

THE AMERICAN AUTOMOBILE INDUSTRY IN THE FIRST WORLD WAR

Until the United States itself entered the war, the automobile industry was largely unaffected by the conflict. It was absorbed in the introduction of the assembly line, the reorganization of General Motors, and the appearance of important new cars like Chevrolet and Dodge. Henry Ford's "Peace Ship" expedition in 1915 was a matter of personal idiosyncrasy, as was his announcement that his company would refuse war contracts. Neither had any relationship to the conduct of the automobile business. Production for the civilian market continued unabated right through 1917. There were exceptions. The White Motor Company built 18,000 trucks for the Allies, doing so well that it decided to give up the manufacture of passenger cars altogether, a decision that proved to be fortunate for the future of the company.

For the "business-as-usual" attitude, responsibility has to be placed chiefly on the government because of its unwillingness to recognize that some bolstering of the nation's defenses was desirable when the rest of the world was at war. Serious industrial mobilization began only after the declaration of war, so that with due allowance for the delays and confusion inevitable in this process, accentuated by the fact that this was a new experience for the United States, it was many months before tangible results emerged. Passenger-car production continued without restriction until well into 1918, when the War Industries Board ordered output for the rest of year reduced to half of what had been built during the corresponding months of 1917. This goal was approached (925,388 passenger cars in 1918 as compared with 1,740,792 for 1917), but the reduction was due more to shortages of materials than to mobilization planning.

Nevertheless the job was done. While the manufacture of pleasure cars was being curtailed, production of trucks doubled. Automobile firms in addition made such items as shells, guns, recoil mechanisms, gun carriages, tractors, and aircraft engines. The Ford Motor Company also built forty-three submarine chasers of a type known as Eagle boats. This achievement, which was overrated because the Eagles were of limited value in service, offered evidence that Henry Ford had withdrawn his objection to war work. Instead he announced that he would refund to the government all profits on war contracts, although he seems to have forgotten about it later.

The war also provided for the United States an impressive demonstration of the value of highway transportation. The road system still left much to be desired, but it was imperative that it be used as much as possible in order to relieve the congestion on the railroads. This task was handled by Roy D. Chapin as head of the Highway Transport Committee of the Council for National Defense. His outstanding achievement was to halt the wasteful employment of rail facilities involved in hauling finished trucks from the Middle Western factories to the Atlantic seaboard. Careful plotting of feasible routes and invoking the co-operation of local authorities to keep them open made it possible for thousands of army trucks to be driven to their ports of embarkation, each carrying a load of freight and thereby further assisting the over-burdened railroads. It was a significant demonstration for the future, showing as it did that highways could be kept in operation the year round and that motor trucks could successfully undertake long hauls.

The least successful of the automobile industry's wartime operations was its foray into aircraft manufacturing. There were extenuating circumstances. Despite the fact that the airplane was an American achievement the country did almost nothing to stimulate aviation before the war, with the result that an aircraft industry practically did not exist. As late as 1915 the country's total output of military aircraft was twenty-six. There was, moreover, among political leaders and the general public, as well as among automobile men, a happy assumption that the facilities and techniques that produced motor vehicles in quantity could do the same for airplanes. Before we become condescending or critical about this error, it is as well to remember that precisely the same illusion persisted twenty-five years later and with less reason.

At any rate, no airframes rolled down the automobile production lines, although automobile men had a hand in building the considerable number that were actually produced. John N. Willys acquired control of the Curtiss Aeroplane and Motor Company, with encouragement from the government because Glenn Curtiss was more interested in design than production; the other major manufacturer of airframes, the Dayton-Wright Company, was the creation of a syndicate from the automobile industry headed by Edward A. Deeds of Delco. The fact that Deeds subsequently was put in charge of aircraft production gave rise to much of the ensuing recrimination about the lapses, real or alleged, in the aviation program. That he made mistakes is certain; it would have been miraculous if he had not. More serious charges were made against him, but none was ever proved, and in retrospect it seems that Deeds was the scapegoat for failure to attain unrealistic expectations. In those more innocent days, Americans still had to learn that military goods cannot be conjured into existence overnight.

There was a different story with aircraft engines, which were still sufficiently similar to automobile engines so that it was practical to build them in existing automotive engine plants. The obvious method of getting into production rapidly was to use tested Allied types, but on investigation this solution did not turn out to be so simple as it looked. The drawings supplied by the Allied governments presupposed a substantial amount of hand machining by skilled craftsmen and were not suitable for American methods of production. Accordingly, while Bugattis and Hispano-Suizas were eventually made in some quantity in the United States, the basic decision was to design an engine capable of being turned out immediately by American techniques and in existing facilities.

The result was the famous Liberty engine, designed mainly by E. J. Hall of the Hall-Scott Motor Company and J. G. Vincent of Packard. They immured themselves in a Washington hotel room for three days at the end of May, 1917, under instructions to come up with an engine that embodied only devices already tested and proved and that was adapted to quantity production. The Liberty therefore emerged as an excellent but very conventional engine, initially eight-cylinder but later raised to twelve and with a horse-power rating starting at 220 and increasing to 440. In all, 24,475 Liberty's were built during the war, almost entirely by automobile firms. The 300,000 cylinders needed for these engines were a Ford contribution, representing a major achievement in the application of mass production techniques to an item that had hitherto required elaborate hand machining.

In short, the concept that the productive capacity of the automobile industry could be the foundation for a massive aircraft program was sound enough once the nature of the problem was fully understood. For engines there was no alternative; of the 42,000 aircraft engines built in the United States during the war, 30,000 came from the automobile industry. The most serious error was the failure to realize that military aircraft could not be turned out in thousands of identical units like automobiles. Provision for changes of design based on combat experience and advances in aeronautics had to be incorporated into the process of production, but it was done belatedly and thereby caused confusion and delay. Had the war continued into 1919, most of the difficulties would have been seen for what they really were—the results of ignorance, inexperience, and neglect of advance planning, rather than of incompetence or corruption.

RETURN TO PEACE

Since the American automobile industry was never completely converted to war production, the sudden cessation of hostilities caused no great disturbance—nothing, for example, to compare with the disaster that struck the nascent aircraft industry when war contracts were cancelled practically overnight. To be sure, there were difficulties. In the wake of the war came the influenza epidemic, labor unrest that included severe strikes in the coal and steel industries, shortages of materials, and uncertain rail service while the nation's railroads disentangled themselves from their emergency wartime operations. Despite these handicaps, motor-vehicle production in 1919 was slightly ahead of the 1917 figure, and in 1920 it passed the two million mark for the first time.

Behind this achievement was an accurate assessment by the leaders of the automobile industry that there would be a great expansion in the demand for passenger cars and in commercial highway transport after the war. Planning for this eventuality was actively pressed by those with the foresight to envisage the opportunities. The most dazzling prospect, of course, was to invade successfully the mass market for low-priced cars preempted by Henry Ford. As of 1919 the leading contender was John N. Willys, whose Overland, priced at about $800, was the second best selling car in the United States. Willys contemplated offering the Overland for $500, including electric starting and lights and a spare tire, luxuries that had not yet appeared on Tin Lizzie. In preparation he had put together in 1917 a combination of car and parts manufacturers loosely controlled by a holding company, the Willys Corporation. Besides the Overland, Willys built the Willys-Knight, the most prominent American car to use the Knight engine.

The Hudson Motor Car Company also had its eye on the mass market. While Roy D. Chapin was managing the highway transport program in Washington he contrived to find time to plan with his business associates for the introduction, after the war, of a low-priced car named the Essex. This step was taken after careful estimates of production problems and assessment of market potential, so that the Essex avoided the hazards of the immediate postwar inflation and depression. Not until 1922 did Chapin present his boldest innovation, the offering of a closed car for only $100 more than the touring car. This step began a new era in American motoring by offering to the public the possibility of riding with style and comfort in all weathers without having to pay luxury prices.

Meanwhile, at General Motors, Durant's Second Empire was in full career. In 1918 the organizational monstrosity represented by Chevrolet control of General Motors was removed by the creation of the General Motors Corporation, which absorbed both the General Motors Company and Chevrolet along with another Durant promotion, a combination of parts manufacturers called the United Motors Corporation. One of the participants was Delco, and so Charles F. Kettering was brought officially into the General Motors fold. Still more important, United Motors included the Hyatt Roller Bearing Company, whose president, Alfred P. Sloan, Jr., became head of United Motors and would in time outshine Billy Durant as the builder of General Motors.

A graduate of the Massachusetts Institute of Technology, Sloan went from college to work for the Hyatt Roller Bearing Company, founded by John Wesley Hyatt, the inventor who created celluloid because he wanted a substitute for ivory as a material for billiard balls and who was now trying to market a tapered roller bearing. Hyatt, however, was no businessman. The company was saved from extinction by a loan of $5,000 from Sloan's father, and Sloan replaced Hyatt as president. He found a lucrative outlet for his bearings in the fast-growing automobile industry and built Hyatt into a large-scale enterprise, until, as Sloan himself pointed out, it became too big to be independent. When Durant proposed that Hyatt join United Motors, Sloan was reluctant, but on thinking it over he realized that his company would be in serious trouble if both Ford and General Motors should decide to manufacture their own bearings. He had to have a guaranteed market with one or the other. So Sloan went into United Motors, and in the 1918 reorganization he became a General Motors vice-president.

Durant also managed, at least temporarily, to hold on to Walter Chrysler. Nash and Storrow had tried to persuade Chrysler to join them, and he had been strongly tempted, but Durant offered him a salary of $500,000 a year to stay at Buick—a remarkable increase in just five years. Then, with the administrative structure of General Motors apparently settled, further expansion proceeded in characteristic Durant fashion. Some of his acquisitions turned out very well. The Fisher Body Company was certainly worth the $30 million General Motors paid for it. It was the creation of six brothers who had initially been wagon and carriage builders in Norwalk, Ohio, but sensibly decided in 1908 that there was a brighter future for them in designing and manufacturing automobile bodies. Frigidaire was picked up for just $56,366.50, the amount Durant personally paid for the Guardian Frigerator Company, a one-man operation run by Alfred Mellowes, who had designed his first electric refrigerator in Dayton, Ohio, in 1915. He then moved to Detroit to manufacture his product. When Durant bought the business, it had sold less than forty refrigerators in two years, all in the Detroit area and all personally serviced by Mellowes. In the process the company had lost some $34,000. Durant changed the name to Frigidaire and in 1919 sold the property to General Motors for what it had cost him. When his fellow directors asked what an automobile manufacturing firm was doing making electric refrigerators, he replied that the two products were similar—each was a box containing a motor. Another innovation of this period, the General Motors Acceptance Corporation, showed a realistic appreciation of the financial problems of mass marketing of motor vehicles.

With this much to his credit, Durant was entitled to some mistakes, and he made them. Some weak automotive properties were taken into General Motors, but the worst blunder was a venture into the manufacture of tractors and farm machinery, taken against Walter Chrysler's advice, and abandoned in 1920 after General Motors had poured $30 million into it. In addition, the construction of the General Motors Center in Detroit had been started; this operation is not to be classed as an error, but it did impose an additional heavy financial burden at a time when the company's resources were already far extended. Durant was gambling that the postwar boom would continue.

So, for that matter, was Henry Ford. Like everyone else in the industry, he saw ahead a rising demand for cars, and in particular a demand for Fords beyond the capacity even of his comparatively new Highland Park factory. Planning was begun in 1916 for a vast plant on the River Rouge in Dearborn, to incorporate the most up-to-date mass-production techniques and to include among other things its own steel mill. Some preparatory work was carried on during the war, and with the coming of peace the project was rapidly pushed to completion. The total outlay on the Rouge installation was more than $116 million, by itself well within the means of the Ford Motor Company. At the same time, however, Ford found himself obligated for $8 million in back dividends and voluntarily assumed the $100 million burden of buying out his stockholders. To get the funds, Henry Ford had to borrow $75 million from Boston and New York banks, much against his will. However, with the primacy of the Model T still almost uncontested—three-quarters of a million were sold in 1919 for profits of more than $70 million—the Ford Motor Company's margin of safety seemed ample.

This period, indeed, was the high noon of Henry Ford's career. His feat in revolutionizing motor-vehicle production was still reasonably fresh, and there was so far no near rival. To the great bulk of the American people (and many others) he was the mechanical wizard with the Midas touch, the Horatio Alger hero who had climbed from farm boy to billionaire by his own unaided genius. He became a sort of Paul Bunyan figure, for whom no task was too great. The most vivid illustration of the Ford legend appears in a Pullman smoking-room conversation during the early twenties, overheard and reported by Frederick L. Smith, former president of the Olds Motor Works, in *Motoring Down a Quarter of a Century*.

"Who invented the automobile anyway?"
"Henry Ford. Started as a racer by beating Barney Oldfield on the ice

at Detroit. Right after that he built a plant to turn out the same kind of car in fifty thousand lots."

"Doesn't he own the Lincoln now?"

"Yeah, owns the Lincoln and the Packard, Cadillac, Buick—all the big ones and a lot of the little ones besides."

"Is it true about his taking over the Detroit City Hospital?"

"I'll say it's true. Bought it and runs it for his employees. Charges everybody a fixed rate for every job and makes it pay."

Among the inaccuracies, the reference to the hospital does less than justice to the Henry Ford Hospital in Dearborn.

It is now a forgotten item of American history that Henry Ford was a Democratic candidate for the office of United States senator from Michigan in 1918 and lost by a narrow margin to Truman S. Newberry, who was subsequently deprived of his seat because of election frauds. Had Ford won, the Senate in 1919 would have been divided equally between Democrats and Republicans, 48–48, so that with the tie-breaking vote of Vice-President Marshall the Democrats would have controlled the chamber. In this situation the chairman of the Committee on Foreign Relations during the debate on the Versailles Treaty and the League of Nations would have been a Democrat and not Henry Cabot Lodge the elder. In this respect it was a significant election; what Henry Ford would have been like as a senator otherwise has to be left to speculation. As a popular idol he was inevitably mentioned as a presidential prospect, and in the early 1920's an organized movement came into existence to give him the Republican nomination in 1924. This however was stopped, after some hesitation, by Ford himself.

For Henry Ford, and still more for his family and friends, the attraction of public life was markedly lessened by his experience when he sued the *Chicago Tribune* for libel for calling him "an ignorant idealist" and "an anarchistic enemy of the nation." The objectionable editorial appeared in 1916, when the *Tribune* and Ford were in sharp difference over the desirability of military preparedness, but the case did not come to trial until 1919. Henry Ford was put on the witness stand for a pitiless exposure of his ignorance of non-automotive subjects. He did not, however, actually say "History is bunk." What he did say was that when he was in school he thought that history was bunk, which is quite a different thing and in fact a fairly common educational experience. Yet, however unpleasant this incident might have been, it did not diminish the glamour of the Ford name in the least. If anything, the effect was just the opposite. The intelligentsia might sneer, but they made their usual blunder of believing that what they thought was public opinion. The average American knew just as little history as Henry Ford and had much the same opinion of it. Ford's deficiencies made him more than ever a figure with whom the common man could feel an affinity: clearly a titan, but equally clearly molded from common clay. Aldous Huxley meant it as satire, but he was hitting very close to the mark when he made Ford the deity of *Brave New World.*

THE CRISIS OF 1920–21

For the American economy as a whole the panic of 1920 ranks as a minor depression. It was sharp but short and was rightly regarded as a readjustment in the wake of the war boom. For the automobile industry, however, it was a major crisis. The market for new cars collapsed, and after a brief effort to hold the line, so did prices. In late September, 1920, Henry Ford cut his touring car from $575 to $440, and the rest of the industry promptly conformed. This was a routine business reaction, but now for the first time both manufacturers and distributors became acutely aware of the problem of the used car. It was bound to come. By the end of 1920, motor-vehicle registrations in the United States passed ten million. So far the steady accumulation of actual or potential secondhand vehicles had not obstructed the sale of new cars, but now, under depression conditions, the effect of the used-car market became a matter of concern. No one had a really satisfactory solution, but the problem of used-car competition was largely responsible for the general adoption during the 1920's of the practice of introducing a new model each year, with enough changes in appearance or technical features, it was hoped, to make secondhand cars definitely out of style. This policy was subsequently termed "planned obsolescence."

The panic struck at the two extremes of the automobile industry. The medium sized companies with good management, like Hudson, Packard, and Studebaker, had little trouble riding out the storm. On the other hand, the big firms—Ford, General Motors, Maxwell, Willys—were caught dangerously overextended and had to resort to drastic measures to avoid disaster. At the other end of the scale the depression shriveled the prospects of the many newcomers who tried to ride the postwar boom into a place in the automotive world. Most were strictly ephemeral; a few achieved distinction. The first of these clearly was the Lincoln, creation of the man who previously had made the Cadillac one of the world's outstanding cars. Henry M. Leland left Cadillac and General Motors in 1917 at the age of 72, largely because he wanted to devote himself to making aircraft engines for war use, but also because of distaste for another Durant regime. With his son he organized the Lincoln Motor Company, which built 6,500 Liberty's. (The name Lincoln was chosen to honor the man Leland most admired and for whom he had cast his first vote in 1864.) When the war ended the Lelands decided to return to the automobile field with a new luxury car. The market collapse caught them just getting into production and short of liquid capital, partly because of an erroneous tax assessment, which failed to allow for depreciation the company was legally entitled to. Before the error was corrected, Lincoln was in receivership.

At this point Henry Ford entered the picture and bought the property for $8 million, to the accompaniment of a fanfare of publicity conveying the impression that he was generously helping out an old friend. A heated and still unsettled argument followed. The Lelands claimed that Ford had promised to leave them in charge and to recompense both their creditors and their stockholders. Ford did pay the Lincoln debts but he denied assuming any other obligations. Since any agreements made were verbal, there is no proof and no definite explanation of why Ford chose to deviate from his policy of concentrating on one model. It seems likely that Edsel Ford was mainly responsible for taking over the Lincoln. He was now officially president of the Ford Motor Company and was trying to persuade his father to give up the Model T, but he had little real authority and seems to have hoped that he would have a free hand where the Lincoln was concerned.

Another prominent casualty of the depression was C. H. Wills. In 1919 Wills and John H. Lee, who had succeeded Dean Marquis as head of the Sociological Department, left the Ford Motor Company along with several other prominent executives. Wills and Lee joined forces to build a car of their own, and since one was generally credited with being Ford's engineering genius and the other the labor relations expert, this news caused a good deal of excitement. Wills announced that he was going to build a car ten years ahead of its time, and unfortunately for himself he did. The Wills Sainte Claire was a beautiful and magnificently designed car, still cherished in the memories of automobile enthusiasts. Its trouble was that it was simply too good. It was high-priced and it was expensive to maintain because no ordinary mechanic could repair it. It appeared on the market squarely in the middle of the depression and could not be sold in sufficient numbers to keep the company solvent, and in this instance there was no rescuer.

Although the big companies had serious difficulties, all managed to survive. Ford had the easiest time, essentially because he dumped his burden on his dealers. The second half of 1920 saw Ford with falling sales, the heavy obligations previously described, and the $75 million bank loan coming due early in 1921. Wall Street eagerly anticipated the Ford Motor Company's being compelled to put some of its stock on the market, but the bankers underestimated Henry. He cancelled his orders for materials and supplies, worked off the inventory on hand, and in January, 1921, shipped some 125,000 cars to his dealers and closed down for six weeks. The dealers were told that this was their first consignment for the new year and that in accordance with their contracts they must accept the cars on the customary cash basis or forfeit their franchises.

It is a striking tribute to the dominant position Ford then occupied that practically all of the 17,000 Ford dealers complied, some at considerable loss to themselves. A Ford franchise was too valuable to be abandoned without a major effort to preserve it. So Ford triumphantly paid off his note and emerged from the crisis seemingly stronger than ever. To the general public, the folk hero had outwitted the bankers. Even in informed business circles there was a tendency to overlook the rather sloppy management of finances that had preceded the crisis—that is, the piling on of obligations with no clear accounting technique to balance them against the company's probable earnings. Nor was much attention given to the steady attrition of top personnel in the Ford Motor Company. Couzens was gone, his successor, F. L. Klingensmith, went out in 1919 along with Wills and Lee, and two years later came the departure of William S. Knudsen, which would prove to be the most damaging blow of all.

The General Motors situation was more complex. The company emerged from the war with a revised corporate structure, an ambitious program of expansion, and stronger financial backing than it had previously enjoyed. With good management there was every reason to anticipate a bright future, and there was first-class managerial talent available in men like John J. Raskob, treasurer of the Du Pont Company, who supervised finances, Walter Chrysler, and Alfred P. Sloan.

The trouble was that there was no co-ordination of the sprawling General Motors structure. William C. Durant was a man of tremendous dynamism and drive, but he either could not or would not concentrate on keeping the affairs of General Motors in order. He swung irregularly between ignoring his subordinates and interfering with them, and much of his time and effort was devoted to stock market operations. He was estimated to have had at least seventy separate brokerage accounts. Chrysler stood it until early in 1920, when the farm machinery fiasco proved too much for him and he quit. Sloan, also disturbed by the mismanagement, or rather non-management of the company, submitted a reorganization plan to Durant at this time, basically the one he himself was to apply later. Durant approved the plan but did nothing about it. Sloan then took a trip to Europe to think things over. He decided to resign when he returned, but the depression caught up with Durant first.

When the panic arrived, Durant's finances were badly tangled. He tried to hold the line on car prices and to keep General Motors stock from dropping. He was committed well beyond his resources, although he himself did not know how far. On his own he might have been able to keep his losses short of the disaster point, but he felt that he had to support the market to discharge an obligation to friends who had bought General Motors stock on his recommendation.

Meanwhile the corporation was having its own troubles. In the optimistic mood that preceded the slump many divisions had accumulated excessive inventories at boom prices. They had been warned to cut back early in 1920, but because of the lack of effective control at the top the warning had not been enforced. In addition, some of the expensive parts of the expansion program were not halted as promptly as they should have been. Not all these mistakes were Durant's. There is clear evidence that even before the stock market collapse he wanted to reduce the corporation's heavy commitments by curtailing work on the General Motors Center but was dissuaded by Raskob.

Nevertheless, Billy was the danger point. In the fall of 1920 he was sliding rapidly toward bankruptcy, and if that had occurred, the shock to public confidence might well have brought General Motors down with him. Consequently, when reports of Durant's financial difficulties reached Pierre S. Du Pont, he became deeply alarmed. An inquiry to Durant brought the disturbing admission that Billy simply did not know where he stood. A series of conferences followed in which Durant's indebtedness emerged as approximately $30 million, whereupon a Du Pont–Morgan syndicate was formed to bail him out in exchange for his two and a half million shares of General Motors and his resignation as president. Pierre Du Pont took his place, not because he particularly wanted to but because he had the confidence of the financial community. His executive vice-president, who clearly would actually run the business, was Alfred P. Sloan.

Durant himself was by no means out of the automotive world. Within a month after his expulsion from the company he had founded, he succeeded in raising $7 million from a group of sixty-seven friends and was at work putting together a new combination called Durant Motors. There can be no doubt that he had to leave General Motors. It was his concept and creation, and he started it on its way to greatness, but twice he almost ruined it by his recklessness. Still, it seems a pity that in later years, when Billy's fortune was gone and he was old and ill, all that General Motors could do for him was give him a place on the platform when the corporation celebrated the production of its 25-millionth car in 1942.

Ford and General Motors were able to remain solvent and preserve their organizations intact; General Motors, in fact, emerged from the panic strengthened. Their principal competitors, Willys and Maxwell, were less fortunate. Both had managerial problems. Like Durant, John North Willys had permitted his interests to become so dispersed that he was unable to exercise proper supervision over his automobile business. At Maxwell, authority was divided. The company had previously taken over the Chalmers Motor Car Company, and so the board chairman was Hugh S. Chalmers, former supersalesman for the National Cash Register Company, who knew a lot about selling but very little about production, and the president was Walter E. Flanders, who knew production but evidently not much about engineering. His earlier automotive offering (EMF) had been nicknamed "Every Mechanical Fault," and the Maxwell of 1919–20 had an unhappy propensity for breaking its rear axle.

Interested banking houses brought Walter Chrysler into both companies to take charge of reorganization. The Willys Corporation was put through receivership and liquidated, its component parts resuming their corporate independence. Since it had never had any real cohesion, there was probably nothing more Chrysler could do, although the possibility has to be considered that he might have fought harder if he had been sure that he was fighting for himself rather than for the still powerful figure of John N. Willys. Willys did, in fact, make a spectacular recovery. With the aid of business friends in Toledo he regained control of the Willys-Overland Company and subsequently built another Willys empire. With the Overland continuing to be one of the popular low-priced cars, Willys appeared to have surmounted his difficulties, but events would show that he had passed his zenith as a power in automotive world.

Maxwell was a different matter. There Chrysler had no rival approaching his own stature, and despite the defects in the current models, the Maxwell name still carried weight with the motoring public. If Chrysler wanted his own company, as he did, here was a made-to-order foundation. He was by this time at work with a trio of bright young engineers (Carl Breer, Fred Zeder, and Owen Skelton) on a design for a new passenger car that would take advantage of what had been learned from aviation about high-compression engines and that would bear the Chrysler name. So the Maxwell Motor Car Company went into receivership in 1921 and was reorganized with Chrysler in control, retaining the Maxwell name for another four years until the Chrysler car had been offered to the public and had proved a success. Then the Chrysler Corporation was created to take over the entire Maxwell property.

By late 1921 the panic was over and the automobile was starting a climb to new heights of production and use. On the surface it appeared that this depression had been merely a temporary and not very serious interruption of the growth of the automobile industry; some of the weaker firms had been wiped out, a few of the stronger ones had been shaken up, and that was all. The expanding flow of motor vehicles had not been retarded in the least; the number of cars and trucks on the highways rose from nine million in 1920 to ten and one-half million in 1921. In a general sense this optimistic view was accurate enough. What the depression of 1920–21 left behind was a shift of strength, imperceptible at the time, within the automobile industry. It would take a few years to become apparent and it would not in any way affect the advance of the automobile to its dominant position in American life, but it would determine who provided the cars and to some extent what kind of cars would be offered to the American public.

CHAPTER 6

Coming of Age

As America moved into the "Roaring Twenties," the automobile came into its own. Motor-vehicle manufacturing was by then the largest industry in the country and was still growing rapidly. The continuing expansion of the production and use of motor vehicles was one of the most important factors in the boom of the 1920's, perhaps the most important if its effect on other industries, on highway construction, and on automobile-connected retail and service enterprises is taken into consideration. Automobile production figures rose from two million in 1920 to five and one-half million in 1929. Registrations passed twenty million in 1925 and reached twenty-six and one-half million in 1929, with trucks and buses representing about an eighth of the total. By the late twenties a point was reached at which it was possible to move the entire population of the United States by road at one time, since there was close to one motor vehicle for every five people. Employment in automobile factories was a quarter of a million in 1922 and in excess of four hundred thousand in 1929; during the same period the amount of wages paid doubled, from $400 million to $800 million. About three times as many people were employed in industries dependent on the automobile.

The sale of this swelling flood of cars was made possible by two factors. First, until the mid-twenties there was a downward trend in automobile prices, reaching its lowest point in 1926 when a new

Model T touring car could be bought for $290. Secondly there was a liberal extension of credit to both consumers and dealers. The big companies went into the financing of sales on a large scale, General Motors through its Acceptance Corporation and Ford through a subsidiary, the Universal Credit Corporation (sold in the 1930's to avoid possible antitrust action). The other manufacturers relied on independent finance companies such as the Commercial Credit Corporation and Commercial Investors Trust, and on banks, which were attracted to the opportunities in underwriting installment buying of automobiles. The result was that by 1925 three-fourths of all sales of motor vehicles, new and used, were made on time-payment plans, and the technique was rapidly becoming the accepted method of selling all types of durable consumer goods.

The automobile manufacturers also attempted to regulate the used-car market, but with only qualified success. General Motors, followed by most of the industry, recommended to its dealers that trading in used cars should be managed so as to encourage the sale of new cars. Ford as usual was the exception. Since purchasers of Model T's were usually buying their first car, they were likely to trade in the Ford for a higher-priced model, new or used. Conversely, people who bought a more elegant car in the first place seldom traded it for a "flivver." Dealing in used cars, consequently, did little to stimulate the sale of new Model T's, and Ford dealers were expected to handle their used-car business so that it would pay its own way.

THE AUTOMOBILE AND THE BUSINESS BOOM

This process of expansion promoted a widespread business boom. The motor vehicle was now consuming annually 90 per cent of the country's petroleum products, mostly in the form of gasoline, 80 per cent of the rubber, predominantly tires, 20 per cent of the steel, 75 per cent of the plate glass, and 25 per cent of the machine tools. To these must be added the multitudinous repair and service facilities the automobile had brought into being, as well as the substantial business operations in the manufacture and sale of automotive accessories. In addition, a new Federal Highway Act in 1921 provided further aid to states for road construction, with the specific objective of promoting the development of a national system of highways. Under this act each state highway department (the 1916 Road Aid Act required a state to have a highway department in order to be eligible for federal aid) was to designate up to 7 per cent of its non-urban road mileage as "primary." These roads were planned as links in interstate routes, and for them federal assistance was given on a fifty-fifty matching basis. Initially about two hundred thousand miles of trunk highways received federal support.

Beyond this mileage, the multiplication of automobile owners clamoring for better roads stimulated a greatly increased volume of construction by state and local authorities, especially after the interesting discovery was made that highway users could be made to pay for their roads by the simple and apparently painless method of taxing the sale of gasoline. Oregon led the way in 1919 by imposing a levy of one cent a gallon. Ten years later every state had a gasoline tax, and the average had risen to three cents a gallon. Expenditures on roads during this decade averaged over $2 billion a year from all sources. The federal aid program also led to a uniform system of highway numbering and marking (odd numbers for north-south routes; even for east-west). Thus the motorist no longer had to stop at every crossroad to try to decipher a welter of signs and determine which of several obscure villages lay in the direction he wanted to take.

The figures tell only part of the story. The qualitative effect of the automobile on American industry was fully as important as the quantitative. The continuous-strip mill for rolling sheet steel and the continuous-process technique for manufacturing plate glass were both introduced in the early 1920's for the specific purpose of meeting the heavy requirements of the automobile industry. Henry Ford, in fact, went into the glass business because the established firms were skeptical about continuous process and Ford saw it as the only remedy for the increasingly short supply and high price of plate glass. Safety glass appeared at this time in response to one of the less pleasant features of the automobile, the hazard of shattered glass in the event of accident.

The rubber manufacturers vied with each other in improving the quality of tires. Most of the advances were gradual and unspectacular, such as the general adoption of cotton cord as the base fabric, improvements in the weave of the fabric and the quality of the rubber so as to give better wearing qualities, and more efficient design of treads to give greater traction. The outstanding change was the introduction of the low-pressure balloon tire, riding on thirty pounds of air as against the sixty of its predecessor and adding greatly to the smoothness and comfort of automobile travel.

The petroleum industry continued to search for more and better gasoline. New techniques, first catalytic cracking and then hydrogenation, were developed to replace the Burton process and increase refinery yields. In 1922 Charles F. Kettering and Thomas H. Midgley achieved the outstanding single qualitative advance by discovering after long experimentation that the mixing of tetraethyl lead with gasoline reduced engine knock—this after Kettering had been subjected to a good deal of ridicule for suggesting that the cause of knocking might be in the fuel and not in the motor. He had been stimulated to work on this problem in the first instance by insinuations that Delco's battery-operated ignition system accentuated knock. The octane scale for gasoline was introduced by Graham Edgar in 1926. "Boss Ket" broke another major bottleneck in automobile production in 1923 by developing, this time in co-operation with Du Pont, quick-drying finishes. The chemical industry was also called upon to provide antifreeze solutions superior to the ordinary alcohol that was the earliest and most common protection against winter temperatures. Millions of Americans in those days learned the elementary lesson that alcohol has both a low freezing and a low boiling point.

Road construction was virtually revolutionized by the replacement of gravel and cobblestone with smooth, hard surfaces of asphalt or concrete and by constant improvements in highway design to permit traffic to move with greater speed and safety. Highway development had the unforeseeable effect of touching off a race between road and vehicle that is still in progress, with the vehicle consistently ahead. Not only was the number of cars on the highways steadily increasing, but as roads got better, owners of motor vehicles were encouraged to use them more freely. Old roads were rebuilt and new ones were added; the result seemed to be merely that traffic got progressively heavier. In addition, better roads encouraged automotive engineers to design faster cars and heavier trucks so that a new highway was likely to be obsolescent by the time it was finished.

Not everyone benefited from the automobile boom. The automobile industry gave the railroads a substantial volume of freight traffic; on the other hand, the products of the industry began in the 1920's to cut heavily into the railroads' business. Motor-truck competition made itself most severely felt at first in local hauls and light loads and was not yet a matter of serious concern to the major trunk lines. Passenger traffic offered a more immediate challenge. The number of passengers carried by American railroads reached its peak in 1920 and declined steadily thereafter except for a resurgence during the Second World War. Buses accounted for some of the loss, although like trucks they competed most effectively at first in local rather than long-distance travel. The really irreparable damage to rail passenger traffic, however, was inflicted by the private automobile. Trips, long and short, that in former years would have been made by train if they had been made at all, were now taken in the family car. It was more convenient, as a rule it was cheaper, and the motorist was independent of someone else's schedule. The railroads were badly handicapped in meeting these new competitors. Apart from the greater flexibility and generally lower cost of highway transportation, the railroads were subject to rigorous federal and state regulation, whereas road traffic, commercial or private, was very loosely controlled by state authority where it was under any control at all.

The railroads survived the onslaught of the motor vehicle, with some lasting damage but also with compensation in the form of the freight generated by the automobile industry. City transit systems and interurban electric lines suffered more devastating losses with no offsetting benefits. Most of them gradually withered away, the interurbans first and then the trolley lines on the city streets. The rail transit systems that continued to operate were generally confined to the larger cities and most had to be subsidized in one way or another. Where streetcars remained in existence they were increasingly regarded as an encumbrance to automobile traffic.

The Automobile and Social Change

The total effect of the motor vehicle on American life has still to be measured, if indeed such measurement is even possible. Certainly the automobile brought major social changes, and some of these were becoming evident with the widespread extension of car ownership in the 1920's. It would be an exaggeration to say that the automobile made Americans a mobile people; the people who made their way across the American continent while the motorcar was still a dream were far from static. It would be more accurate to say that an already mobile people was given the means to travel farther, faster, and more freely.

There was no great folk migration involved. Cars were used instead of public transportation to get to and from work, to go shopping, or to visit friends. As the volume of motor-vehicle traffic on city streets rose, the problems of congestion and parking made their appearance and have remained unsolved. In justice to the automobile it should be pointed out that it found rather than created congestion in the larger cities, and that its own advantages of speed and maneuverability were wasted because city streets were not designed for motorized traffic. As with intercity highways, improvements could not be made fast enough to keep pace with the rising torrent of motor vehicles.

On weekends the cars sallied out into the country carrying families bent on recreation, sightseeing, or merely the pleasure of riding in a car. This last practice gave rise to the species termed the "Sunday driver," who wandered aimlessly along the highway, in no hurry because he (or she) was not going anywhere in particular, and frequently displaying a blithe disregard for other traffic. On Sunday evenings the returning travelers converged on the cities, with the result that the narrow roads of the period became choked with long lines of cars, endlessly starting and stopping, overheating, running out of gas, and more often than not taking hours to cover the last few miles.

The vehicle that took the city dweller into the country functioned just as effectively in the opposite direction—to take the farmer into the city. Students of American society may well conclude sometime that the most important influence of the automobile on American life has been alleviating rural isolation and breaking down the age-old distinction between the country and the city dweller. This process was just in its preliminary stages in the 1920's, and a good deal of improvement in both highways and cars would be required to make it really effective. Nevertheless it was in progress. At the beginning of the decade Sinclair Lewis's *Main Street* could focus on the drabness and barrenness of small-town life. The distinction between the small town and the city would have been harder to draw ten years later, although it would still have been there.

Long-distance journeys by motor vehicle were becoming less a major adventure and more an accepted and normal method of travel during the 1920's, although severe handicaps still existed. The mileage of good hard-surface road was growing steadily, but the bulk of it was still in the Northeast. Automobile manufacturers were emphasizing the romance of motoring in their advertising, an outstanding example being the "somewhere west of Laramie" advertisement devised by Edward M. Jordan (1882–1958) of Cleveland, builder of the Jordan car. It used the lure of the West, plus a pretty girl driving a Jordan "Playboy" sports car, as its appeal, but the motorist who actually ventured west of Laramie in those days was likely to conclude that the journey might better have been made by covered wagon. The express highway, moreover, had not yet appeared. Main roads ran directly through the centers of villages, towns, and cities, and there was invariably opposition from local merchants to suggestions that civic centers be bypassed. The motorist who averaged thirty miles an hour in actual driving time, excluding even stops for meals, was doing remarkably well.

Nevertheless the volume of long-distance highway travel was increasing, and with it came a growth of service facilities that represented significant economic and social change. As a matter of course, filling stations and garages sprang up wherever automobile traffic existed in reasonable volume. So did roadside restaurants. More interesting was the fact that the downtown hotel by the railroad station held little attraction for the motorist who had to think about parking his car, wanted to avoid city traffic, and was likely to be reluctant to pay the varied costs of hotel accommodation. Residents of the smaller towns discovered that there was money to be made by renting their spare bedrooms to tourists or, more ambitiously, by building cabins on a convenient piece of vacant property.

The cumulative effect of these changes was strikingly brought out by R. S. and H. M. Lynd in 1929 when they made their study of the typical American community in *Middletown*. At all income and social levels, they found, "ownership of an automobile has now reached the point of being an accepted essential part of normal living." Some families insisted that they would cut down on food and clothing rather than give up their car. The family car was a social rather than an economic need—frequently, indeed, it was a financial burden. It was defended as a means of relaxation and recreation; the family could go for a drive after working hours or take a vacation trip it could not have afforded otherwise.

Not all the social consequences of the automobile could be

regarded with approval. Some of Middletown's residents voiced concern because people were spending their Sundays on the highways instead of going to church and because the automobile appeared to be weakening family life by making it easier for individuals to disperse to their separate interests. Across the nation the motor vehicle was charged with being an encouragement to crime because it enabled criminals to get away rapidly from the scene of their misdeeds. It was also accused of fostering moral laxity because it provided young people with an easy method of escaping parental supervision and at the same time a convenient place to indulge romantic inclinations. In addition, there was a natural concern about the increase in highway accidents—the death toll approximately doubled during the decade, from about fifteen thousand in 1922 to thirty-two thousand in 1930—and there was a human inclination to charge the instrument with the responsibility for this unhappy situation.

All this criticism exemplified man's propensity to blame his technology rather than himself for whatever evil consequences it might produce. The vehicle that took people away from church could equally well take them to it. The automobile itself was not responsible for the materialistic, secular mood of the 1920's any more than it was responsible for crime and moral laxity. If it was used for the wrong purposes, the fault was with the users. After all, motorcars could be employed to enforce the law as well as to break it; and to offset the carnage on the highways was the fact that medical assistance, for illness as well as for accident, could get to where it was needed far more rapidly than in the days of the horse and buggy. The one thing certain was that the motor vehicle was effecting a social as well as an economic revolution in the United States, and revolutions invariably have both good and bad features.

THE AUTOMOBILE INDUSTRY IN TRANSITION

While the automotive conquest of American society was in progress, the automobile industry was undergoing fundamental changes in structure. The day was gone when an individual with technical skill, a little capital, and some business acumen could set out to make cars with some prospect of succeeding. After the First World War the handicaps facing the newcomer were so great as to be insuperable. To break into the mass market required not only a tremendous capital outlay in manufacturing facilities but also an elaborate and widespread dealer network, and even if these were created there was a growing consumer reluctance to buy unknown makes. The buyers of low- and medium-priced cars were becoming habituated to think in terms of trade-in value when they made their purchases, and were inclined to shy away from potential "orphans." The luxury-car field might have offered brighter prospects for a new arrival except that this market was too limited to support the firms that were already competing for it.

Consequently, although several attempts, some under fairly impressive sponsorship, were made to enter the automobile industry during the boom period of the 1920's, none survived. For example, there was the Rickenbacker Motor Car Company, named for and headed by the American aviator of the First World War and promoted by two veteran automobile men, Walter Flanders and Barney Everitt. Despite the combination of experience with the glamour of the Rickenbacker name, the company lasted only five years (1921–26). The Gray Motor Company, managed by former Ford business manager Frank L. Klingensmith, for a time seemed to be making a place for itself in the low-priced market, but it disappeared after just four years of operation (1922–26).

Among the established firms in the industry there was a series of historic shifts in position, with the result that a clear pattern of oligopoly emerged from what had previously been a structure approximating the classical model of free competition. The most momentous change came at the top, where General Motors replaced Ford as the leader of the industry. It was by no means a foreordained development. At the beginning of the boom period of the 1920's, Ford's preeminence was unchallenged and seemingly unchallengeable; in 1921 the Ford Motor Company made three-fifths of all the motor vehicles manufactured in the United States.

General Motors, on the other hand, had just been on the verge of disaster, its strength rested on two of its five models, Buick and Cadillac, and it possessed nothing approaching the glamour of the Ford name. The company's eventual place in the automotive firmament was far from certain.

Henry Ford's contributions to his own defeat were considerable. He stubbornly refused to see that his own great achievements with the assembly line and the Model T were merely a step in the progress of the automobile and not the culminating stage. Consequently he continued to turn out Tin Lizzies essentially unchanged from their prototype of 1908, oblivious to the fact that more attractive and more comfortable cars were available for two or three hundred dollars more than the Ford, or indeed at comparable prices if the customer chose to buy in the used-car market. Since Henry Ford was in no way an economist, he may be pardoned for missing the point that the automobile was introducing a fundamental change in American buying habits: to wit, in consumer decisions price was only one of several determinants and not necessarily the most important.

In the contest with General Motors the decisive factor was that Henry Ford, with his casual attitude toward organization, was pitted against one of the great organizing geniuses of American industry in Alfred P. Sloan, Jr., who became president of General Motors in 1923. Sloan gave to the corporation the coherent structural plan he had proposed to Durant, whereby a clear distinction was made between the operating divisions, which were self-contained and autonomous within the framework of the general policies of the corporation, and the central policy-making and planning bodies. Behind this structure was Sloan's philosophy of business organization, whose principal features may be summarized thus. No one man could successfully manage a corporation the size of General Motors. Policies should be formulated by group judgment based on careful analysis of the data, and although the lines of authority should be clearly defined, authority itself should be decentralized as much as possible. Since subordinate officials ought to be encouraged to make decisions, they had to be given the power to do so.

The Sloan reforms extended well beyond corporate structure and the top-level administrative echelons. Every sector of the General Motors organization came under close and careful scrutiny. For instance Sloan was aware that the sellers' market in motor vehicles was a thing of the past, and that particular attention was needed in the region where General Motors came into contact with the buying public—in the dealers' establishments. He himself spent much time on the road, visiting not only dealers' meetings but individual dealers, sometimes four and five in a day. The result was a strengthening of the General Motors sales organization through improved mechanisms for liaison between the corporation and its dealers and for hearing and adjudicating dealer complaints, more elaborate provisions for financial assistance, and more generous discounts—24 per cent as compared with 17 for Ford dealers.

The difference between General Motors and Ford was strikingly illustrated in the matter of personnel. In contrast to the ruthless battling for power and continuous attrition of executive and technical talent that characterized the Ford organization, Sloan built at General Motors a co-operative and efficient team, including William S. Knudsen, who gave to General Motors the genius for production he had formerly given to Ford and who would in time be Sloan's successor. Knudsen's greatest achievement at General Motors was to rehabilitate the Chevrolet Division, which had slumped so badly after the First World War that Pierre Du Pont seriously considered abandoning it altogether.

When Knudsen took charge Chevrolet was a languid competitor not only of the Model T but of such popular cars in its own price range ($500–$1,000) as Dodge, Essex, Overland, and the Durant Motor Company's Star. It rapidly pulled ahead of the field to become the principal challenger to Ford's supremacy. Ford fought back by trying to dress up Tin Lizzie with frills like spare tires and electric starters, but for all these she still remained Tin Lizzie. General Motors, on the other hand, made the annual model change a definite sales technique, aimed at meeting competition not only from the aging Model T but also from the secondhand car, and this example was followed by most of the rest of the industry. The principal exception was Packard, whose management took the position, quite successfully at the time, that ownership of a Packard conferred sufficient prestige by itself to make tinkering with the appearance and design of the car unnecessary.

Thus the consumer was being offered increasingly sophisticated cars at moderate prices. Lines were smoother, six-cylinder engines replaced fours and the eight was moving out of the luxury class, and items that had recently been accessories were now standard equipment. In the face of this kind of competition Ford's share of the market inexorably declined, until Henry Ford at last recognized the inevitable.

On May 31, 1927 the last Model T (No. 15,007,003) rolled off the assembly line and all Ford manufacturing operations came to a prolonged halt. Chevrolet took first place in car sales and retained it thereafter with only occasional exceptions. Henry Ford appears to have acted in a fit of pique, because he had no replacement for Tin Lizzie in sight when he closed down. Yet faith in his genius remained high; it was taken for granted by the American public that Henry had gone into seclusion in order to work another automotive miracle. Most Ford dealers and many of their customers simply waited patiently for the miracle to occur. What they got was the Model A, put on the market late in 1928. It was a good car, with enough of the Ford spell on it so that it outsold Chevrolet in its first year, but it was not significantly different from its competitors and certainly not superior to them.

At the next level below Ford and General Motors when the 1920's began was an assortment of apparently well-established companies with at least the potential of ranking among the leaders of the industry: Hudson (including Essex), Studebaker, Dodge, Maxwell (later Chrysler), Willys-Overland, Nash, Packard, and Durant Motors. Of these, Durant had the financial instability its founder seemed unable to avoid, and Willys-Overland never really recovered from its collapse in 1921. Packard chose to stay, for the time being, in the prestige-car market. From the rest Chrysler emerged to form what became the Big Three of American automobiledom.

This was the result of a conscious decision on Chrysler's part, along with an ability to grasp opportunities. He was aware that, despite its promising start, the Chrysler Corporation would be a minor and possibly short-lived participant in the automotive world unless it could get established in the mass market. But the manufacturing resources taken over from Maxwell were too limited to enable Chrysler to produce a low-priced car competitively, and the company still lacked the financial strength to build a new plant on the scale that would be required. An extensive marketing organization would also be needed. The solution to the problem was found when the Dodge Brothers Manufacturing Company was put on the market in 1928. John and Horace Dodge had been victims of the influenza epidemic that followed the First World War, and their heirs subsequently decided to get out of the automobile business.

Consequently, after some dickering Dodge was absorbed by the Chrysler organization. The assets acquired by Chrysler were considerable: a first-class manufacturing plant with a well-equipped foundry and other facilities for large-scale production; a car with a well-known name and an established position in the medium-priced market; and a dealer network some twelve thousand strong that could be used as an outlet for other Chrysler products. The Dodge sales organization was considered to be one of the best in the country, and Chrysler's autobiography makes it clear that he wanted the Dodge dealers as much as the Dodge manufacturing capacity. With these resources at his disposal Chrysler was able to introduce the Plymouth in 1928, a step neatly timed to take advantage of Henry Ford's temporary disappearance from the mass market.

With the rise of Chrysler the developing structure of the American automobile industry became clearly discernible. At the top were General Motors and Ford, between them outproducing all the rest of the industry put together. Both were also international automotive powers. Ford had established manufacturing subsidiaries in Europe before the First World War and had regional assembly plants throughout the world. General Motors bought the British Vauxhall and the German Opel companies during the 1920's. Chrysler was well behind the leaders but definitely ahead of the rest of the field. As of 1928 Durant Motors, which was producing a variety of models in the customary Durant manner, was superficially a fourth major power in the industry. However, except for the low-priced Star, which sold one and a half million units over a period of ten years, Billy Durant's third bid for automotive leadership was largely an assortment of rejects and misfits that nobody else wanted, and Durant Motors was coming unstuck well before the boom period ended.

Next in line, sharing 15 to 20 per cent of the automobile market, were Hudson, Nash, Packard, Studebaker, and Willys-Overland. Behind them, struggling for the less than 10 per cent of the market that remained, was a diminishing assortment of smaller concerns. Some bore famous names in American automobile history: Reo, Peerless, Franklin, Hupmobile. Special mention might be made of the splendidly engineered Marmon, whose twelve- and sixteen-cylinder models matched the Rolls-Royce in luxurious smoothness, and the Stutz, whose "Bearcat" roadster was preeminently the sports car of the Jazz Age. During the 1920's Stutz was controlled by the steel tycoon Charles M. Schwab, but his talents were apparently not transferable to automobile manufacturing, as the company steadily declined. On the other hand, one minor concern appeared to be on the way up. This was the Auburn Automobile Company of Auburn, Indiana, a modest producer of high-priced cars since 1903, which in 1924 came under the control of Errett Lobban Cord (b. 1894), a salesman, promoter, and former racing driver and mechanic. Under his management Auburn sales rose from 2,500 in 1924 to 15,000 in 1927. Simultaneously Cord took charge of the Duesenberg Motor Company, founded in 1920 by two brothers, Fred and August Duesenberg, who had got their start as builders of high-powered engines for racing cars and then for airplanes during the First World War. The Duesenberg was the first American passenger automobile to have a straight-eight engine, and it introduced the four-wheel hydraulic brake invented in 1918 by Malcolm Loughead (Lockheed), a member of a family better known as aviation than as automobile pioneers.

But the Duesenbergs were better engineers than businessmen and so their company eventually was merged with Auburn, to the accompaniment of a pronouncement by Cord that he would build the world's most expensive passenger automobile. In 1929 Cord combined an assortment of automotive and aircraft interests as the Cord Corporation and added to his automobile line a car bearing his name and equipped with front-wheel drive. The Cord was an interesting car technically, its one major drawback being that the front-end drive was a complicated mechanism to service and repair. Unfortunately for its promoter, it made its appearance at the worst possible time, just when the market for high-priced cars disintegrated.

In general, the outlook for the small-scale producer was gloomy well before the onset of the depression. Between 1923 and 1927—that is, when the recovery from the 1921 panic was well under way and before there were any signs of the 1929 crash—the number of firms engaged in motor-vehicle manufacturing shrank from 108 to 44. The casualties included historic names like Haynes and Winton, which went back to the birth of the industry. Winton himself had long since lost interest in automobile manufacturing and remained in business as a designer and builder of diesel engines. Among the survivors, those with the best prospects were firms like White, Autocar, and Mack, which had chosen to concentrate on trucks, buses, and other specialized vehicles. In fact, the Fageol brothers of Kent, Ohio, after selling one successful commercial vehicle enterprise to American Car and Foundry, were able to start over again in 1927 with the Twin Coach Company and revolutionize bus transportation. Their design changed the motor bus from an elongated passenger car to a vehicle specifically designed for commercial passenger carriage, with the engine underneath so that the whole body space was available for payload and the driver right in front in the best position to handle his vehicle in traffic.

This, however, was a special situation. In the mainstream of automobile production, whether of passenger cars or standard-type trucks, competitive conditions favored the big company, as they were bound to do when the motorcar became an article of mass production and mass consumption. No one has ever managed to build a hundred thousand cars a year in a machine shop. If automobiles are to be produced in quantity and at low unit cost, the techniques of mass production must be used, and this requires a large-scale operation. These conditions do not necessarily apply to high-priced cars produced in limited numbers, but even in this field the big companies were in a superior competitive position before the end of the twenties. General Motors and Ford could make just as luxurious cars in the Cadillac and the Lincoln as could any of the smaller firms—Pierce-Arrow or Moon, for example—with the advantage of being able to spread some of the overhead cost over their larger organizations.

While the technology of production has to be given first place, there were other factors contributing to the inexorable progression of the automobile industry toward oligopoly. The advantages of size extended to marketing as well as manufacturing, and in the 1920's selling replaced production as the industry's principal problem. Besides being able to finance their selling operations in the way described at the beginning of this chapter, the big companies could maintain larger sales organizations and support more numerous dealers than the small ones, so that as a matter of simple arithmetic they could reach more of the potential buyers. The regional distributors of earlier years disappeared during the 1920's. Selling was far too critical for the manufacturers' sales departments to want any intermediate authority between them and their dealers.

The big producers, moreover, were far better able to advertise extensively in mass media, and because they also had many more dealers who were doing their own local advertising, their appeal to the buying public was stronger and more persistent than that of the small firms. The return from this kind of effort was calculable and striking. Market surveys of this period demonstrated that three-fourths of all prospective purchasers had decided on the make of car they wanted to buy before they arrived at the dealer's salesroom.

In marketing as in production, unit cost declined as volume increased. At the end of the 1920's the advertising and other direct marketing costs incurred in selling approximately a million Chevrolets was about twenty-five dollars a car, which was at least five dollars less than the cost of selling a Gardner or a Reo or a Chandler. In short, whether in building or selling automobiles the small company had to contend with handicaps that had become inherent in the nature of the business.

Finally, as Billy Durant had foreseen twenty years before, the big concerns could accept losses that would be fatal to their smaller rivals. This point was about to be vividly and painfully demonstrated.

CHAPTER 7

Prosperity and Adversity

As with most other elements of American economic life, 1929 was a watershed in the history of the automobile. Production of motor vehicles in that year reached 5,337,087, a million more than in the previous year and a record that would not be surpassed or even matched for another twenty years. The economic cataclysm that followed the stock market collapse not only curtailed drastically the demand for new cars but had other and more lasting effects on the automobile industry. The decline in production was sharp but temporary; output dropped to a low of 1,331,860 in 1932, but after that conditions slowly improved. On the other hand, the depression accelerated the extinction of the independent producers and brought the United Automobile Workers into existence; these were permanent changes in the structure and functioning of the industry.

In these respects the experience of the automobile industry was in no way unusual, but the impact of the Great Depression is only one reason for picking 1929 as a watershed—the most obvious and probably the most important. There are others worth pointing out. It was a single generation since the first crude Duryea car had made its appearance; the Duryea brothers in fact were still living in 1929, along with other pioneers such as Charles B. King, Freelan O. Stanley, Ransom E. Olds, Henry M. Leland, Alexander Winton, and even George B. Selden. In that time the motor vehicle grew from a dubious experiment of little conceivable value except as a "rich man's toy" to become the bellwether of the American economy and perhaps the most important single influence in American social life. When Herbert Hoover accepted the Republican nomination in 1928, he could announce "two cars in every garage" as an objective shared by his fellow countrymen generally.

During these thirty-odd years before 1929 the automobile changed much more radically than it would do in the same span of time afterward. Had a motorist of 1899 been transported thirty years forward in time and placed in an automobile of that year, he would have been helpless. Vehicles, roads, traffic conditions would all have been radically different from anything in his experience. On the other hand, had the same time machine dropped a 1929 motorist into a car in 1959, he would have felt reasonably at home and would have needed only a little practice to get along.

By the end of the 1920's, in short, the automobile had evolved the mechanical and structural form it would thenceforth retain, subject to improvement and refinement, until some completely new automobile technology replaced it. This is said in full awareness of the introduction after 1929 of the automatic transmission, power steering and braking, streamlining, and other technical advances. These all fall into the category of "improvement and refinement," and practically all had been thought of and experimented with earlier.

The typical new passenger automobile of 1929 was a closed car; the ratio of closed to open cars was nine to one, exactly reversing the corresponding figures for 1919. It was gasoline-powered; at the National Automobile Show in 1924 it was noted that for the first time not a single electric or steam model was displayed. Four-wheel brakes were standard equipment, with mechanical braking systems predominant in the lower price ranges and hydraulic in the upper. Radios and heaters were beginning to appear as optional luxury items.

Engines, as stated before, were mostly six cylinders in the popular models, with a growing trend toward eights. But the advances of the 1920's in motor fuels and the improvement of engine design to give higher compression ratios resulted in greater gains in performance than the mere increase in the number of cylinders would suggest. For instance, the Model A Ford had a four-cylinder engine as did Tin Lizzie, but it had twice the horsepower. Finally, the 1929 car had the low body line of its successors instead of rising high off the ground as had most of its predecessors. The lowering of the center of gravity made it easier to take curves and reduced the risk of the vehicle's turning over. This change was made possible by two developments. One was the introduction of hypoid gearing, first used by Packard in 1927, which permitted lowering of the driveshaft and the rear axle and consequently of the chassis and body also. The other was simply that by 1929 the mileage of hard-surfaced road had become so extensive that it was practical to design and build low-slung cars. It could be assumed that an automobile would normally be operated on a reasonably smooth, hard pavement; it was no longer necessary to design the car so that it could negotiate the deep ruts and other hazards of poorly maintained dirt roads.

The evolution of the automobile industry to 1929 has already been described. It had not yet acquired completely its subsequent oligopolistic form, but the trend was unmistakable. To look at it in a different light, in its first thirty years the American automobile industry grew from a dubious and highly speculative offshoot of machine shops and bicycle manufacturers to the point where its bigger companies ranked among the world's largest manufacturing enterprises and were occasionally extending their operations into other fields. This process was more illuminating of the growth of the automobile industry than significant in its own right. American motor-vehicle manufacturers were usually reluctant to venture outside the automotive area, largely because the phenomenal expansion of their own industry gave them enough to do without looking for additional activities.

Nevertheless, there were some gestures at diversification. Ford got into the tractor business as early as the First World War and, subject to some interruptions, was the only automobile firm to stay in it. General Motors' entry into refrigeration was a whim of Billy Durant's that paid off. In the middle and late twenties there was a flurry of interest in aviation on the part of some automobile companies, stimulated by the advance of aeronautics and the assumption of a close relationship between the two industries because both were based on the internal-combustion engine.

Ford started by buying control of the Stout Metal Airplane Company in 1924 to the accompaniment of much speculation that Henry Ford was going to produce a flying Tin Lizzie. For some years the company built the famous Ford trimotor, the Tin Goose, but it was strictly a transport plane and not an aeronautical Model T. Ford and William B. Stout disagreed on aircraft construction, and finally Ford lost interest and discontinued the operation in 1932. In 1929 General Motors decided that it should be in a position to take advantage of possible commercial developments in aviation and consequently acquired control of the Fokker Aircraft Corporation and a 24 per cent interest in the Bendix Aviation Corporation. Fokker, founded by a Dutch aeronautical engineer who became famous in the First World War, was later renamed the General Aviation Corporation and was absorbed by North American Aviation in 1933. This transaction gave General Motors a 29 per cent interest in North American. By that time the prospect for an immediate, phenomenal boom in aviation had evaporated and General Motors made no further commitment to the airframe business, although it retained its stock holdings in North American and Bendix until 1948.

In addition, the American automobile industry dominated the world market. In the late 1920's the United States built 85 per cent of the world's motor vehicles. About a tenth of the output was exported, this above and beyond what was produced by American-owned firms in foreign countries. The figures become more meaningful when it is appreciated that the number of American cars exported was, for example, approximately twice the total motor-vehicle production of the United Kingdom during this period.

Despite the highest wage scales in the world (Ford was now up to a base rate of seven dollars a day) the American manufacturers were able to compete internationally because of their enormous superiority in the organization and technology of production. For instance, Morris Motors, the biggest of the British firms, did not install a moving assembly line until 1934—not because of any lack of ability to use the technique but simply because demand was too limited to justify the investment. The principal handicap American cars had to encounter in the world market was tax structures based on horsepower, which put a heavy burden on the big American vehicles.

THE ONSET OF DEPRESSION

For the history of the automobile, the first noteworthy feature of Great Depression of the 1930's is that it demonstrated conclusively how firmly imbedded in American society the motor vehicle had become. Between 1929 and 1932, as we have seen, the annual production of new cars in the United States declined 75 per cent. On the other hand, in the same period motor-vehicle registrations dropped only 10 per cent, from 26,500,000 to 23,877,000. In other words, while the American public was deciding that it could not afford to buy new cars, it was contriving to keep those that it had. Economic crisis or no, the family car was not a luxury to be jettisoned during the storm; it was a household necessity which, if it could not be replaced, had somehow to be kept running until better times arrived.

This situation, where an automobile was in effect part of one's household goods, was a novelty in the history of civilization. In the main Americans took it for granted; others did not. As an illustration, when John Steinbeck's novel *The Grapes of Wrath* was made into a moving picture, the film was welcomed by the Communists and exhibited throughout the Soviet Union as an example of the horrible conditions that existed under American capitalism. After about six weeks, further showings were canceled. Russian audiences, it became evident, were less impressed by the plight of the Joads than by the fact that these supposedly downtrodden victims of capitalist oppression owned a motorcar. It may have been a dilapidated jalopy, but it was still a possession beyond the reach of the common man in proletarian Russia.

The preservation of old cars, however, was of little value to an industry that depended on the sale of new ones. The dropping-off of sales from their 1929 peak hit all the automobile companies hard, but what was a difficult period for the big companies was irretrievable disaster for most of the small producers. A few managed to survive by getting out of the passenger-car business. Reo, again managed by R. E. Olds after a few years of retirement, became a manufacturer of trucks exclusively in 1936. Marmon went out of operation in 1933 but in the meantime the Marmon family had joined forces with Arthur W. S. Herrington to form the Marmon-Herrington Company for the manufacture of all-wheel-drive trucks. These were designed by Herrington as a result of his experience as a military transport officer in the First World War. The Hupp Motor Car Company, later reorganized as the Hupp Corporation, became a manufacturer of automotive parts and eventually diversified its operations into such fields as kitchen appliances and electronics.

These, however, were exceptions. Under the blight of depression one famous name after another disappeared from the American automotive scene: Franklin, Moon, Pierce-Arrow, Kissel, Gardner, Peerless, Stutz, Cord. Of these, Peerless had a remarkable record. It began in the late nineteenth century as a manufacturer of clothes wringers, then turned to bicycles and subsequently to automobiles. When the company had to abandon automobile manufacturing in 1931, it was reorganized as Peerless Corporation and three years later transformed its plant into a brewery. E. L. Cord went out characteristically in a confusing flurry of corporate relationships. The Cord Corporation was absorbed by the Aviation Corporation, subsequently known as AVCO, but in the process Cord himself emerged in control of AVCO. Then, however, the whole aviation industry was thrown into a turmoil when the federal government professed to find irregularities in the award of airmail contracts, and in the ensuing reorganization of AVCO, Cord got into a quarrel with the Securities and Exchange Commission and in disgust gave up both his automotive and his aeronautical interests. With his departure manufacture of the Auburn, Cord, and Duesenberg ceased.

A still more spectacular casualty was William C. Durant. Already in trouble before the stock market crash, Billy tried desperately to keep going, but his technique was shopworn. The money market had seen the show twice; it was not impressed by flamboyant announcements of projected new combinations, which failed to materialize, or of the appointment of allegedly top-ranking managerial talent, which turned out to consist of Dodge executives displaced by the merger with Chrysler. The depression provided the coup de grâce. Durant Motors was liquidated in 1933, and two years later Billy, then 75 years old, declared himself bankrupt, listing liabilities of $914,000 and assets of $250 (his clothes).

He was still not finished. In 1935 he started a supermarket in Asbury Park, New Jersey. When an enterprising newspaperman saw him helping to clean up in preparation for the grand opening, the story was published that the founder of General Motors was reduced to sweeping floors for a living. He then started to promote a chain of bowling alleys, designed to take bowling from the cuspidor and sawdust atmosphere in which it then existed and make it a family recreation—in short, to do what others would do later. Durant's aspirations were frustrated by ill health and the shortage of materials caused by the Second World War. He died in 1947, leaving behind the memory of a colorful, likable man who had risen to spectacular heights and then inexorably fallen like the hero of a Greek tragedy. His former business associate, Frederick L. Smith of the Olds Motor Works, summed him up accurately:

It would be a poorly posted analyst who failed to list W. C. Durant as the most picturesque, spectacular, and aggressive figure in the chronicles of American automobiledom. He certainly made some capital mistakes—but the man who makes no mistakes rarely makes anything at all on a large scale.

The medium-sized automobile firms had mixed fortunes. Like everyone else Packard and Nash saw their sales shrink, but they remained solvent. Nash even expanded its area of operations by merging with the Kelvinator Corporation in 1936 as Nash-Kelvinator, thus following General Motors in combining the manufacture of automobiles with electric refrigerators. Both Packard and Nash conceded to the depression by bringing out lower-priced models, with qualified success. Packard in fact appears to have permanently impaired its prestige value by allowing the concept of a "cheap" Packard to get established. Hudson avoided bankruptcy by a monumental effort on the part of Roy D. Chapin, recalled to deal with the crisis after serving briefly as Hoover's Secretary of Commerce. The effort probably cost him his life; he died of pneumonia just as it became clear that the company was safe.

Willys-Overland and Studebaker both had to undergo receivership. For John N. Willys this was his second experience. After his disaster in 1921 he had put together another assortment of automotive companies, producing the popular Overland and a line of higher-priced cars using the Knight engine. In 1929 Willys himself retired from active management to become ambassador to Poland. The crisis brought him back, but there was nothing he could do to keep his company solvent. Before his death in 1933 he did have the satisfaction of seeing it on the way to reorganization, minus its Knight-engined models, which should have been abandoned earlier. Willys was the last major manufacturer to use the sleeve-valve motor, and it seems clear that this was a blunder. By the 1930's the poppet-valve engine had been refined to the point where the extra cost and complexity of the Knight could no longer be justified.

The Studebaker catastrophe was the direct consequence of tragic blunders by president Albert R. Erskine (1871–1933). Here was a long-established firm with an unbroken record of success as a vehicle manufacturer, which should have had as good a prospect as

ORIGINAL PRODUCTION CHRYSLER SIX

This car, Chrysler's first production model, appeared in early 1924.

THE FIRST PLYMOUTH

Introduced in 1928, the Plymouth confirmed Chrysler's position as one of the Big Three.

HENRY MARTYN LELAND, 1843–1932

RANSOM ELI OLDS, 1864–1950

WILLIAM C. DURANT, 1860–1947

HENRY FORD, 1863–1947

(Courtesy The Chrysler Corporation)

WALTER P. CHRYSLER, 1875–1940

(Courtesy General Motors Corporation)

ALFRED P. SLOAN, JR.

(Chase Ltd. Photo, courtesy UAW)

WALTER P. REUTHER

(Courtesy Office of the Governor, Lansing, Mich.)

GEORGE ROMNEY

AUTOMOBILE
STYLING
1896–1965

This series of pictures of Ford
products strikingly illustrates men's
changing notions, over a span of
nearly seventy years, of what an
automobile should look like. For
the first half of the period motorcars looked pretty much like what
they were often called, machines.

From top to bottom on this page
are Henry Ford in his quadricycle,
1896; the first production Ford,
Model A, 1903; the Model N, 1909;
a Model T sedan, 1922, and the
Model A of 1929.

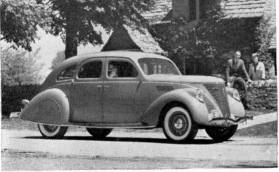

On this page from top to bottom: the V-8 model of 1934; the streamlined Lincoln-Zephyr, 1936; the first true postwar model, 1949; a "Fairlane 500" hardtop, 1957; and a Mustang of 1965.

(All photos these two pages courtesy Ford Motor Company)

EARLY BODY DROP

On a General Motors assembly line of about 1920 the tonneau of an automobile is lowered onto the chassis, a process involving a good deal of hand labor.

THE SAME PROCESS TODAY

In forty-five years, the basic task has not changed, but the methods have become almost completely mechanized.

SHOPPING BY AUTOMOBILE

More than five thousand automobiles have brought shoppers to this retail complex at Columbus, Ohio. The development of such suburban shopping centers is one of many economic and social changes brought about by the automobile.

(Picture by Michigan State Highway Department, courtesy Automobile Manufacturers Association)

FREEWAY INTERCHANGE

The requirement in modern superhighway design that automobiles join a stream of moving traffic only when they are already going in the same direction and traveling at highway speed necessitates the construction of elaborate interchanges such as this one near Detroit.

anyone of weathering a prolonged depression. Erskine had been president since 1915 and had handled the company's affairs with competence and judgment. At the peak of the boom, however, he seems to have developed a streak of overoptimism. He tried to expand by buying the Pierce-Arrow Motor Car Company, which proved to be worthless. Then when the depression came, Erskine was convinced that it would be brief. He shared this view with many others, but when he carried his beliefs so far as to pay dividends out of capital in order to maintain confidence, his optimism was clearly running away with his judgment. Events of course proved him disastrously wrong. A desperate last-minute effort to avert bankruptcy by arranging a merger with the White Motor Company failed, and Erskine committed suicide. For a time it appeared that Studebaker would go out of business altogether, but the company was successfully reorganized by Harold S. Vance and Paul G. Hoffman, although it never recovered its previous stature.

Thus the middle group of automobile manufacturers survived the depression, along with one of the smaller producers, Graham-Paige, and the stronger of the truck manufacturers. Nevertheless the status of the independents was perceptibly weaker. Their share of the market dropped from the 25 per cent of 1929 to 10 per cent in 1939. This decline occurred in the face of strenuous efforts to appeal to the buying public in every possible way: styling, colorful names, new technical devices. Essex, for instance, offered a new model called the "Terraplane," which sold well enough to help the Hudson Motor Car Company remain solvent. Studebaker, on the other hand, got nowhere with a low-priced car called the "Rockne," after the famous Notre Dame football coach.

One interesting feature of the response to depression conditions was a renewal of emphasis on the mechanical qualities of the car. These had been the prime subject of advertising when the automobile was young, but in the lush days of the twenties, styling took precedence over engineering. In the thirties, however, the desperate competition for markets turned the manufacturers to the sales appeal of devices that could be claimed to enhance economy or efficiency of operation. Studebaker led the way by offering free-wheeling in 1930, and the rest of the industry promptly followed. Freewheeling, which put the transmission in neutral when the power was cut off, was presented as a fuel-saving technique. But since it sacrificed the braking power of the engine, it cost about as much in extra wear on brake shoes as it saved in gasoline consumption, and it was an additional driving hazard. It was generally abandoned after a brief trial. Overdrive, first introduced by Chrysler in 1934, was a better method of economizing on fuel.

The trouble with this kind of competition was that whatever the smaller companies could do, the big ones could do just as well—frequently better, because they had greater resources for development, testing, and marketing. Chrysler was not only first in the field with overdrive but introduced three-point engine suspension on rubber mountings in the 1931 Plymouth. Reo offered a car with automatic transmission in 1934, but this was one of the last Reo passenger cars, and it was left to General Motors to revive automatic transmission as a feature of the Buick and Oldsmobile in 1937. None of these techniques, it should be understood, was "invented" at this time although the advertising might have given this impression. Practically all had been experimented with earlier, but the 1930's first saw them introduced on regular production models.

There were also valid technical reasons for these changes being made at this time. Automatic transmission may be taken as a sample. Both the torque converter and the hydraulic coupling were tried experimentally on marine engines before the First World War, and the other essential of the automatic transmission, the epicyclic gearbox, was used in the 1890's by the great British automotive engineer F. W. Lanchester, and later by Henry Ford in the transmission of the Model T. It was not until the 1920's, however, that torque converters or hydraulic couplings were refined to the point of being usable for motor vehicles. Another ten years of development, in the United States carried out largely by General Motors, was required to design an automatic transmission suitable for installation on production models. Thus the automatic transmission could hardly have been introduced as a commercially practical device before the late 1930's. It might well have been held up even longer except for the competitive pressure: the company that first put out a car with a workable automatic transmission could expect a definite sales advantage.

The Big Three in the Depression

It should not be thought that the giants of the automobile industry went through the depression unscathed. General Motors, Ford, and Chrysler all shared in the agonies of the period, with production curtailed and revenues diminishing. Nevertheless there was a fundamental difference between the experience of the Big Three and that of their smaller competitors in that the former were at no time threatened with extinction.

It is easy to get the impression, however, that the survival of the Ford Motor Company was more a matter of habit than of any conscious planning. Ford provides an excellent illustration of the fact that a really large business organization can withstand a surprising amount of mismanagement. The company was run by an aged despot, who despised systematic organization and who believed in keeping his executives, including his own son, constantly in conflict with each other. In this policy he was abetted by Harry Bennett (b. 1892), a former prizefighter who made his way into Henry Ford's confidence, apparently by working on his fears for the safety of his grandchildren—this was the time of the sensational kidnapping and murder of Charles A. Lindbergh's infant son. Bennett was made head of a Service Department, with vague powers over all Ford personnel. It was not a revival of the old Sociological Department; Bennett's employees were more likely to be ex-convicts than welfare workers, and the Service Department functioned on the lines of a totalitarian secret police. This was the era when Ford executives were liable to discover that they had been dismissed by finding their offices barred and their effects thrown into the street. Edsel Ford disliked Bennett and disapproved of his methods; Bennett protected himself by using every opportunity to promote friction between father and son. Bennett also had charge of labor relations; how these were handled will be described in the next chapter.

It is difficult to believe that there could have been achievement under such conditions, but there was. The Ford Motor Company produced in 1932 the first low-priced car with a V-8 engine, a feat characterized by Charles E. Sorensen, Ford's production manager and Bennett's principal rival for power, as "the elder Ford's last mechanical triumph." Mass-producing a V-8 engine at low cost was made possible by innovations in foundry technique permitting the entire block and crankcase to be cast as a unit. The V-8 temporarily put Ford ahead of Chevrolet in sales, but Ford management was not equal to the task of holding the lead against its efficiently organized competitors. The lasting effect was a general increase in horse-power among the low-priced cars. In just six years Ford jumped from the 20 horsepower of the Model T to the 65 horsepower of the V-8, although the comparison has to be qualified by the fact that two systems of calculating horsepower are involved. The rating of the Model T engine is a nominal horsepower computed by a formula based on bore measurement and the number of cylinders. This method has been generally employed where motor vehicles are taxed according to horsepower. The figure for the V-8 engine represents brake horsepower, arrived at by measuring engine out-put at a given number of revolutions per minute with a dynamome-ter and almost universally used for American cars because it gives a higher and more impressive-sounding horsepower rating. In any event the advance in Ford performance was unmistakable. A Model T in ordinary running condition had a top speed of about fifty miles an hour, whereas the V-8 could match most of the other cars it met on the highway.

This accomplishment was the only bright spot in the Ford picture. Henry Ford continued to deteriorate and a stroke in 1938 further impaired his powers, but he persisted in trying to control the company, although his efforts increasingly became mere capricious interference. An example was his pushing the company into a vague verbal arrangement with an Irish engineer named Henry George Ferguson for the manufacture of tractors using some of Ferguson's designs. Fordson tractors had not been made in the United States since 1928, such production as there was being carried on by the Ford plants in England and Ireland, but the idea of a cheap tractor had always been a passion of Henry Ford's, and in 1938 he imposed it on a reluctant management. At the time the operation lost money, and in later years the company had to pay close to $10 million in patent claims because of the casual nature of Henry Ford's agreement with Ferguson.

Bennett's influence over his nominal chief continued to increase, until it became impossible to tell who was actually issuing the orders. Ford's bitter opposition to unionization hurt the company's popularity and to some extent its sales. It is fair to say, indeed, that during the depression years the Ford Motor Company, except for the V-8 achievement, lived largely on its past reputation: specifically on the existence of a solid core of dealers and customers who remained loyal to the Ford name.

The extent of the Ford decline was such that from 1933 until 1950 the company dropped to third place in total sales. The number of Ford cars produced remained comfortably ahead of the number of Plymouths, but the entire Chrysler line (Chrysler, Dodge, De Soto, Plymouth) consistently outsold the combined Ford-Lincoln output. The introduction of the Mercury in 1938 was an effort sponsored by Edsel Ford to improve his company's competitive position.

The Chrysler record was an impressive achievement. In the pit of the depression the Chrysler Corporation was operating at 40 per cent of capacity, but careful management preserved the company's fiscal health and strengthened its market position, as we have seen, by being first in the field with important technical innovations.

When economic conditions started to improve, the corporation was able to pay off the $60 million indebtedness it had incurred when it bought Dodge. With his company solidly established and clear of debt, Walter Chrysler retired in 1935. He died five years later.

Like the others, General Motors saw its business decline sharply after the stock market collapse. In contrast to its previous crises, however, this time there was accurate financial planning and efficient management to prevent any repetition of the conditions of 1910 and 1921. General Motors, indeed, not only rode through the depression safely but was even able to expand into new areas of operation.

The first of these was diesel engines. For General Motors the impetus to enter this field came predominantly from Charles F. Kettering, who had been experimenting for some time to find out why an engine with the advantages of high thermal efficiency and low fuel cost was not more widely used. The basic problem was that the diesel engine had a very high weight-to-power ratio because of the solid construction required to withstand compression of 500 pounds per square inch. Consequently diesels could not be used efficiently for locomotion on land. The same problem was being worked on in Cleveland, Ohio, by the Winton Engine Company and the Electro-Motive Corporation, the latter a firm engaged in designing railroad equipment propelled by an internal-combustion engine with electric drive. On Kettering's recommendation General Motors bought both companies in 1930.

From this activity came a revolution in transportation. The weight-power difficulty was resolved by adopting two-cycle operation (this idea seems to have originated with Kettering), and major improvements were made in the fuel-injection and cooling systems. The impact of these changes first made itself felt on the railroad system, where in an astonishingly short time the diesel locomotive drove the "iron horse" off the tracks it had dominated since the days of George Stephenson. Adapting the diesel to highway vehicles called for still more refined engineering; diesel-powered trucks and buses were beginning to appear at the end of the thirties, but they came into widespread use only after the Second World War.

The second of General Motors' new ventures was into the manufacture of aircraft engines. This step originated with purchase of the Allison Engineering Company of Indianapolis as part of the acquisition of aviation properties by General Motors in 1929. It was a minor transaction—$592,000 for the entire company—but it was the only one to remain in the General Motors organization. Allison had originally been a machine shop making parts for racing cars and had moved into the manufacture of bearings for aircraft engines. During the 1930's it turned to the design and building of liquid-cooled aircraft engines, and with the coming of the Second World War it expanded to become and remain a major producer in this field.

In 1937 Alfred P. Sloan resigned the presidency of General Motors to become chairman of the board. His successor was William S. Knudsen, who had only four years in the office before he was called to Washington to take charge of war production. When Sloan stepped down, General Motors made 40 per cent of the motor vehicles built in the United States and 35 per cent of the total world output, and it was an important producer of electric refrigerators, diesel locomotives, and aircraft engines. It had five American passenger cars: Cadillac (which also built a slightly lower-priced model, the La Salle, at this time), Buick, Oldsmobile, Pontiac (which replaced the Oakland during the depression), and Chevrolet, consistently the nation's best seller. There was a separate division which made GMC trucks and buses, and Chevrolet also built light trucks. Overseas, General Motors made the Vauxhall in England and the Opel in Germany. It was not only the world's biggest privately owned manufacturing enterprise; it was an industrial empire such as the world had never seen before. The largest single stock ownership was Du Pont, with about 23 per cent. This was not an individual holding, however, but represented a composite of stocks owned by the Du Pont Company and by members of the Du Pont family as individuals. Sloan himself, although a substantial stockholder, had nothing approaching a controlling interest.

Changing the Guard

The change of top management at General Motors and Chrysler and the progressive decline of Henry Ford's ability to manage his company were evidence of the fact that the first generation of automotive leadership was passing from the American scene. During the thirties, Charles W. Nash and Ransom E. Olds also gave up the presidency of their respective companies, bankruptcy eliminated William C. Durant from the automobile business, and death took other outstanding figures such as Roy D. Chapin, Hiram Percy Maxim, John N. Willys, Henry M. Leland, and Alexander Winton. Founding automobile companies seems to have promoted longevity. Leland died at eighty-nine and Winton at seventy-two. Durant and Ford both died in 1947, aged eighty-seven and eighty-four respectively; Nash followed them a year later at the age of eighty-four and Olds was eighty-six when he died in 1950.

These were colorful individuals whose achievements over the span of a single generation were breathtaking. They represented a cross-section of American society. Maxim and Henry B. Joy were millionaires' sons; Chapin, Sloan, and Durant came from middle-class business and professional families; Chrysler and Ford were farm boys; Nash personified "rags to riches"; Winton and Chevrolet were immigrants. Considering the period in which they grew up, there was a surprisingly large proportion of college graduates: Chapin, Maxim, Sloan, Kettering (who seldom admitted it), Haynes, Packard. The others came up chiefly as mechanics or salesmen, but we have to include, as we have seen, such varied occupations as the manufacture of bathtubs, photographic plates, bird cages, and washing machines.

It is always easy to say, "There were giants in those days." In this instance it happens to be true, but it would be unfair to draw the conclusion that the next generation of automotive leadership was inferior. Pioneering usually looks more glamorous than running the going concern afterward. In any event, the management that was taking over in the 1930's had a very different set of problems to face. Their predecessors worked under conditions of unrestricted competition and in an environment where the overmastering task was to meet an apparently insatiable demand. In the early days, to quote Alfred P. Sloan, "Selling the cars was easy enough; the insistent problem was how to produce." In the depression era precisely the opposite situation prevailed; the automobile industry could produce far more cars than the market was willing to accept.

Moreover, until the coming of the depression the management of the automobile industry had little concern with government other than to urge more funds for better roads. Before the First World War there was also an inclination to press for tariff protection for American cars, but the development of the large export trade of the twenties changed this attitude. Whatever residual support there was for protection vanished after the Smoot-Hawley Tariff of 1930 provoked reprisals in other countries and provided a convincing demonstration that the industry had far more to lose from the closing of its export markets than from the competition of foreign cars in the United States.

The depression and the New Deal brought with them the novel situation of massive intervention by public authority. They also brought labor unrest and an irresistible drive for union organization. The times required a different approach on the part of management from what had been needed previously. Whether the automotive old guard could have adapted to unfamiliar conditions is impossible to determine. Sloan could and did. Ford could not. Most of the others were involved only partially or not at all. It was sheer coincidence that the guard should have been changing at a time of major social and economic upheaval, but perhaps it was better that way.

CHAPTER 8

The Automobile and the New Deal

Because of the key position the automobile had come to occupy in both the economic and the social structure of the United States, it was of necessity deeply involved in the great changes introduced into American life during the period of the New Deal. It was self-evident that the nation's biggest industry and its variety of ancillary enterprises must be restored to health if economic recovery was to be achieved, but there were complicating factors. The automobile industry was a focal point for the Roosevelt administration's ambitious recovery program as expressed in the National Industrial Recovery Act (NIRA). If it worked with the automobile industry it would with others.

In addition, the consequences of the depression in widespread unemployment and wage reductions for those who kept their jobs produced deep-seated labor unrest, which inevitably became channeled into pressure for unionization. This pressure was accentuated when a federal administration came into power committed to the promotion of collective bargaining and strongly sympathetic to the labor side of the bargaining process. The achievement of unionization, however, was complicated not merely by the opposition of the companies but also by interunion rivalries and the fact that the assembly-line worker did not fit the pattern of the predominantly craft-oriented organizations that comprised the American Federation of Labor.

THE AUTOMOBILE CODE

When, to the accompaniment of fanfare, parades, and lavish display of blue eagles, the American economy was urged to organize itself under the code provisions of the NIRA, the automobile industry was in a unique position. Apart from the issue of unionization, which will be considered later, the objectives of the codes in stabilizing production and prices and promoting equitable trade practices did not excite the automobile manufacturers because they believed their industry to be already well enough organized for these purposes. The system of putting a new model on the market each year required that production schedules be geared closely to sales forecasts, so that there was not much a central supervisory authority could do to control production. Prices were administered by the manufacturers, and as far as the low-priced cars were concerned—the bulk of the market—prices still followed Ford's lead at this time. The kind of price competition—uncontrolled price-cutting—which the New Deal wanted to stop was not particularly a problem for the automobile manufacturers. The small independent producers who might have posed such a threat had largely disappeared by 1933, and the few surviving firms had no interest in a form of competition which could only result in everyone's getting hurt. In fact, a formal price structure under an NRA (National Recovery Administration) code was more likely than not to cause trouble, since the other producers could accurately anticipate that Henry Ford would continue his maverick ways and refuse to subscribe to any agreement that would restrict him from doing as he pleased.

Moreover, the industry already had a powerful trade association in the National Automobile Chamber of Commerce, which administered the cross-licensing of patents. It also functioned as a clearinghouse for information on trade practices such as relationships with supplier firms and dealers. These relationships were reasonably uniform throughout the industry and were likewise something the manufacturers preferred to leave undisturbed. The dealers were less well satisfied. The pressure for sales that had been manifest in the late 1920's was greatly intensified by the depression. Both manufacturers and dealers were struggling desperately to hold what they could of a declining market, and in this situation the dealers became acutely aware that the franchise system put control of sales policies and practices, and indeed life-and-death power over the dealer's business, completely in the hands of the manufacturers. As some of them bitterly expressed it, the only right the dealer had under his contract was to buy cars at a discount. The dealers complained of the issuance of new franchises without consideration of the territorial rights of existing distributors, of unrealistic sales quotas, of being forced to take unwanted cars, and of arbitrary cancellation of franchises. The result was an extensive investigation by the Federal Trade Commission, which elicitated much information but produced little in the way of tangible results. No evidence of collusive price-fixing or limiting of production on the part of the manufacturers was found, and although the dealers' grievances were adjudged valid, there was no acceptable legislative remedy. By the time the commission finished its report in 1939, most automobile firms had taken steps to correct the worst abuses, and the revival of business had muted the dealers' complaints.

In any event, in early 1933 there was no urgency in the industry to adopt a code. On the other hand, the administration saw the automotive industry as the critical factor in its recovery program, so that President Roosevelt took a strong personal interest in the formulation of an automobile code and the head of the National Recovery Administration, General Hugh S. Johnson (Old Iron-pants) demanded compliance with standards that did not yet exist. Consequently the leaders of the automobile industry concluded that they had better draft their own code rather than have one imposed on them by governmental fiat.

A committee of the N.A.C.C. was appointed to draft a code, including a representative of the Ford Motor Company. It completed its work late in July, 1933. As adopted, the automobile code included only the vehicle-manufacturing firms and their subsidiaries. Independent parts manufacturers and distributors were excluded. These groups subsequently worked out their own codes, which was probably the most sensible way to handle the problem. Dealer codes, for example, contained provisions against price-cutting on new or used cars, a practice that was far more directly the concern of the dealer than the manufacturer, since the manufacturer got his list price less dealer's discount anyway. At the same time, given the complex interrelationships of the automotive world, separate codes inevitably meant areas of overlap and friction. During its brief and stormy existence the NRA was constantly bedeviled by bickering among automotive code authorities.

The basic automobile code predictably made little change in the industry's trade practices. It sanctioned the already accepted procedure of offering next season's models in the fall, in the hope that there would be two buying periods (fall and spring), a situation that would reduce the highly seasonal character of automobile production. The major code provisions dealt with wages and hours of labor. The standard work week was set at thirty-five hours; a maximum of forty-eight hours was permitted during peak production periods as long as the annual average was held at thirty-five. Minimum wages were set at forty to forty-three cents an hour, depending on locality. The framers of the code were able to claim that these provisions matched and in some instances bettered the standards of the President's Reemployment Agreement, a temporary measure that employers were invited to sign pending approval of their codes. Indeed, most of the employed automobile workers were at least at the minimum wage scale by the time the automobile code was adopted.

Labor relations were another matter. The industry leaders hoped to avoid unionization and would have preferred to disregard Section 7(a) of the NIRA, giving labor the right to organize and bargain collectively through agents of its own choosing. But Section 7(a) was in the law and had to be included in all codes. The industry consequently tried to take the position that the law did not require ("coerce" was the term actually used) labor to organize. The fate of this interpretation will be discussed later.

The automobile code, like most NRA codes, was never very effective. For one thing, Henry Ford ignored it altogether. Under the law the Ford Motor Company was bound by the code provisions whether it signed the document or not, and it did in fact meet code requirements for wages and hours. Technically, however, the company was guilty of non-compliance, and like the other automobile manufacturers, it was vigorously resisting Section 7(a). Yet the government rather than the company backed away from a showdown. Only half-hearted attempts were made to stop governmental purchases of Ford cars, and no attempt whatever was made to challenge Ford's open defiance of the NRA. Henry Ford was still a great folk hero to large numbers of Americans, and neither Franklin D. Roosevelt, for all his popularity, nor General Johnson, for all his bluster, chose to force an open break. The impasse lasted until the entire code system was brought to an abrupt end on May 27, 1935, by the Supreme Court's unanimous decision in the Schechter Chicken Case (*Schechter Poultry Corp.* v. *U.S.*)

LABOR UNREST

The problem of labor discontent would not vanish quite as readily. Before the Great Depression, the record of the automobile industry in the field of labor relations was mixed. During the era of Henry Ford's greatest achievements there had been the five-dollar day and the Sociological Department as evidence of concern for the welfare of the Ford workers. The rest of the industry did not imitate Ford's paternalism but conformed generally to his wage policy, probably because there was no option if Ford's competitors were to keep their best workers. The high wage rates survived; in 1928 the average hourly wage of automobile workers was seventy-five cents, about twenty cents higher than the average for manufacturing industries as a whole.

This figure, it should be noted, applied only to the automobile firms. Wages and working conditions were uniformly poorer in the independent parts manufacturing companies, which were under the pressure of the oligopolistic trend in the industry. The supplier firms, that is, found their market increasingly limited to a few large automobile concerns, most of whom had their own parts-making affiliates and subsidiaries, so that the independent suppliers were competing with their own customers. This situation explains why the manufacturers preferred that the parts makers should have their own NRA code. It also was a prolific source of disagreement and friction when the issues of labor relations eventually came to a head, since one of labor's complaints was that the automobile firms evaded NRA restrictions by passing on to suppliers work that they could just as well have done themselves.

Until the arrival of the New Deal the automotive industry was predominantly open-shop, a state of affairs entirely satisfactory from the point of view of management. However, although the automobile companies supported antiunion organizations like the Detroit Employers' Association, the failure of the automotive workers to organize has to be attributed primarily to other causes. The most important was that assembly-line production created a type of worker who simply could not be fitted into the categories of existing labor-union organization. He was not a craftsman in the accepted sense of the term; neither, on the other hand, was he an unskilled manual laborer. Only about a tenth of the jobs in the automobile industry required more than one year of training, but at the other end of the spectrum only a fourth of the jobs called for no training at all. Even the term semiskilled is too loose for the majority of the automotive workers, since their skills ranged from jobs that could be learned in a few days, or even a few hours, to those that needed several months.

The response of the American Federation of Labor to this novel industrial situation can be described best as one of monumental ineptitude. A few halfhearted attempts at unionization of the automobile industry were made before the First World War and again in the 1920's, but, along with other handicaps, they received negligible support from the federation. The leadership of the AFL was obviously more concerned with protecting the jurisdictional rights of existing craft unions than with developing an organizational structure that would meet the needs of the automobile workers. At the beginning of the century there had been an active union of carriage and wagon makers that had logically tried to extend its operations to the automobile industry, but it ran into implacable hostility from AFL craft unions and was ruined. By 1930 it had degenerated into a minuscule organization whose sole function was to provide a base of operations for Communist organizers.

Yet even the aggressive IWW made no headway whatever in the automobile industry. The automobile workers simply lacked interest. They had grievances, or at least they had grievances pointed out to them. Because of the seasonal nature of automobile production, the high hourly wage rates became less impressive when they were translated into annual income, which is estimated to have averaged between $1,600 and $1,800 during the boom period of the twenties. There was also a growing awareness that assembly-line production had created a new problem in industrial relations; namely, the effect on the individual worker of prolonged monotonous repetition of the same operation. The evidence of considerable emotional as well as physical strain was fairly impressive, but until the stock market crash the people most directly concerned showed little disposition to complain.

The explanation for this apparent apathy lies in the fact that much of the automotive labor force was made up of newcomers to the American industrial scene. More than half the automotive workers in Detroit in 1930 were immigrants or Negroes, drawn to the promised land of the assembly line by the lure of five and six dollars a day for work that could be performed with a minimum of previous skill or training. If they were disillusioned, they were afraid to show it because they were too easily replaceable; and the few who were even aware of the possibility of organization could have seen little hope of relief from that quarter. In any case, the extent of labor dissatisfaction in the automobile industry during the prosperous years of the 1920's is difficult to measure. Seasonal as employment might be, the aggregate earnings undoubtedly represented a greater cash income than most of the assembly-line workers had previously enjoyed, and it may be doubted whether they were as much bothered by monotony and routine as the people who studied them. To most of them a job was just a means of making a living; its dullness would not matter much—certainly not so much as it would to a member of the intellectual class, especially one with an ideological axe to grind.

The arrival of the depression brought a radical change. Employment dropped along with production, and in time wage rates fell off also. The companies did their best to spread out the available work, but the overall effect of this policy was to create a shorter work week and longer and more frequent layoffs, so that average annual income for those who were employed dropped to about $1,000 in 1932. As conditions deteriorated, grievances that had existed previously but had been ignored now tended to become acute. There were complaints, unquestionably well founded, of arbitrariness and favoritism on the part of foremen. Workers became acutely aware that they had no security in their jobs, that there was no recognition of seniority rights.

Unfortunately there was no machinery for handling problems of labor or even discussing them. A strong, well-established, responsible union would have been a godsend at this juncture to both labor and management, but no such thing existed. The automobile workers were left angry, frustrated, unorganized, and leaderless—a made-to-order situation for the Communists who controlled the tiny Auto Workers Union, the relic of the old carriage and wagon makers' organization. On March 7, 1932, this group staged a march of the unemployed to the Ford River Rouge plant, selected because Henry Ford was the personification of American capitalism. The demonstrators clashed with the Dearborn police and four were killed. Harry Bennett himself was involved in the fighting and was injured—lack of physical courage was not one of Bennett's deficiencies—but there is no indication that he or his service force started the trouble. The Communists did that; it was the whole purpose of the march. Bennett in fact seems to have been honestly trying to prevent the violence from spreading, and subsequent investigation cleared the Dearborn police of anything except possible errors of judgment in handling the mob. A second Communist-inspired march on the Rouge a year later was a failure.

By early 1933 there were sporadic strikes in the automotive industry: spontaneous, almost purposeless expressions of discontent, probably a blind reponse to a feeling that with the election of a new president things ought to be changing. Significantly, in view of the acknowledged disparities in working conditions, these strikes broke out in parts factories rather than in the automobile plants, the worst occurring in the Briggs Manufacturing Company of Detroit, which made bodies for Ford. The strike achieved nothing. The depression was at its depth, the Roosevelt administration was an unknown quantity and not yet in office, and the AFL gave no support.

The NRA Period

The arrival of the New Deal and the enactment of the NIRA changed the situation completely. Management's apprehensions about Section 7(a) were matched or exceeded by labor's expectations. In contrast to its earlier indifference, automotive labor was now eager and anxious to be organized. But what did 7(a) mean? Were company unions acceptable as bargaining agents? Was it obligatory for a minority to accept the choice of the majority? These and other questions had to be worked out, and the process generated further conflict, not only between labor and management but within the ranks of labor itself.

The interpreting and administering of Section 7(a) was ultimately the responsibility of the federal government, but this function was exercised through a complex structure of agencies. The following all had a hand in labor relations in the automotive industries while the NIRA was in effect: (1) the Conciliation Service of the United States Department of Labor; (2) the National Labor Board, established to deal with labor problems under the general provisions of the NIRA; (3) the Labor Advisory Board, created to consult on drafting the automobile code; (4) the Compliance Boards of the NRA; and (5) the Automobile Labor Board, created to deal with the specific problems of the automotive industries. It was a typical New Deal arrangement; Roosevelt seems to have believed that administrators worked best under highly competitive conditions.

These assorted agencies had to deal with constant conflict between management and labor and within the ranks of labor. The automobile companies fought Section 7(a) either by trying to organize company-controlled unions or by resisting unionization altogether. The latter policy was followed by the Big Three, all of whom set up espionage systems within their plants to root out union sympathizers. On the labor side, the existence of a friendly national administration and legislative endorsement of collective bargaining, plus the obvious determination of the automobile workers to be organized somehow, finally moved the AFL to action. It was spurred on also by the more aggressive leaders of its own membership—John L. Lewis, Sidney Hillman, David Dubinsky—who felt that this opportunity must not be lost, not only in automobiles but in steel, rubber, and the other great non-unionized industries.

The federation's trumpet, however, still blew somewhat uncertainly. It would not create a union for automotive workers. Instead, it set up a network of "United Automobile Workers Federal Unions," which were locals under strict control of the parent body. Membership was open to automobile workers who could not be assigned to other AFL unions. It was an unsatisfactory provisional arrangement whose primary function was to protect existing jurisdictional rights and in which the people most directly concerned, the automobile workers, had the least to say on matters of policy. It is surprising that comparatively few automotive workers turned to the competing attractions of the Communist AWU and the IWW.

In the circumstances, with feelings running high and no accepted or effective procedure for negotiation or arbitration, industrial conflict was unavoidable. Strikes and walkouts erupted in unending succession, culminating in an angry outbreak at the Electric Auto-Lite Company of Toledo, Ohio, in May, 1934, which required the intervention of the National Guard. As a rule the grievances cited were questions of wage rates, working conditions, hours, discrimination against union members, and allegations of "speed-up" of assembly lines; but always the paramount issue, whether expressly stated or not, was union recognition. On this front some gains were made among the smaller companies, a few very minor advances were registered at General Motors and Chrysler, but not a dent was made on the Ford Motor Company. As far as establishing collective bargaining was concerned, the NIRA appeared to have been an exercise in futility, with responsibility for this ineffective performance distributed among the vagueness of the law, the chaotic disorganization of the machinery for enforcement, the inertia of the AFL, and the determination of the principal companies not to be unionized.

THE RISE OF THE UAW

The whole problem of labor relations, however, was much too important a national issue to permit efforts at a solution to lapse, or to be dissipated in administrative confusion and fruitless bickering. Likewise, it was politically and economically embarrassing to have constant disturbance in the industry which the administration hoped would lead the way to recovery, preferably along the route chosen by the New Deal. Thus it came about that in the year that saw the end of the NIRA, other developments of considerably longer-range significance were in train. First was the passage of the Wagner-Connery, or National Labor Relations Act, designed to establish conclusively the right of collective bargaining and provide for more rigorous enforcement than had been achieved under the NIRA.

At about the same time the AFL reluctantly issued a charter to the International Union, United Automobile Workers of America. The federation had little choice if it was to hold the automobile workers at all, since many of them were withdrawing in disgust from their "federal union" locals and were establishing independent organizations of their own. The UAW's orientation was definitely toward the industrial union principle, so that when the Committee for Industrial Organization was formed by the Lewis-Hillman-Dubinsky group and soon afterwards separated from the AFL, the UAW went with it. Thereupon most of the independent automotive unions joined it.

The task facing the new organization was great. The AFL federal locals contributed about 23,000 members and the independent unions probably twice as many—in all, perhaps 15 per cent of the approximately 400,000 workers in the automobile and parts industries. Not more than 1,200 members altogether were in Big Three plants. It was hoped that the new National Labor Relations Act would strengthen the hand of the union, but at that juncture the likelihood of the Wagner Act's being sustained by the Supreme Court was dubious and employers were generally ignoring it.

The AFL attempted to provide the leadership for the new organization, but this phase of the UAW's existence was brief. Control of the union was quickly taken by aggressive-minded newcomers to labor organization, such as Homer Martin, a former Baptist minister with a propensity to let his enthusiasms run away with his judgment, and the Reuther brothers, Walter (b. 1907) and Victor (b. 1912), young men in their twenties but ambitious and eager for power. Some of the top figures of the UAW were suspected of being markedly left-wing in their political and economic views, and some undoubtedly were, although the union was never Communist-dominated as were some of the others formed at this time.

Its leaders, however, were prepared to take drastic steps in the face of the stubborn resistance of the Big Three automobile firms. They imported the newly devised European technique of the sit-down strike, in which the labor force stopped work but remained in the plant, so that strikebreakers could not be brought in to keep production going. At the end of 1936 most of General Motors was closed down in this way, and despite court orders and occasional attempts at eviction, the strikers held out. Governor Frank Murphy of Michigan, later a justice of the United States Supreme Court, refused to use force to restore the plants to their owners, preferring to mediate in the hope of avoiding bloodshed. In the end the company gave way. On February 11, 1937, a landmark date in the history of the automobile industry, General Motors accepted the United Automobile Workers as the bargaining agent for its members. Two months later, after a similar experience with sit-down strikes, Chrysler capitulated also. The sit-down strikes were not, of course, the whole story behind the UAW's success. The sweeping victory of Roosevelt and the New Deal in the election of 1936 undoubtedly predisposed Alfred P. Sloan and Walter Chrysler to resign themselves to unionization as inevitable.

Henry Ford was another matter. Apparently convinced that his employees were antiunion and that public opinion would support him, Ford refused to deal with any union, and to Edsel's consternation, put labor relations completely into the hands of Harry Bennett. What this policy meant was dramatically demonstrated in the notorious "battle of the overpass" on May 26, 1937. On that date Walter Reuther and several other UAW organizers were brutally beaten by members of Bennett's Service Department while they were distributing handbills on an overpass leading into the River Rouge plant. Company spokesmen, including the unctuous W. J. Cameron, former editor of the *Dearborn Independent* and at the time spokesman on the Ford Sunday Evening Hour, a radio program of classical music, attributed the attack to "loyal" workers who resented this outside interference. The explanation was unconvincing. Not even the most loyal assembly-line workers habitually carried blackjacks and brass knuckles.

Since the Supreme Court had upheld the constitutionality of the Wagner Act (*NLRB* v. *Jones and Laughlin Steel Co.*) a month before the battle of the overpass, the Ford Motor Company was clearly in violation of the law when it refused to permit its workers to be organized, or even to hold an election to determine if they wanted to be organized. Yet Ford was able to hold out for another four years because the UAW chose this time to plunge into a bitter internal struggle. The immediate issue was dissatisfaction with Martin's leadership. He was accused of being too complacent about Communist infiltration into the union, and he blundered badly by trying to deal on a personal basis with Harry Bennett. Essentially the revolt against Martin was a contest for power among rival leaders, and Martin's defeat was important chiefly because it cleared the way for the subsequent rise of Walter Reuther.

The break at Ford came with dramatic swiftness early in 1941. The UAW, reunited and strengthened, was successfully recruiting members in spite of Bennett's terrorism, and complaints against the company had passed through the ponderous machinery of the National Labor Relations Board and been upheld by the courts. To bolster the union was the fact that Ford was falling behind in competition for defense contracts because of his labor record. On April 1, the discharge of several union members, a familiar enough occurrence during the previous four years, touched off a spontaneous walkout by all but a handful of the company's labor force. Appeals by Henry Ford for protection against violence met with an icy reception from both federal and state authorities; actually the violence was limited to fist fights between pickets and non-strikers trying to leave the Rouge factory, plus occasional and understandable grasping of opportunities to settle old grievances against Harry Bennett's boys.

Henry Ford and Bennett wanted to resist, but Edsel threw his weight on the side of negotiation. The strike was halted, and an

NLRB election produced an overwhelming majority for the UAW. It was a bitter disappointment for the elder Ford, who still cherished the illusion that his workers were contented and anti-union. He spoke about shutting down the entire operation and letting the government take over the Ford factories if it so desired, but this was simply petulance from an ailing old man. At any rate, his wife talked him out of it.

So the union conquest of the automobile industry was completed after almost ten years of conflict. The effect was not to solve all the problems of automotive labor, but at least some of the worst abuses that had crept in were ameliorated. There was recognition of seniority rights and restriction on the arbitrary speed-up of assembly lines. On the other hand, nothing much could be done by a labor organization about the seasonal nature of automobile manufacturing. Whether a wage system could be worked out that would offset the irregularity of employment was a problem for the future. For the present the UAW had gained its first requisite—recognition—and the rising war boom permitted, in fact required, the deferment of less urgent issues.

THE TURNPIKE COMES BACK

The influence of the New Deal extended beyond the problems connected with the manufacture of motor vehicles. It is an interesting phenomenon of response to depression that the 1930's should have seen more rather than less activity in highway construction than did the prosperous decade of the twenties. The reason is simple enough. Road-building was an obvious and acceptable method of using public funds to combat unemployment. In Germany the Hitler regime was doing the same thing by promoting a national system of express highways, the *autobahnen*, except that the Germans had an element of military planning in locating their roads that was not present in the American program.

As a matter of fact, what existed in the United States was not, properly speaking, a program at all. It was an assortment of

unrelated activities, more concerned with providing jobs and prim-
ing the economic pump than with creating an integrated highway
system. The Civilian Conservation Corps built access and fire roads
in remote areas, the Public Works Administration financed highway construction and other substantial projects such as new bridges
and the elimination of grade crossings, and the Works Progress
Administration engaged extensively in local road improvement.
The Tennessee Valley Authority also did a good deal of highway
building and relocation in its area. Meanwhile the regular federal
aid program under the Highway Act of 1921 continued, temporarily reduced early in the decade as an economy measure but
restored when the emphasis switched to recovery.

This multiplicity of agencies, plus the work of state and local
authorities, makes it difficult to estimate just how much road
construction and improvement was done during the New Deal era,
but it does not mean that there was very much unnecessary
duplication of effort. The United States had slightly over three
million miles of roads, exclusive of city streets, and somewhat less
than half was rated as improved, that is, with as much as a gravel
surface capable of all-weather use. There was plenty to be done,
and the activities of the alphabetical agencies had the merit of
putting needed effort into the betterment of the byways as well as
the highways. The significant change of policy was reflected in the
expanded role of the federal government. Where federal contributions had previously accounted for about 10 per cent of the total
national expenditure on roads, during the New Deal the federal
share rose to between 40 and 50 per cent. To a large extent this
increase was a matter of necessity, since state and local governments
came through the depression with badly depleted finances, but once
a grant-in-aid policy has been expanded, it seldom shrinks again.

Most of this highway activity, however, was palliative not only
for economic purposes but also as a means of providing for the
future of automotive transportation. What was needed most was
not the construction of additional mileage of roads of existing types
but new roads designed and built for high-speed motor vehicles,

with traffic flow channeled to provide for the minimum of interruption and to eliminate conflicting streams of traffic. The direction
to be taken was clearly indicated by the Italian *autostrade,* begun in
the 1920's, and the German *autobahnen,* as well as by the parkway
developments around some American cities. The main roads of the
future would be multilane express highways, with limited access,
no cross traffic at grade, and separate roadways for traffic moving in
opposite directions.

The heavy cost of this kind of construction was a severe deter-
rent, but it was bound to come. The Commonwealth of Pennsylvania led the way by converting a long-abandoned railroad right-
of-way between Harrisburg and Pittsburgh into the nucleus of an
express highway across the state. The projected railroad dated back
to a power struggle of the 1870's between the New York Central
and the Pennsylvania. It was graded and ready for tracks to be laid
when the combatants came to terms, and there it lay for sixty years,
complete with tunnels (nine of them, of which seven were used by
the Turnpike) through the Alleghenies. The state, seeking to
combat unemployment, took advantage of this ready-made route;
and to finance the project, Pennsylvania returned to the tollroad
system of an earlier era. It established a Turnpike Authority to
build and operate the highway, with power to issue bonds and to
meet its expenses by collecting tolls. The Pennsylvania Turnpike
was opened to traffic between Harrisburg and Pittsburgh in October, 1940. It eventually stretched 360 miles across the state without
an intersecting road or a traffic light; it had no grade greater than 3
per cent; and its curves were designed for speeds as high as ninety
miles an hour. It proved to be successful both financially and as a
carrier of high-speed traffic.

As could be expected of this first express highway, experience in
its use revealed unanticipated defects in design. Median strips
needed to be wider and divider fences stronger. The comparative
absence of curves proved to be a quite unexpected hazard, in that
continuous high-speed driving on long straight stretches of road
produced the condition known as highway hypnosis. Nevertheless

the Pennsylvania Turnpike was clearly the prototype for the highway of the future, and other states prepared to follow Pennsylvania's example. The coming of the Second World War, however, interrupted almost all building of new roads, so that these plans had to be deferred.

Motor Carrier Regulation

Finally, the New Deal succeeded in bringing interstate highway traffic under some degree of federal regulation. This step was also depression-inspired, although it had been advocated for some time by the railroads, which were losing business to the combination of more and better motor vehicles operating on more and better highways. The onset of depression won over the larger trucking concerns to a policy of regulation also. What happened was that thousands of people, many of them truck drivers who had lost their jobs, went into business as highway carriers with equipment usually consisting of a secondhand truck bought on credit. The result was merciless and uncontrolled rate-cutting. These individual operators were satisfied if they could meet day-to-day expenses, and they seldom bothered with luxuries like insurance.

To the desirability of reducing the chaos on the highways was added the hope of alleviating the plight of the railroads, whose overall financial position during the depression was so desperate that even the relief that might be afforded by eliminating a handful of fly-by-night truck operators was not to be disregarded. There was some suggestion that co-ordinated systems of transportation—rail, road, air, water, pipeline—might be the most promising remedy, but in the end the established policy of regulating each medium of transportation separately was retained.

The regulation of commercial interstate highway traffic was embodied in the Motor Carrier Act of 1935, placing certain categories of highway carriers under the jurisdiction of the Interstate Commerce Commission. Vehicles carrying farm products were exempted from the operation of the law, and private trucks, owned by firms not engaged in the business of transportation and used exclusively to carry freight for their owners, were subject only to ICC regulations regarding safety, marking of vehicles, and accounting. Effectively the commission's authority was restricted to common and contract carriers engaged in interstate commerce. (Common carriers are trucks and buses serving the general public; contract carriers operate only under specific agreements or charters.) For these the commission was empowered to issue "certificates of convenience and necessity," giving the right to run on specified routes. Rates were to be "fair and reasonable"; in general, with these particular carriers the ICC had supervisory powers with respect to rates, records, security issues, and so forth similar to those it possessed over the railroads.

The principal immediate effect of the Motor Carrier Act was to eliminate the shoestring operator insofar as he was engaged in interstate commerce. But if the sponsors of the Act expected a comprehensive control of highway carriers, they were disappointed. The great bulk of highway traffic has remained outside the scope of the Motor Carrier Act. Even in commercial transport, only about a third of the interstate business is subject to the route- and rate-making authority of the ICC.

CHAPTER 9

Arsenal of Democracy

It was fortunate for the nation that a reasonable degree of internal peace, if not harmony, had been established in the automobile industry before the full force of the Second World War struck, because this industry and its affiliates constituted the country's largest single resource in manufacturing capacity. The nature of this need was at best vaguely appreciated before the war came. The National Defense Act of 1920, attempting to capitalize on wartime experience, had authorized the drafting of detailed plans for industrial mobilization, but in point of fact very little had been done. The military services spent most of the interwar period in a state of near poverty, and detailed studies of the possible conversion of industrial concerns that had little interest in military production was an activity that could be deferred.

For industry there was no particular incentive to take any independent initiative. The military market was scarcely adequate to support the firms that were organized for it, and in the prevailing mood of the period they had to bear the stigma of being popularly considered "merchants of death." There was therefore no reason for automobile manufacturers, with their enormous civilian market, to be concerned about the problems of making military materials. Until the outbreak of hostilities none did, except to the extent that General Motors had its interests in aviation. The government was still more complacent. As far as the administration anticipated the problem, it assumed that given the continuation of depression conditions, there was ample excess plant capacity and labor, so that wartime needs could be met without disturbing the normal course of the economy. Thus, when war came, both government and industry had to learn their production roles from scratch.

THE EARLY PREPARATIONS

When the German blitzkrieg in the spring of 1940 brought a belated awareness that the threat of a Nazi conquest of Europe was far greater than most people had realized, the United States government began to press more energetically for military preparations. Except in the matter of aircraft production, which will be discussed later, industrial mobilization was still half-hearted. In May, 1940, it was put under the supervision of an advisory committee of the Council of National Defense, and it was a clear indication of where the bulk of the expected production was to come from that the chairman of this committee was William S. Knudsen, president of General Motors. At this time, however, Knudsen had no authority. He could persuade but he could not compel.

After a year's experience had demonstrated the ineffectiveness of this approach to industrial mobilization, President Roosevelt created an Office of Production Management, with Knudsen and Sidney Hillman, president of the Amalgamated Clothing Workers, as joint heads. It was a fantastic administrative arrangement; the only reason it worked at all was that both Knudsen and Hillman were responsible, patriotic individuals. Not until after the United States itself became a belligerent was there an effective organization to control production. In the meantime, getting anything at all accomplished depended entirely on voluntary co-operation on the part of industry, and fortunately this co-operation was forthcoming. Progress was slow and halting for many months; first of all it was necessary to determine what had to be done, and after that to figure out how to do it. There was also the fact that except for a few leaders of government and industry who were aware of the true seriousness of the war situation, there was no great sense of urgency in the twilight era before Pearl Harbor. Even among those who were most committed to aiding the anti-Axis nations, there was a tendency to assume that American "know-how" and productive capacity would produce the necessary rabbits out of an as yet non-existent hat. As it turned out they were ultimately right, except that instead of sleight-of-hand, the trick was performed by a great deal of unappreciated hard work.

The manufacture of motor vehicles continued very much on a "business-as-usual" basis through 1940 and 1941, reaching a total of 4,400,000 and 4,800,000 units in each of these years respectively. This was done despite growing shortages of materials, and at Knudsen's request the industry suspended major model changes so that the resources of the machine tool industry could be devoted to military needs. At the time, or rather on the basis of second-guessing shortly afterward, the automobile manufacturers were criticized for using as much as they did of materials that were becoming scarce and might otherwise have gone into armaments. It seems unfair to hold the industry responsible for the government's failure to formulate a clear-cut production policy or to establish and enforce a rigorous system of priorities. The automobile men must have developed some sympathy for their counterparts in aviation, who until the outbreak of war were excoriated for making military aircraft at all, and then were equally bitterly assailed from the same sources for not making them fast enough.

Yet despite the handicaps there was progress. It was of course a simple matter to make trucks for military as well as civilian use, and before the end of the war more than two and a half million would be turned out. The manufacture of trucks was less glamorous than some of the other war activities engaged in by the automobile industry, but in its contribution to the final victory it probably rates as high as any. The "Red Ball Express," which kept the Allied armies in France supplied after the breakout from the Normandy beachhead, was merely the most spectacular of many occasions on which truck transportation kept advances moving when by ordinary logistic calculations they should have been brought to a halt because of the destruction of rail lines.

There was likewise no major production problem involved in manufacturing the jeep, which was perhaps the most distinctive contribution of the American automobile industry to the war effort and would survive the war to find widespread adoption as a peacetime vehicle. The design of the jeep was the work of Captain Robert G. Howie of the United States Army, working in co-operation with Colonel Arthur W. S. Herrington, who was mentioned previously as cofounder of the Marmon-Herrington Company for the purpose of developing all-wheel-drive vehicles. A prototype was put on display at Fort Benning, Georgia, in March, 1940. Initially the jeep was to be built by the American Bantam Car Company, a firm that had been trying without much success to put a small car on the American market. Within a short time, however, the demand outran this company's production capacity, and the assistance of Willys-Overland and Ford was invoked. With Willys as the principal producer, some 660,000 jeeps were built for war use.

It was also logical that the War Department should turn to the automobile industry for help in building tanks. This was a more complicated production problem than making military trucks or jeeps. Tanks could not be built on automobile assembly lines; they required the construction of new factories, run by men who for the most part had never seen a tank before. The first automobile company to be approached on tank manufacture was Chrysler. It undertook the task in June, 1940, beginning by sending a selected team to the Rock Island Arsenal to examine a tank and take 186 pounds of blueprints back to Detroit. Ground was broken for a new plant in September, and regular production was achieved in the following April. This was just the start; other automobile manufacturers were rapidly drawn in, although Chrysler remained the principal builder of tanks.

A tank was at least a motorized vehicle. Simultaneously the automotive industry was turning its skills and techniques to completely novel and unfamiliar products; artillery and shells, gun mountings, machine guns, fire-control systems, small-arms ammunition, fuses—all the complex equipment of twentieth-century war. The scope of this diversity can be gauged by the fact that of General Motors' eventual $12 billion worth of military production, two-thirds was in items the company had never made before. For the time being however, in 1940 and 1941, most of the effort had to go into planning and preparation, somewhat to the disappointment of an impatient public, which had come to expect miracles from the automobile manufacturers and had no idea of the unavoidable delays incurred in starting from nothing to design and build weapons of war.

THE AUTOMOBILE INDUSTRY AND AIRCRAFT PRODUCTION

Among the wartime activities of the automobile industry, the one that was most highly publicized and drew both the most lavish praise and the sharpest criticism, was the industry's participation in the quantity manufacture of airplanes. Of all the knotty problems to be solved in the mobilizing of industry, this was beyond all question the knottiest. Because of a superficial resemblance between the power plants of the automobile and the airplane, the two industries were widely regarded as related enterprises, but in their techniques of production they were about as far apart as they could be.

Aircraft manufacturing was not and could not have been a mass-production operation. Its highest peacetime output was some five thousand units in 1939; of these more than half were small private planes, representing about one-fifth of the year's production measured in dollar value or airframe weight. The airframe and aircraft engine builders were accustomed to working with small lots, a much higher degree of precision than was required in motor vehicles, and frequent changes in design, whereas the automobile manufacturers changed their models once a year and then concentrated on turning out thousands upon thousands of identical units.

Yet there was a complacent assumption on the part of public opinion, government officials, and even a large segment of the automobile industry that the techniques and facilities that poured out motor-vehicle engines and chassis could easily be switched to aircraft engines and airframes. The experience of the First World War was misunderstood and misleading. There was, for example, a reasonably close relationship between an automobile engine and the 400-horsepower, in-line, twelve-cylinder Liberty of 1918; the same could not be said for the 2,000-horsepower, eighteen-cylinder, air-cooled radial engine of 1940.

Nevertheless the crisis of 1940 made it abundantly clear that the two industries must join forces to build airplanes—more airplanes than anybody had hitherto dreamed of. President Roosevelt picked a figure out of the air and called for 50,000 (the best guess is that he simply took Woodrow Wilson's figure of 25,000 and doubled it). The precise number to be aimed at was unimportant. What mattered was that, although the democratic powers were short of every kind of military material in that desperate summer of 1940, their most acute and vital shortage was aircraft, and if this one was to be remedied in time to do any good, the American automotive industry would have to carry a major share of the load.

The automotive people were perfectly willing to assume the burden and complacently certain of their ability to carry it. Henry Ford blandly announced that there would be no difficulty in turning out a thousand planes of standard design a day if he was left to do it unimpeded by government requirements or labor unions. It was no doubt possible, except that to concentrate on a standard design for aircraft to attain maximum production would have been a good way to lose the war. On their side the aircraft manufacturers were willing to accept assistance, with reservations. First, they were skeptical about the applicability of automobile production methods to their business. Second, while they were accustomed to a feast-or-famine existence, they had no desire to accentuate the inevitable postwar famine by having automotive firms get into aviation and stay there. Automotive companies might be admirable as subcontractors, but that was as far as they should be encouraged to go.

These difficulties caused less trouble than might have been expected, essentially because both industries were staffed by men who realized that there was a vital job to be done. The automobile manufacturers were able to convince their aeronautical associates that they were willing to help build airplanes as a patriotic duty but that their real preference was for building motor vehicles as a long-range occupation. There was a certain amount of patronizing about each other's techniques of production, but that evaporated when experience in co-operation demonstrated that each could profitably learn from the other.

Not that everything went smoothly; that was hardly to be expected under conditions where big and unfamiliar tasks were being undertaken in an atmosphere of emergency. The first appeal to the automobile manufacturers was for help in making aircraft engines, including an arrangement with the Ford Motor Company in June, 1940, to build Rolls-Royce engines for the Royal Air Force. Edsel Ford and Charles E. Sorensen approved, but before anything could be accomplished, Henry Ford's isolationist pacifism flared up and he announced that his company would have nothing to do with building engines for Britain. No appeal would move him, and the Rolls-Royce engines were eventually made by Packard. Later in the year, however, Ford joined with General Motors in a contract to build Pratt and Whitney engines.

By the fall of 1940 it had become evident that automotive resources would have to be employed in the quantity production of fuselages, wing sections, and every other kind of airplane part as well as engines. Military missions to Britain brought back the information that production estimates for two- and four-motored bombers, the most difficult types to fabricate, must be revised sharply upward and production time drastically reduced. The attainment of these goals required the fullest possible co-operation of all participants, and in response to an appeal from William S.

Knudsen, the Automobile Manufacturers Association (formerly the National Automobile Chamber of Commerce) sponsored the Automotive Committee for Air Defense. This organization formally came into existence on October 30, 1940, and terminated its work at the end of March, 1941.

What it did can best be summarized in its concluding report to Major James H. Doolittle of the Army Air Corps, who at this juncture was described as "the man who was trying to promote a peacetime wedding of the aircraft and automobile industries without benefit of a shotgun." In its six months of existence the ACAD reported that it had:

1. Conducted an educational exhibit of aircraft components visited by 2,067 representatives of 1,018 companies.

2. Assisted in placing $1 million worth of orders in the Detroit area for machine shop and tool-and-die work to assist the aircraft manufacturers.

3. Assisted the Air Corps to place "educational orders" for aircraft parts to determine if the firm in question could do the work.

4. Co-ordinated a program whereby Ford would manufacture assemblies for the four-motored Consolidated B-24 "Liberator" bomber; General Motors for the North American twin-engined B-25; and Chrysler, Hudson, and Goodyear Tire and Rubber for the Martin B-26. The plan was that the final assembly should be done by the aircraft companies in new plants to be built by the government, with 75 per cent of the total work being done by the automotive firms.

This program was still in its preliminary stages when the bombs dropped on Pearl Harbor, but at least a start had been made. When war came to America, precious time had been saved—just barely enough if we consider the critically thin margin by which the Axis powers were held in 1942. The aircraft program was able to expand so that President Roosevelt's apparently visionary request was almost met. Output for 1942 was 47,000 aircraft of all types; the 50,000 quota would have been reached if emphasis had not shifted to big bombers. Subsequently this total would be surpassed.

It was not done without delays and disappointments. The outstanding example was the Ford Motor Company's venture into the manufacture of B-24 bombers. For this a vast factory was begun in 1941 at Willow Run in Ypsilanti, Michigan, under the general supervision of Charles E. Sorensen and with ambitious plans for using mass-production techniques on a scale never previously attempted in aircraft manufacturing. These plans caused prolonged disagreement between Consolidated and Ford engineers, and although the Consolidated people eventually adopted some of the Ford proposals in their own plants, they were antagonized by Sorensen's obvious attitude that they were ignorant when it came to production. Moreover, along with the unavoidable problems of shortages of materials and trained labor, the Willow Run operation became entangled in the internecine troubles of the Ford Motor Company: the power struggle between Sorensen and Bennett, the elder Ford's unpredictable interference, and the company's still unsatisfactory labor relations. As late as September, 1943, the Air Force was seriously considering asking the government to take charge of "Will-It-Run."

This solution would have been gratifying to a group of left-wing spokesmen both in and out of the government, who fundamentally wanted to see all war production nationalized. They had been identified with the so-called "Reuther Plan," a proposal made by Walter Reuther late in 1940 whereby idle automotive plants would be devoted to aircraft manufacturing under a joint management arrangement including the government, the automobile companies, and the UAW. The idea found little general support and gradually withered. Its sympathizers, however, continued to hope that the exigencies of war would provide a wedge for nationalization, and they would have liked nothing better than to begin with the Ford Motor Company, since Henry Ford was of course anathema to those of socialist sympathies.

As it happened, by late 1943 Willow Run was over the hump. In the following year the plant was pushing out Liberators at the rate of four and five hundred a month. It was at last a triumph of the mass-production technique, although it seems a pity that all this effort should have been expended on an airplane like the B-24, which Air Force pilots found hard to handle and which was obsolescent by the time Ford got it into full production. However, the decision on what to build was the Air Force's, not Ford's, and it undoubtedly made sense to concentrate on what was available.

The principal casualty of Willow Run was Sorensen. To the extent that he insisted on doing things his way, he contributed to the delay in getting into production, but it was unfair to blame him for troubles that were due to the war itself, and his methods were vindicated in the end. But too much had been expected too soon. Someone had to be the scapegoat, and "Cast-Iron Charlie," his hold on Henry Ford's confidence undermined by Harry Bennett, was it. He had served Henry Ford for forty years as an able, hard-driving, ruthless, and cordially disliked production man, a longer tenure than any other official in the history of the company; now he was tossed aside as casually as any discharged assembly-line worker. He became president of Willys-Overland briefly and then went into retirement.

TOTAL WAR

The aftermath of Pearl Harbor brought with it the startling realization that automotive transportation in the United States was now subject to drastic limitations. For the duration of the war the American automobile owner would no longer be able to indulge his well-established freedom to get into his car at any time and go wherever he chose. It was not just that all production of motor vehicles was stopped early in 1942 in order to conserve steel and other vital materials for war purposes, so that if the family car wore out, the old simple procedure of turning it in for a new (or newer) model could no longer be followed. There were other troubles to be faced as well.

To begin with, the Japanese invasion of Malaya and the Netherlands Indies abruptly cut off almost the entire supply of natural rubber. This possibility had been anticipated, but with the prevailing tendency (pre–Pearl Harbor) to underestimate the Japanese, it had not been taken very seriously. A little stockpiling had been done, but not much, and facilities for making synthetic rubber were still in the pilot stage. There was also some effort to revive rubber growing in Brazil, which had once produced the bulk of the world's raw rubber, but no relief could be expected immediately from this source. The government was compelled to prohibit all non-military use of rubber, so that even if the family car stood up mechanically, it faced the prospect of being immobilized if its tires wore out. A very distinguished special committee (Bernard Baruch, Karl T. Compton, and James B. Conant) urged rigorous measures to conserve rubber and pointed out that the nation's greatest reserve of the product was the tires on its 35,000,000 motor vehicles.

Hard on the heels of the rubber crisis came a shortage of petroleum products in the northeastern states. In this instance the sources of supply were untouched, but submarine depredations along the Atlantic seaboard and in the Gulf of Mexico during the first half of 1942 caused a wholesale destruction of the tankers that normally carried the gasoline and oil to the densely populated, heavily industrialized Northeast. The first claim on tanker tonnage had to be for military needs; after these had been met there was not enough left to provide for the ordinary civilian demand. The railroads performed heroically, but they were already overburdened, and although pipeline construction was pressed, shortages of labor and materials made it evident that relief from this quarter was far in the future.

Yet automobile transportation had to be kept going. It was not just that many of the normal activities of American life had become dependent on the motor vehicle; the war effort itself would be seriously retarded if people were unable to use their cars. The new defense plants and military bases that were springing up were frequently located where there was neither housing nor public transportation. There were valid reasons for picking these sites, and it had never occurred to anyone that people might be unable to come and go by car as usual.

The government's first response to this situation was to establish a national speed limit of forty miles an hour in May, 1942, subsequently reduced to thirty-five. The primary purpose of this measure was to conserve tires. Six months later, a year after the nation had gone to war, a nationwide system of gasoline rationing was adopted. The gasoline shortage remained localized in the Northeast, but it was considered undesirable to discriminate against one section of the country in imposing rationing. In any event the purpose was not only to conserve gasoline but to curtail needless use of automobiles in order to save both vehicles and tires. At the height of gasoline rationing the basic allotment, for pleasure driving only, was two gallons a week; supplemental allowances were made for various necessary uses of cars. In particular, special allowances were given to encourage the formation of car pools by people who had to drive to and from work. The total number of gasoline ration books issued exceeded 25,000,000. There were regrettably widespread abuses of the system, but it worked well enough to keep essential highway traffic moving for the duration of the war.

Upon entry of the United States into the war the automobile industry's defense production activities greatly increased. No longer was there any conflict between the civilian and the military market or any uncertainty of direction and purpose. Instead, an industry with a deep-rooted tradition of free and vigorous competition voluntarily pooled its resources to meet the challenge. Three weeks after the attack on Pearl Harbor the Automobile Manufacturers Association sponsored the formation of the Automotive Council for War Production, for the purpose of facilitating the utilization of the full resources of the automotive industry in the prosecution of the war. Alvan Macauley (1872–1952) president of both the AMA and the Packard Motor Company, became chairman of the ACWP, and another AMA official, George Romney (b. 1907) then, was appointed managing director. Romney, that is, was the executive officer responsible for seeing that the council's functions were carried out.

The council's operations provide the best and indeed the only survey of the automobile industry's multifarious war activities that is at once comprehensive and concise. It functioned through twelve divisions. Three were for industrywide service:

1. Machine Tool and Equipment Service, which listed all machine tools in automotive plants (the total exceeded 350,000) and arranged for interchange so that there would be maximum use of every machine.

2. Tooling Information Service, which performed a similar function for all types of equipment available for making gauges, tools, dies, and jigs.

3. Contract Information Service, which expedited subcontracting.

The nine product divisions reveal the scope of the industry's participation in war production. They were: (1) Aircraft Engines; (2) Airframes; (3) Ammunition Components; (4) Artillery; (5) Small Arms; (6) Marine Equipment; (7) Military Vehicles; (8) Propellers; and (9) Tanks and Tank Parts.

The most useful feature of the automotive industry's wartime performance was not so much the scale on which it could operate, important as that was, as the ability of the automobile men to apply to military equipment the ingenuity in production techniques that had been so spectacularly successful in the making of motor vehicles. An unending list of such achievements could be compiled; the following are samples taken from the reports of the ACWP.

A passenger car producer, getting an anti-aircraft gun of foreign design into production seven months after receipt of the order, cut four months from the time required by the company that invented the gun— time and cost were saved when the military endorsed the company's suggestion that the barrel could be broached instead of processed by traditional rifling methods. This cut the manufacturing time for this part to fifteen minutes from three and one-half hours.

Ingenuity on the part of automotive engineers [engaged in tank manufacture] was outstanding. One company, for example, adopted a flame-cutting process to form the steel sprockets which transfer the engine's power to the caterpillar track. This method allowed twelve sprockets to be turned out every six minutes. About eight hours were formerly required to make only one.

To cut down on welding operations, one company adapted huge presses —formerly used to stamp out automobile body panels—to the forming of armor plate. These presses eliminated sixty-four inches of welding in two places on the tank hull.

On an aircraft wing-panel operation, use of automotive-type machines and tools saved 75 per cent of the time previously required and cut the cost of the wing by $1,000.

Aircraft engine parts, formerly ground one at a time by hand, were grouped into special jigs and automatically ground out fourteen at a time.

It is fair to point out, and it does not detract from the achievement, that these methods could have been employed just as well by the armament industries if they had been engaged in quantity production, but until 1940 they were not. The fact remains that when the need came, the automobile industry was the country's greatest reservoir of "know-how" and skill in the technique of making, accurately and reliably, the largest possible number of items in the shortest possible time. Its record is shown in the accompanying table, which is given in full because it shows more

TABLE 2
PRODUCTION TOTALS, SECOND WORLD WAR

The following list of products produced by motor vehicle, body, parts and accessories companies, is as comprehensive a tabulation of the automotive industry's production for World War II as has been possible to obtain. Compiled in 1947, it is incomplete because it does not embrace all of the end products made by automobile, body, and parts factories, nor does it take into account the huge volume of components, such as vehicle and aircraft sub-assemblies and parts.

4,131,000 Engines

Aircraft	455,522
Marine	168,776
Tank	257,117
Military Trucks	3,250,000

5,947,000 Guns

Carbines and Rifles	3,388,897
Machine Guns	2,276,204
Anti-Aircraft	156,313
Other Guns	125,527

2,812,000 Tanks and Trucks

Tanks....................................	49,058
Amphibian Tanks..........................	5,115
Gun Carriages (Tank Type).................	24,147
Gun Carriages, Other; and Armored Cars....	126,839
Military Trucks (1940–46).................	2,600,687

27,000 Complete Aircraft

Airplanes...............................	22,160
Helicopters.............................	219
Gliders.................................	4,290

Other Items

Trailers................................	529,647
Aircraft Propellors.....................	255,519
Jettison Fuel Tanks.....................	981,358
Small Arms Ammunition...................	12,500,000,000
Shells..................................	245,300,000
Shot....................................	1,800,000
Bombs...................................	5,150,000
Anti-Sub Ammunition.....................	780,000
Rockets.................................	2,850,000
Torpedoes...............................	5,289
Mines...................................	2,480,000
Buzz Bombs..............................	1,292
Atomic Bomb Equipment...................	—
Rocket Motors...........................	1,177,000
Fuses...................................	274,000,000
Cartridge Cases.........................	315,000,000
Containers, Shell, etc..................	7,788,000
Ammunition Boxes........................	2,080,000
Rifle Clips.............................	58,500,000
Ammunition Belt Link....................	2,620,000,000
Link Loading Machines...................	64,000
Mine Parachutes.........................	55,000
Mine Anchors............................	28,000
Ammunition Hoists.......................	415
Shell Extractors........................	1,228,000
Drop Boxes..............................	28,000
Sand Bags...............................	1,000,000
Squad Tents.............................	11,000
Comforters..............................	390,000
Helmets.................................	20,870,000
Helmet Liners...........................	10,000
Identification Discs....................	50,000
Buckles.................................	150,000,000
Field Ranges............................	62,200
Cook and Stock Pots.....................	76,000
Air Raid Sirens.........................	347
Airplane Landing Mats, sq. ft...........	50,136,000
Heat Exchangers.........................	304,577
Fire Pumpers............................	39,539
Fire Extinguisher Pumps.................	2,196,000
Fire Extinguishers......................	252,000

Searchlights	97,216
Binoculars	207,400
Periscopes	16,500
Indirect Vision Devices	648,400
Radios	118,000
Radar Computers	2,600
Wire Reels	4,753,000
Marine Tractors	8,418
Motor Tugs	3,025
Life Rafts and Floats	13,000
Pontoons	9,002
Gas Cylinders	1,460,000
Water and Gas Cans	4,313,000
Submarine Nets (miles)	100
Gyro Compasses	5,500
Gyroscopes	300,000
Climb Indicators	5,400
Electric Motors	5,059,000

Automotive Industry Percentage of Total War Output

Complete Airplanes	10%
Machine Guns	47%
Carbines	56%
Tanks	57%
Armored Cars	100%
Scout Cars and Carriers	92%
Torpedoes	10%
Land Mines	10%
Marine Mines	3%
Army Helmets	85%
Aircraft Bombs	87%

SOURCE: *Freedom's Arsenal: The Story of the Automotive Council for War Production* (Detroit, Mich.: Automobile Manufacturers Association, 1950), pp. 199–201.

lucidly than anything else the astonishingly diversified uses to which the industry's productive resources were applied. In all, by the time the Second World War came to an end, the American automotive industry manufactured $29 billion worth of military materials, constituting one-fifth of the nation's entire output of such commodities.

This performance was brought to a halt rapidly but on the whole smoothly. One of the functions assumed by the Automotive Council for War Production was that of intermediary in negotiations for contract termination. At the outset these terminations were predominantly caused by shifts in military requirements as the war situation changed. Then, when the course of events brought eventual victory in sight, both government and industry began to plan for the resumption of peacetime production. They were castigated for doing so by the zealots who insisted that it was improper to think about peace until the war had been won; for dramatic effect these should have been the same people who shrilly denounced planning for war before the shooting actually started, but they probably were not. The fact remains that when the war did come to an end, the advance preparations permitted the enormous production machine to turn from swords to plowshares with far less confusion and disruption than most authorities had feared. The automobile industry faced the postwar world with much happier prospects than its aeronautical cousin. When the reconversion process was accomplished, there was a market for motor vehicles; airplanes in 1945 were definitely a surplus commodity.

The American public demonstrated emphatically what one of its first priorities was going to be. Gasoline rationing officially ended on August 15, 1945. Unofficially it ended the day before, when Japan formally surrendered. On that day the streets of every American community were littered with the scraps of gasoline ration books, while owners leaped into their cars, with the rebuilt motors and the retreaded tires, and drove joyously about until they were ready to head for their dealers and place orders for new cars, deliverable when the assembly lines should catch up with the accumulated demand of four years.

CHAPTER 10

Peace Has Its Problems

When the victory celebrations came to an end and the American automotive world could take stock of its future prospects, its mood was preponderantly one of optimism, with some reservations. For the manufacturers the market outlook was excellent: it would in fact be necessary to go back before the First World War to find a comparable situation, one in which there was a demand for cars beyond the immediate ability of the producers to supply. The demand side is easy to explain. From its 1941 level of 3,250,000 (the highest since 1929), passenger car production dropped to 223,000 in 1942, exactly 139 in 1943, 610 in 1944, and 700 in 1945. In the meantime registrations dropped by four million as automobiles became inoperable for one reason or another and could not be replaced. It is a safe guess that at least as many more passenger cars were ready for the scrapheap by the time the war ended.

Meeting this pent-up demand required time. The war contracts were liquidated satisfactorily enough, but it was no more possible to switch the assembly lines overnight from military matériel to civilian automobiles than it had been to do the opposite five years before. Apart from the necessary reorganization and retooling, there were still acute shortages of materials and other difficulties left behind in the wake of war. It was late 1946 before the government lifted priorities, and price controls remained rather haphazardly in operation for a year after that.

The result was an unparalleled seller's market. Any vehicle that would roll under its own power was salable. (The writer can testify personally to a 1935 Ford bought for $100 in 1941 and allowed a trade-in value, despite worn-out bearings, of $75 in 1946.) The prospects of the automobile business, indeed, were so alluring that for the first time in twenty years there was a determined effort by an important newcomer to break into the ranks of the automobile manufacturers. As an added attraction, a great boom in highway construction was clearly in the making, as projects which had been deferred for the duration of the war were revived. When the new cars arrived, there would be new roads for them to use. Along with this encouraging outlook for the automotive future, there were various imponderables in the situation that would affect the response of the automobile industry to its opportunities. Among them were: whether the trend to oligopoly would continue, or whether the independent producers would survive in the postwar world; whether, among the automotive giants, the Ford Motor Company would be able to find its way out of the chaos into which it had been plunged by the continued vagaries of its founder, Edsel's sudden death, Bennett's machinations, and the firing of Sorensen. The greatest of all imponderables, however, was labor. The aftermath of a great war is usually a period of labor unrest, and the late 1940's conformed to the pattern. In the automobile industry the UAW, now led by Walter Reuther, announced that it expected for its members the same high level of earnings in peacetime as they had enjoyed in war, along with other benefits, some of them attainable only by a drastic revision of management-union relations.

The Postwar Industry

Among the established passenger car manufacturers, General Motors was the best equipped to make the transition from war to peace. It lost Knudsen, who during the war was given the rank of lieutenant-general and devoted himself to expediting the production of military materials. He died in 1948, worn out by his efforts for his adopted country. His successor at General Motors was Charles E. Wilson (1890–1961), later Secretary of Defense in the Eisenhower administration. He was known to the business world as "Engine Charlie" to distinguish him from another Charles E. Wilson, who was president of General Electric and accordingly identified as "Electric Charlie." General Motors, with its flexible organization and its diversity of operations, was in excellent condition to maintain its automotive leadership.

Chrysler likewise made a satisfactory adjustment. It had no change of management; K. T. Keller (b. 1885), who became president when Walter Chrysler retired, remained in this post until 1950. In addition, Chrysler's role as the country's leading manufacturer of tanks was interrupted only temporarily. The independents—Hudson, Nash, Packard, Studebaker, and Willys—emerged from the war with high hopes for the booming motor-vehicle market of the future. Studebaker, in fact, was the first of the manufacturers to get back to full-scale operation, with a car whose design was apparently inspired by a ferryboat, in that it gave the impression of being double-ended. While the postwar shortage lasted the independents did reasonably well, climbing to 50 per cent of the passenger car market in 1949, but once the Big Three got their assembly lines rolling normally, the inability of the small-scale producer to compete again made itself manifest. It was significant that the independents abandoned the low-priced car market. Even Hudson, whose Essex and Terraplane had had an established position in this market, made no effort to return to it. Willys-Overland perhaps should be considered an exception because it continued to manufacture jeeps for peacetime use, but the jeep was a special case. It was not really competitive with the conventional passenger automobile, and in any event it did not sell well enough to restore Willys-Overland's former glory.

In the immediate postwar years, however, the major question marks in the management of the automobile industry were personified by two Henrys—Henry Ford II (b. 1917) and Henry J.

Kaiser (b. 1882). With the former, the problem was whether he could rehabilitate the Ford Motor Company. Even though he had much to work with, it was not going to be easy. The starting point for this story takes us back to May 26, 1943, when Edsel Ford died, the tragic victim of his father's prejudices. Stomach ulcers, beyond question the consequence of frustration and persecution by the elder Ford and Harry Bennett, turned to cancer, which in turn was aggravated by undulant fever brought on by drinking non-pasteurized milk from the family farm. The company's historians, Allan Nevins and Frank E. Hill, sum up Edsel's death as "stomach cancer, undulant fever, and a broken heart."

The vacant presidency was taken by the eighty-year-old Henry Ford, already the victim of two strokes. It was an arrangement satisfactory to no one except Bennett, who seems to have been maneuvering to secure the presidency for himself. There was consternation in Washington over what might happen to the needed productive capacity of the Ford Motor Company; it was about this point, indeed, that the suggestions of nationalizing the company became loudest. Instead, Henry Ford II, the oldest of Edsel's sons, was released from service in the navy to assist in the management of the company.

He was made vice-president late in 1943, but for a time it seemed to be an empty title. His attempts to exercise authority were blocked by his grandfather's interference, or by what Harry Bennett claimed were the elder Ford's wishes. Young Henry was unable, and more than likely unwilling, to prevent Sorensen's downfall. But the Ford picture was brighter than it looked. Henry Ford II may have come to the company without experience in its management, but both at college (Yale) and in the navy he had made a point of keeping himself as fully informed about its affairs as he could. Bennett made the mistake of underestimating him. In addition, Henry II had allies against whom Bennett's techniques were useless: to wit, the women of the Ford family. Mrs. Henry Ford, the elder, had not interfered in the operation of the business while her husband was in possession of his faculties, but now that he was palpably failing she had no intention of standing aside while her grandson walked the road that her son had been compelled to tread. Mrs. Edsel Ford was the implacable foe of the man who had caused so much misery to her husband and whom she held responsible for his untimely death.

It took time and effort to wear down old Henry's reluctance to surrender his control, but it was finally achieved, and on September 21, 1945, Henry Ford II was elected president of the Ford Motor Company, with a free hand to manage it as he chose. Harry Bennett received his walking papers the same day, although he was given a month to wind up his affairs, which was a greater courtesy than he had extended to the innumerable victims of the Bennett ascendancy. The founder of the company went into complete retirement for the two years more that he had to live, a senile invalid with his great days far behind him.

It was a tragic end to a phenomenal career. For good or ill, Henry Ford *was* the image of America to millions of people throughout the world, and on balance it was a favorable image. He was not just the poor boy who became enormously rich; he was the prophet who struck the rock of mass production and brought from it a stream of plenty for rich and poor alike, who made luxuries like motorcars accessible to the common man, and who saw the secret of prosperity in wages high enough to leave the wage-earner with disposable income. If he was a despot, in his early days he was a benevolent one, and for his great achievements he could be forgiven some foibles and eccentricities. Had he been willing to turn over real authority to Edsel and retire along with the Model T, his reputation would be unassailable. Instead he stayed on, dominated by the prejudices of his rural boyhood and unable to adapt to a fast-changing industrial society which he had done as much as anyone to create; unwilling to let anyone else run his company and progressively less able to do it himself. It is not really surprising that the news of his death startled a good many people because they were under the impression that it had occurred some time before.

The new president of the Ford Motor Company must have been

staggered by what he found when he actually took charge. Conditions were markedly worse than he had envisioned. The Ford Motor Company was losing money at the rate of about $9 million a month. The administrative structure, as far as one could be said to exist, seemed designed to prevent anyone from exercising responsibility, and the legacy of Harry Bennett was present in an atmosphere of mistrust and suspicion and an unwillingness to display initiative or independence of judgment. The accounting system was a joke. One department is credibly reported to have estimated its costs by weighing its invoices. (This is a valid procedure under some conditions. The great mail-order houses can base much of their day-to-day planning on the weight of the morning mail, but it has never been recognized as an acceptable method of cost accounting.)

Ford sensibly decided that he needed help, and furthermore that the logical place to go for assistance in reorganizing an automobile company was General Motors. The man he wanted was Ernest R. Breech (b. 1897), at this time president of the Bendix Aviation Corporation. He had previously been president of North American Aviation, so that his principal executive posts had been in aviation rather than automobiles, but he had held various offices, mainly financial, in General Motors and was thoroughly familiar with its organization. It took a good deal of negotiating to persuade Breech to leave a secure position for a company he knew to be in bad shape, but the challenge of trying to rehabilitate the Ford organization won him over. He became executive vice-president and later moved up to the presidency.

Aid also came from a different and unexpected source. Ten air force officers, ranging in age from twenty-six to thirty-four, who had been concerned with logistics and especially with financial and statistical controls and who wanted to remain associated in peacetime, applied in a body to the Ford Motor Company and were accepted, with no more definite assignment at first than to study and report on various phases of the company's operations. They were promptly dubbed the "Whiz Kids," and they provided the

Ford Motor Company with some high-powered administrative talent. Their leader, Charles B. (Tex) Thornton, left after a year or so to go into the electronics business in Los Angeles and became the founder of the highly successful Litton Industries. The others contributed several vice-presidents and two presidents (Robert S. McNamara and Arjay Miller) to the Ford Motor Company, and McNamara became Secretary of Defense for Presidents Kennedy and Johnson.

The transfusion of new blood had the desired effect. The structure of the Ford Motor Company was comprehensively overhauled. The deficits were replaced by profits, and in 1950 Ford finally recovered from Chrysler second place among automobile producers. When the fiftieth anniversary of the company arrived in 1953, it could celebrate its past with the assurance that it also had a future. By comparison, Studebaker was simultaneously observing its hundredth year as a vehicle manufacturer, but it was an open question how much longer it would be able to continue.

The crisis and convalescence of the Ford Motor Company were only partially matters of public knowledge. Far greater attention was being paid to the effort of Henry J. Kaiser to get established as an automobile manufacturer. The effort still deserves attention for what it reveals about competitive conditions in the American automobile industry as it began the second half century of its existence.

Kaiser was a colorful figure, a California businessman with a variety of interests who rose to national prominence during the Second World War by impressive production performances, especially in shipbuilding. By intensive use of prefabrication, so that the shipyard itself became in effect an assembly plant, he was able to set records of tonnage and speed in turning out merchant ships. The technique was borrowed immediately from the automobile industry; no one thought to give credit to the Venetian shipwrights of a bygone era. Kaiser was also instrumental in starting steel manufacturing on the Pacific Coast, aided by the wartime demonstration that it was not only costly and cumbersome but also dangerous to have to haul steel across the United States in a time of national crisis.

During the war Kaiser joined forces with Joseph W. Frazer, president of the Graham-Paige Motor Company, to undertake the large-scale manufacture of automobiles when peace came. In 1945 they formed the Kaiser-Frazer Corporation, which absorbed Graham-Paige a few months later. The new venture was launched under promising auspices. Henry J. Kaiser emerged from the war with the reputation of a latter-day Henry Ford. His career offered ample evidence of entrepreneurial and managerial ability. Manufacturing facilities were acquired at bargain prices by purchase or lease of government-owned plants built for war production and now no longer needed, including Willow Run. Credit was also available from government sources, notably the Reconstruction Finance Corporation, which loaned Kaiser-Frazer $44 million in 1949.

With the market situation as promising as it was possible for it to be, if Kaiser-Frazer could build automobiles, it could sell them. New cars were almost non-existent and, because of the four-year span without replacement, even used cars were scarce. For a time it appeared that this combination of favorable conditions would enable Henry Kaiser to create the first new automotive empire since the rise of Chrysler twenty years before. In 1948 the Kaiser-Frazer line (Kaiser, Frazer, Henry J.) accounted for 5 per cent of domestic new-car sales. But that was high tide. Within five years all three models disappeared from the American market. Kaiser-Frazer became the Kaiser Motors Corporation in 1953 and also the owner of Willys-Overland; two years later the company, renamed Kaiser Industries Corporation, withdrew from the passenger car field to concentrate on jeeps and commercial vehicles, all to be built in Toledo by what was now Willys Motors. Kaiser cars continued to be produced in South American subsidiaries. The great Willow Run plant, which had begun with Ford, finished with General Motors. The latter company bought it from Kaiser in 1953 to be used for manufacturing automatic transmissions after General Motors' own transmission plant had been destroyed by fire.

It would be possible to explain the Kaiser experience in general terms as an illustration of the difficulty of breaking into an oligopolistic mass-production industry. It is certainly true that the obstacles facing a newcomer trying to enter the field of passenger automobile production in the United States are almost prohibitively great. Trucks and specialized vehicles are a different matter; here the newcomer and the small firms have brighter prospects. With passenger cars, however, the whole experience of the automobile industry since the 1920's has been that business survival depends on ability to get and hold a position in the mass market.

To do so, the newcomer is faced with a tremendous outlay for the plant and tooling needed for mass poduction, and with the additional heavy expense of creating a marketing and dealer organization—all predicated on the uncertain gamble of breaking into a highly competitive market against firms with established reputations and far greater experience. The worst difficulty, as Kaiser found, is the problem of marketing. Given adequate finances, building the manufacturing facilities is a routine process. Creating a sales organization and finding customers is something else again. Successful dealers cannot be expected to sever their existing connections to join an enterprise whose prospects are speculative at best. The new manufacturer has to recruit from his competitor's discards or from people inexperienced in selling automobiles, and this sales force has to overcome the massive barrier of customer resistance. The American motorist will display an intense interest in a new automotive offering, but he is likely to let someone else take the risk of buying it unless there is an unusual market situation such as existed when Kaiser-Frazer started operations. Normally the American purchaser prefers cars with a reasonably dependable trade-in value in the future. These considerations were fully understood by the business world at the time. It was helpful to Kaiser-Frazer that it had access to RFC financing, but it was also an indication of weakness, because it meant that the private investment and banking community had weighed the company's prospects in the balance and found them wanting.

Yet to write off Kaiser-Frazer as the victim of a general economic pattern is oversimplification. The enterprise began with good prospects, and if it had had something significant to contribute to the automotive world, it might well have solidified its position by the time the output of new cars caught up with the deferred demand. But it soon became apparent that while Henry J. Kaiser's success in his other manufacturing operations was due in part to his drawing ideas on production from the automobile industry, he had nothing to contribute to it in return. The Kaiser cars were conventional, unoriginal designs built by conventional methods. Moreover, while the conversion of war-built aircraft plants provided factory space cheaply, it was a less efficient arrangement than plant specifically designed for the quantity manufacture of motor vehicles. There is a telling comparison in the 1950 records of Kaiser and Hudson. They made almost the same number of cars, 151,000 for Kaiser and 144,000 for Hudson, but where Hudson made $12 million profit, Kaiser showed a $13 million loss. Manufacturing facilities were not the whole story, but it is worth observing that the Ford Motor Company, which had operated Willow Run, considered and rejected an opportunity to buy it from the government when the war ended.

There were other postwar aspirants besides Henry J. Kaiser for a place in the automotive world. The most flamboyant was a Chicago businessman named Preston Tucker, who proposed to produce a rear-engined automobile with sports-car lines, tentatively called the Torpedo. The Tucker Corporation leased a government-built factory in Chicago where the Dodge Division of Chrysler had made engines for B-29 Superfortresses. Tucker, however, ran into financial troubles and went out of business in 1949. A similar effort to market a sports car named Playboy (unrelated to the Jordan Playboy of the 1920's) was even shorter-lived.

A far more interesting experiment in the light of future automotive developments was the Crosley Corporation's attempt to produce what would later be termed a compact. The Crosley was a lightweight car with a four-cylinder engine. It first appeared in 1939, but since it scarcely had time to get on the market before production was halted, it is properly a postwar development. The Crosley had financial substance behind it in that it was sponsored by the manufacturers of Crosley radio and television equipment. It survived until 1952, when the company was bought by General Tire and Rubber and production of the car ceased. It was just a little premature. Had the Crosley still been on the market five years later, when the taste of the American public was turning to compacts, it could conceivably have been a brilliant success.

If it is possible to draw conclusions from these ventures, the evidence indicates that entry into the American automobile industry has become inordinately difficult but not necessarily impossible. Kaiser did after all stay in the motor-vehicle business, although not on the scale initially contemplated. The manufacturers of foreign cars were to demonstrate in the 1950's that the American passenger automobile market could be penetrated. Admittedly they were in a more favorable position than a new domestic producer in that they could exist without American sales, but nevertheless they proved that the American buyer could be wooed away from his accustomed choices. The requisites for a newcomer appear to be: (1) a definite innovation in design or techniques of production; (2) adequate financing; (3) a substantial and well-organized marketing organization; and (4) accurate timing. A ponderous inertia on the part of the existing manufacturers, causing an excessively sluggish response to new developments, may also be essential. The odds against this particular combination of circumstances occurring are certainly heavy, but it could happen.

PRICES AND WAGES

The process of resuming the peacetime manufacture of motor vehicles involved a great deal more than reorganizing factories and waiting for materials to become available. The end of the war was accompanied by a sharp price inflation, which the Truman administration tried rather ineffectually to restrain by continuing the price control structure created during the war. At the same time the inflationary pressures were stimulating demands from labor for higher wages and these demands were resisted still less effectively by an administration which owed a heavy political debt to organized labor.

The immediate consequences in automobile manufacturing offer an interesting commentary on the nature of mass production. After the surrender of Germany in 1945, the industry was authorized to make 200,000 vehicles for civilian use during the rest of the year, if it could find the materials. The collapse of Japan permitted the restriction on numbers to be removed, but material shortages and labor troubles limited the attainable volume of production and forced up unit costs on the vehicles that were manufactured. Mass-production methods will turn out large quantities cheaply; they will not do it for small numbers. The Office of Price Administration, however, used the levels of 1942 to set its ceilings on new-car prices, so that even though the industry was putting warmed-over 1942 models on its assembly lines in order to minimize delays in production, there was a negative relationship between price and cost. The Ford Motor Company, for instance, was restricted to a price ceiling of $780 for a car that cost $1,041 to make. When Henry Ford II pointed this fact out publicly, he was vitriolically assailed by Chester Bowles, then head of the OPA, as a member of a selfish conspiracy to "undermine the American people's bulwark against economic disaster."

The price problem solved itself with the termination of controls in 1947 and the increasing output of new cars to restore the supply side of the market. There was no return to prewar levels; new car prices in the late 1940's were approximately twice what they had been ten years before; but the increase reflected quite accurately the decline in the purchasing power of the dollar.

Labor relations were a more persistent problem. With the

coming of peace there was a near epidemic of wildcat strikes and unauthorized work stoppages both in the automobile companies and in their supplier firms. These were a consequence of the tensions of readjustment to peacetime conditions and could be counted on to subside when a reasonable degree of economic stability was restored. On the other hand, the stand taken by the United Automobile Workers involved basic considerations of long-range policy. During the war there had been a general freeze on wages, but high overtime earnings had given most automotive workers substantial gains in actual take-home pay. The UAW now insisted that this level of remuneration be continued by increased peacetime wage rates. The demand had some merit since prices and living costs were obviously not going to revert to their former levels. The same consideration applied to relatively novel issues in contract negotiations, such as fringe benefits and the tying of wage rates to the cost-of-living index.

The industry, however, was not prepared to guarantee a year-round forty-hour work week or to concede that wage rates should be based on profits. The determination of work schedules and decisions on what to do with profits were regarded as prerogatives of management, and there was a feeling that wage scales should bear some relationship to the productivity of the worker. On this point, the argument that wages should be determined by ability to pay, the UAW prepared to attack General Motors, as the company with the best profit record in the business. If the principle could be established there, it would be a great triumph, although it was never clear how standards established at General Motors could be applied to companies that were having a desperate struggle to survive.

In any event, when a demand for a 30 per cent wage increase was rejected, a strike began at General Motors in November, 1945, and lasted until the following March. The final settlement was for an eighteen and one-half cent raise representing an increase of about 15 per cent, plus some fringe benefits. Negotiations were handicapped by the fact that the UAW was itself involved in a bitter struggle for control between pro- and anticommunist factions. The anticommunists finally won under the leadership of Walter Reuther, but while the fight was on, the contending forces felt obligated to outdo each other in displaying "militancy." Nor was a spirit of compromise stimulated when President Truman publicly endorsed the union's position on the relationship between wages and profits.

The other automobile companies escaped the long agony of General Motors, but they reached approximately similar settlements in the spring of 1946 in the form of a substantial increase in hourly wage rates. At this juncture the union members themselves exhibited a definite preference for straight cash raises rather than greater fringe benefits. The other issues were left in abeyance.

When the next round of negotiations began in 1948, the atmosphere had changed. The manufacturers were anxious to avoid work stoppages. They were getting into full-scale production and were beginning to meet the clamorous postwar demand for new cars. Moreover, they had discovered, as had other industrialists, that higher costs resulting from concessions to labor could be passed on to the buying public without objection from Washington. On its side the UAW was under the chastening influence of the Taft-Hartley Act, passed over President Truman's veto in 1947 in response to an outburst of public indignation against the arrogance and irresponsibility of a number of labor leaders and their unions. In justice to the UAW, it had not been one of the major offenders; nevertheless its leaders had to be aware that there was a need for circumspection.

Once again an agreement with General Motors was to be the criterion for automotive labor standards. This time, however, the bargaining was done in private, by parties who were in a reasonably amicable mood and genuinely wanted to come to terms with each other. The result was a contract of historic importance in American labor relations, since it established a pattern that was widely followed in the next decade. Its most conspicuous features were first, a provision adjusting wage rates in accordance with the cost-of-living index, computed by the United States Department of Labor; second, an annual "improvement factor," calculated to allow for the increased productivity of the worker resulting from advances in manufacturing techniques.

This agreement was to run for two years. When it expired in 1950 it was renewed with some modification for another five years. Meanwhile the UAW negotiated a new contract with Ford in 1949 that incorporated another cherished objective, a company-financed pension plan for hourly wage employees. In the 1949 settlement all Ford employees who had served for thirty years were guaranteed a retirement income of $100 a month, the company making up the difference between that figure and the employee's Social Security benefits.

Because the automobile industry was so much the keystone of the American economy, its labor relations had a peculiar significance. It was not just that disputes and strikes in automobile manufacturing would create a snowballing effect of adverse consequences in other sectors of the economy; it was something more subtle. Consciously or unconsciously the American people had come to look on the automobile industry as the model for others to follow. First it had demonstrated dramatically the possibilities of mass production and mass consumption; then it had led the way in making high wages an American industrial practice; and it seemed to have a limitless capacity for fresh achievements in production and performance. Consequently it was taken for granted that the automobile industry would set the national pattern in labor relations, and this instinctive feeling was largely justified. The cost-of-living formula and the improvement factor were adopted in other industries.

On the whole these labor settlements were beneficial. The automotive workers secured higher real wages and positive gains in job security. On the other side of the picture costs of production were increased and were reflected in higher prices. It seems incontestable that granting automatic pay raises when living costs rose tended to exert a constant upward pressure on the wage-price spiral, since higher wages meant higher costs which in turn had to be met by still higher prices. There was a further consequence, not especially welcome to labor. In a highly competitive industry there was a strong incentive to keep costs down, and the most direct way of offsetting higher wage scales was by intensified mechanization and, as it came to be called, automation.

RECONVERSION COMPLETED

At the midcentury point most of these considerations were still in the future. For the moment there was the comforting prospect that the industry was enjoying internal peace and that the other difficulties of the postwar years had finally been ironed out so that the assembly lines were once more producing at capacity. Output in 1949 rose to more than 5,000,000 passenger cars and 1,000,000 other vehicles, finally surpassing the previous record year of 1929. After the seven lean years the famine had ended. It was once more possible for the ordinary American to go to a dealer and buy whatever kind of automobile, new or used, suited his taste. If it happened to suit his pocketbook also, well and good, but that was a minor question.

If our average American had chosen to buy a new car in 1949 or 1950 and had selected one in the popular-price range, it would have cost him about $1,800. It was most likely to have an eight-cylinder engine rated at about 100 horsepower, although six-cylinder engines were available. Compared with prewar models it had sleeker lines, was slightly longer and lower. It had sealed-beam headlights, and although heater and radio were optional, few automobiles were sold without them. The manual gearshift was still standard equipment but practically all makes now offered automatic transmission if the customer so desired.

Motor-vehicle output in 1950 topped 8,000,000 for the first time in automotive history, but while this record was being made the new era was interrupted by the Communist invasion of the Republic of Korea. American military forces went into action on the other side of the world while at home automobile men patiently put away their plans for expansion of civilian production and began to recall what they knew about the manufacture of tanks, guns, aircraft engines, and wing sections. As it turned out, the Korean conflict did not cause a major disturbance of the civilian economy. There were restrictions on production but nothing on the scale of the Second World War. The manufacture of motor vehicles continued on a somewhat reduced scale, but there was no restraint whatever on their use. The torrent of cars pouring on to American highways went right on rising.

CHAPTER 11

The Broad Highway

In the twenty years that followed the Second World War the outstanding feature of the American automotive world was a great advance in highway design and construction rather than in the evolution of the vehicle itself. Automobiles continued to change, in most respects for the better, but there were no really radical innovations. Roads were a different story. There had been, as we have seen, some parkway and express-highway construction earlier, but it was only after the war that the United States began to get an effective national network of roads built specifically to facilitate the flow of high-speed automobile traffic—roads, in other words, that would encourage rather than obstruct utilization of the potentialities of motor vehicles.

It was high time. In the continuing race between highway and car the latter was emphatically ahead. For all the work that had been done since the first federal highway program in 1916, most American road mileage was still essentially improvement of pre-automotive routes: wagon trails, cart tracks, and cowpaths. U.S. 40, from Washington to St. Louis, followed faithfully the route of the old National Road, which had never been contemplated for use by self-propelled vehicles. U.S. 1, from Maine to Florida, offered a spectrum of conditions calculated to impede rather than assist the flow of traffic. Its northern segment wandered along the Maine coast, offering splendid scenery but also innumerable curves and villages. From Boston to New York it was the Boston Post Road, following the stagecoach route of earlier days and passing through an endless sequence of populous communities. South of New York it took the traveler straight through Philadelphia, Baltimore, and Washington. Eventually it reached the southern tip of Florida, passing en route through a number of localities where justices of the peace and police officials derived much of their income from trapping out-of-state motorists in technical violations of local traffic ordinances.

Even with new roads there had been a tendency to emphasize economy of construction rather than expediting of traffic, so that curves were sharp and grades steep. In an economy where the demand for and production of automobiles was steadily climbing because of the postwar surge in population, accompanied by a general increase in real wages and a rising standard of living, adherence to conventional highway techniques would in a fairly brief span of time have had a seriously retarding effect on both the manufacture and use of motor vehicles. It may be difficult to envisage conditions of worse traffic congestion than actually existed, but such a situation could have developed if there had been shortsightedness in highway planning.

THE TOLLROADS

It was obvious to highway authorities and engineers that what was needed was a network of trunk roads constructed as multilane, limited-access expressways. The technique was well understood; the difficulty was financial, in that such roads were extremely expensive to build. The normal sources of funds for highway construction, even with federal aid increased by the Interstate and Defense Highway Act of 1944, were inadequate for this purpose, particularly in a period when rapidly mounting costs persistently outran revenues. Consequently state after state turned to the example offered by the Pennsylvania Turnpike.

This project had proved to be highly successful both financially and in permitting the smooth flow of a large volume of traffic. There had been grave doubts about the willingness of motorists to pay tolls when alternative free roads were available. The Pennsylvania Turnpike Authority, in fact, had had to have its initial 160-mile section financed by federal funds; 40 per cent of the cost, or $29.2 million, came from a Public Works Administration grant and the rest, $40.8 million, came as a loan from the Reconstruction Finance Corporation.

TABLE 3

TOLLROAD TRAVEL

These are the results of test runs made under the supervision of the Indiana Toll Road Commission to demonstrate the savings on limited-access highways.

Trucks

Chicago–Jersey City round trip via tollroads as compared with U.S. Routes 30 and 22.

Factor	Turnpike Savings	
Elapsed time	29	hours, 54 minutes
Travel time	11	hours, 17 minutes
Gasoline consumption	35	gallons
Speed per hour	8.2	miles faster
Gear shifts	2,339	
Brake applications	696	
Full stops	185	

Passenger Cars

Chicago–New York round trip via toll roads as compared with U.S. Routes 30 and 22.

Factor	Turnpike Savings	
Driving time	10	hours, 34 minutes
Average speed	14.66	m.p.h. faster
Average miles per gallon	0.52	
Gear shifts	834	
Brake applications	741	
Traffic stops	241	

SOURCE: Indiana Toll Road Commission

At the end of the war the atmosphere had completely changed. It was evident that motorists were willing to pay tolls for the privilege of traveling on express highways. For most of them the great attraction was the saving of time. Even with the tolls there was a considerable saving of cost also because of the elimination of frequent starting and stopping. For truck traffic this consideration outweighed the time factor, since non-stop operation and easy grades meant substantial economies in fuel consumption and wear-and-tear on the vehicle. Consequently when the State of Maine began to build a turnpike immediately after the war, it was able to finance the project entirely from the sale of bonds secured by the prospective revenues. The first section of the Maine Turnpike, fifty miles from Portland to Kittery on the New Hampshire border, was opened in 1947.

Once the idea was accepted the arguments in favor of tollroads were impressive. They permitted the building and maintenance of express highways without adding to local taxes; to put it another way, those who benefited from the facility paid for it. The alternative method of placing the burden on the users was to raise the money from gasoline taxes, and this was done in the case of the California freeway systems, which were begun at the same time as the principal tollroads. The objection to gasoline taxes is that their incidence is heaviest on the local population whereas the tollroads found their greatest utility in handling through traffic. If a motorist started at one end of the Pennsylvania Turnpike with a full tank of gasoline, he could complete the 360 miles across the state with one refilling, and out-of-state vehicles have composed half the traffic on the Pennsylvania Turnpike. The California situation was different, indeed unique. There, with a tenth of all the motor vehicles in the country and the majority of these concentrated in the Los Angeles area, the bulk of the traffic was local, so that it was reasonable to finance the freeways from gasoline taxes rather then tolls. Anyone who has driven on a California freeway, moreover, will shudder at the thought of the traffic having to stop for tollgates, especially at rush hours.

The advantages of tollroads, financial and otherwise, were such that an extensive network was projected. At the peak of this twentieth century turnpike boom about twelve thousand miles of tollroads were built, building, authorized, or proposed. About

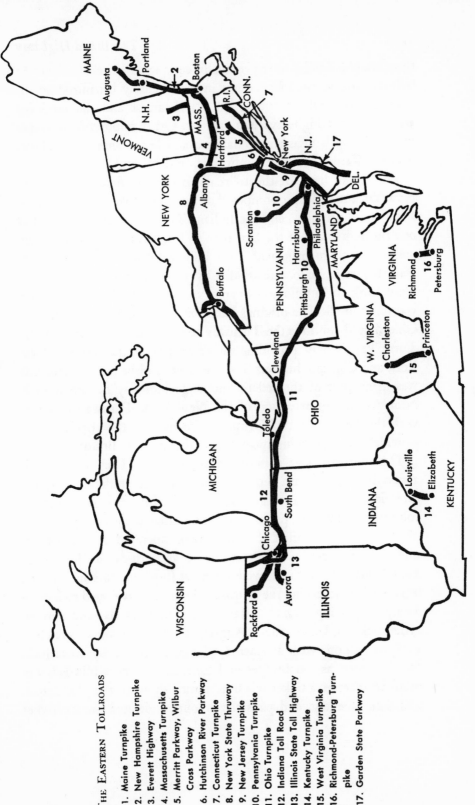

THE EASTERN TOLLROADS

1. Maine Turnpike
2. New Hampshire Turnpike
3. Everett Highway
4. Massachusetts Turnpike
5. Merritt Parkway, Wilbur Cross Parkway
6. Hutchinson River Parkway
7. Connecticut Turnpike
8. New York State Thruway
9. New Jersey Turnpike
10. Pennsylvania Turnpike
11. Ohio Turnpike
12. Indiana Toll Road
13. Illinois State Toll Highway
14. Kentucky Turnpike
15. West Virginia Turnpike
16. Richmond-Petersburg Turnpike
17. Garden State Parkway

three thousand miles were eventually completed at a cost of over $2 billion. Most of the mileage was in the intensely urbanized northeastern states, where congestion was heaviest and the need for arterial express highways was greatest. Other important turnpikes were built in Kansas and Oklahoma and lesser ones in Colorado, Florida, Kentucky, Texas, Virginia, and West Virginia.

The "main line" of the tollroads is the 837-mile stretch from New York to Chicago, composed of the New Jersey, Pennsylvania, and Ohio Turnpikes, and the Indiana Toll Road, all completed as one through route in the late 1950's. The largest turnpike system under a single management is the billion-dollar New York Thruway. Begun in 1950, it extended by the end of the decade from New York to Buffalo and beyond to the Pennsylvania state line, 500 miles in all. The original intention was that Pennsylvania and Ohio should continue the Thruway to a connection with the Ohio Turnpike, thereby providing an alternative route between New York and Chicago, but this link was never finished as a tollroad. It was made part of the federal interstate highway system instead. Near Albany an extension of the New York Thruway connects with the Massachusetts Turnpike, also built in the 1950's, which provides an express highway across the state to Boston.

The tollroads have common characteristics. They are limited-access highways, with separate roadways for traffic in opposite directions, and designed for high speeds. Interchanges generally follow the cloverleaf pattern or some similar design so that traffic streams cannot conflict. Service areas, operated as concessions under the supervision of the turnpike authorities, are located at suitable intervals so that travelers can get food, gasoline and oil, and repairs without leaving the tollroads. Tolls have averaged two cents a mile for passenger cars and have ranged up to twelve and thirteen cents a mile for heavy trucks. Aggregate receipts in 1962 were close to $310 million, with another $186 million added by specialized facilities such as toll bridges and tunnels. On most tollroads the motorist receives a ticket when he enters, showing the place, time, and date of entry, and pays the amount indicated on the ticket when he leaves. Some turnpikes, notably in Connecticut and New Hampshire, follow the practice of having tollgates at intervals across the roadway where traffic stops and pays a fixed amount. This arrangement permits local traffic to make short trips on the turnpike without having to pay toll.

Maximum speeds range from fifty-five miles an hour on heavily traveled sections of the eastern turnpikes to eighty in Kansas. In general the tollroads have had better safety records than the conventional highways. As a rule they are patrolled by their own detachments of state police, but this has not been the sole reason for their good showing. The important lesson of the tollroads has been that properly designed highways make possible high-speed movement of traffic with a minimum of accidents.

As might be expected, the financial record of the turnpikes has varied. In areas where traffic is light, revenues have been insufficient to meet the heavy costs of construction, but these conditions have been encountered on only a small part of turnpike mileage. At the other extreme, in heavily populated regions even a tollroad can become congested. When the Pennsylvania Turnpike reached its twentieth anniversary in 1960, it was handling an average of 80,000 vehicles a day, and on occasions of maximum load such as holiday weekends there were tie-ups at places such as the tunnels, where the four traffic lanes had to be squeezed into two. On the whole, however, the tollroads fulfilled effectively the purpose for which they were intended: that is, to provide up-to-date express highways that would pay their own way.

Yet their reign was destined to be brief. When the Interstate Highway Act of 1956 provided for a nationwide system of toll-free superhighways, to be constructed predominantly at federal expense, the incentive to build additional tollroads was abruptly removed. At the time this act was passed a number of states, ranging as far west as Washington, had authorized or proposed some eight thousand miles of turnpike, above and beyond what was already finished or under construction, but only a fifth of this total was actually built as tollroad. At the same time the existing turnpikes were far from being put out of business. About 80 per cent of them were made part of the interstate system while continuing to operate as tollroads. Important new additions were made to various turnpike systems after 1956, exclusive of the completion of work already in progress, and in the 1960's the senior member of the group, the Pennsylvania Turnpike Authority, was so far from contemplating oblivion that it was building new tunnels to eliminate its worst bottleneck and to upgrade the highway to modern standards of construction by providing separate roadways instead of merely a central divider.

The Interstate System

The origins of the interstate highways go back to the Interstate and Defense Highway Act of 1944, in which Congress attempted to anticipate postwar needs. These were going to be considerable, because during the war the nation's roads had deteriorated. New construction had been almost entirely halted, and maintenance had suffered from lack of materials and manpower. The act was far more comprehensive than its predecessors. It authorized the expenditure of $1.5 billion on roads in the three years following the termination of hostilities, on the equal-matching basis of previous legislation. For the first time urban as well as rural areas were made eligible for federal aid, and 40,000 miles of highway were to be designated as interstate routes, to receive the largest share of the funds.

The act was a bold and well-intentioned step toward a full-scale, coordinated national highway system, and it made possible a substantial amount of urgently needed new construction, but it still proved to be inadequate. The trouble was that given the magnitude of the problem and the soaring inflation of the postwar years, even a sum like $1.5 billion was swallowed up with frightening rapidity. By the time immediate requirements for both urban and rural roads were taken care of, there was not enough left for more than a gesture at the development of a new interstate highway system.

There were two possible solutions: an extensive development of tollroads or a really massive federal highway program. The former, as we have seen, was started but the eventual decision was for the latter. By the Interstate Highway Act of 1956, Congress provided for the construction of 41,000 miles of toll-free express highways, with 90 per cent of the cost to be paid by the federal government. Indeed, since the act made special allowances for states with substantial acreage of tax-free public land and for additional improvements such as prohibition of billboard advertising within specified distances from the right-of-way, it was possible for a state like Nevada to receive 95 per cent of its interstate highway costs from federal funds.

To finance this program Congress imposed excise taxes on motor fuels, tires and tubes, new buses, trucks, and trailers, and a use tax on trucks exceeding thirteen tons weight. The proceeds were allocated to a highway trust fund, to be applied to construction of the interstate routes on a pay-as-you-go basis. The entire system was expected to be completed in 1971, and the initial estimate of cost was $27 billion. As of 1965 the work was progressing on schedule, with about half the interstate network far enough advanced to be open to traffic. The price tag, however, had risen to $46 billion, and it was a safe guess that the final cost would reach twice the original figure.

While the superhighways were in progress a still greater expenditure of money and effort was going into the building and improvement of conventional roads, so that practically every part of the United States was becoming readily accessible by motor vehicle. In 1946 the hard-surfaced road mileage in the United States for the first time equaled the non-surfaced, about 1,500,000 miles each, and the proportion of hard-surfaced roads climbed steadily thereafter, reaching 71 per cent of the total of 3,100,000 miles in 1962. Although the creation of this improved highway network was not the only cause of the tremendous increase in the volume of highway travel that followed the Second World War, it certainly was an indispensable prerequisite.

PLANNED ROUTES OF THE NATIONAL SYSTEM OF INTERSTATE
AND DEFENSE HIGHWAYS

The total projected mileage of the national system of superhighways is
41,000 miles. Of this total about half was open to traffic as the present volume went to press.

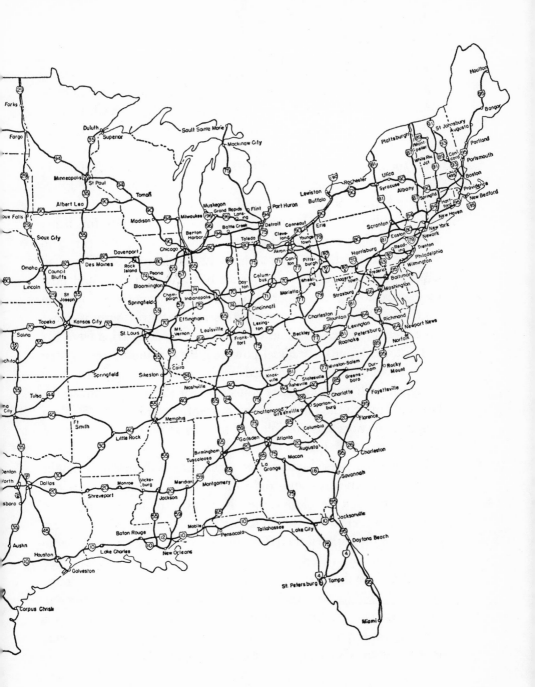

HIGHWAY TRANSPORT

The increase appeared equally in commercial and non-commercial use of the roads. Indeed, it was only now that the potentialities of commercial highway transport began to be fully realized. In 1948 buses carried more passengers than trains for the first time, although in passenger miles the railroads were still ahead and remained so until 1962. As a matter of fact both bus and train travel declined in the 1950's while airlines and private automobiles gained; the difference was that rail passenger traffic lost ground faster.

The railroads can be criticized accurately enough for being willing, with some exceptions, to abandon the passenger field without a contest, but they admittedly had handicaps. They had never been competitive in cost with bus transportation, and now they were losing the superiority they had formerly enjoyed in comfort and speed. The buses of this era were a great improvement over their predecessors. The vehicles used for long trips were big and fast, predominantly diesel-powered. By the middle 1950's they were air-conditioned, provided with washroom facilities, and equipped with reclining seats adjustable for sleeping. In short, the bus could match the railway coach in comfort, and where travel on express highways was possible, it could do as well as the ordinary passenger train in speed.

Highway carriers also increased their share of the nation's freight traffic. Between 1950 and 1960 the volume of intercity freight carried by truck (exclusive, that is, of strictly local hauls) rose from 173 billion to almost 300 billion ton-miles, or from 16 to 22.5 per cent of the national total. Railroad freight traffic fell in the same decade from 597 to 579 ton-miles, a decline from 56 to 43.5 per cent of the total. Like buses, trucks designed for heavy or long-distance hauling underwent striking developments. They became enormous vehicles, capable of carrying loads of twenty tons and with engines requiring sixteen separate gear ratios. For these trucks, as with buses, diesel power was increasingly used.

One of the outstanding features of the 1940's and 1950's was the widespread use of tractor-trailer combinations, in which the load was carried in a trailer detachable from the power unit, so that the tractor could be employed elsewhere when the trailer was being loaded or unloaded. The truck trailer was somewhat of a rarity before the Second World War; by 1960 well over a million were in service. On the open highways of the West, moreover, trailers towed in tandem offered a further development in truck transportation.

When it came to competing for freight traffic, the railroads were by no means disposed to let the contest go by default, as they had done with their passenger business, and the emergence of the truck trailer proved to be a quite unexpected asset for them. A trailer is after all merely a large container for holding goods in transit; it can be moved equally well on its own wheels or on a railroad flatcar. A single train could easily carry a hundred trailers at an aggregate cost less than that of hauling each one over the road separately. So, in spite of protests and court action by the Teamsters Union, "piggyback" transportation was born in the early 1950's. From its improvised beginnings it grew in ten years to proportions that not only won back for the railroads some of their lost ground but also indicated one means of approach to creation of an efficiently integrated transportation network.

Although long-distance, heavy-duty trucks provided the most dramatic and most important aspect of the growth of freight transport by road, they represented a minor fraction, less than 5 per cent, of the total number of trucks in service. Of the 12,000,000 trucks registered in the United States in 1962, three-fifths were classified as "small," carrying loads less than four tons. These were the ubiquitous pickup trucks, panel trucks, multistop delivery trucks, and all the others whose ceaseless comings and goings are taken for granted on American roads and streets. If their operations are added to the intercity freight movements, then since 1954 more tonnage has been carried by motor truck in the United States than by any other medium of transportation. The distribution of business among types is illuminating. The single-unit trucks, the small and medium-sized vehicles, accounted for 60 per cent of truck mileage and carried 25 per cent of the freight. The big trailer combinations logged 40 per cent of the mileage and carried 75 per cent of the freight, calculated in ton-miles.

MASS MOBILITY

Impressive as were the advances in commercial transport, they were minor compared with the outpouring of private automobiles on to the nation's highways. It was not that people by and large traveled farther; the family car consistently averaged between nine and ten thousand miles a year. It was just that there were many more people and cars on the roads. Private automobile registrations in the United States were 25,500,000 when the Second World War ended. They doubled in the next ten years and added another twenty million in the decade after that. By 1960 four-fifths of all American families owned at least one car, an increase of 30 per cent in twenty years. The distribution of automobile ownership among income groups ranged from 57 per cent of the households with incomes below $4,000 a year to 95 per cent of the households with incomes about $10,000.

It would be impossible to itemize all the multifarious uses to which this mass of vehicles was put, but a conspicuous one was to take to the road in search of enjoyment. The growing urbanization of American life seems to have created a backlash in the form of an urge to get out into the open, and widespread ownership of automobiles made it possible for this urge to be satisfied. It was no longer a matter of driving just for the sake of driving. People by the million went by car to beaches, lakes, mountains, and forests, in search of recreation or obeying the long-standing adjuration to "see America first."

The impact of this roving host was considerable. Recreational facilities were inundated, not only in the neighborhood of the big cities but all over the country. Recreation, indeed, became an economic enterprise on a scale which would have been out of the question if people had been limited to the proximity of the great centers of population. Tourist traffic was something to be wooed by public authority as well as by private business. State parks, for instance, were practically non-existent in the 1920's; thirty years later there were more than two thousand, and most states also provided picnic and rest areas along their highways, many of them quite elaborate and attractive installations.

For this volume of travel the tourist facilities of the previous generation were no longer sufficient. The somewhat primitive cabins of earlier days were replaced by motels and tourist courts, more than forty thousand of them, varying from simple structures offering nothing more than sleeping facilities to elaborate establishments with their own restaurants and bars, swimming pools, room telephones, and other luxuries. Whatever their differences, all these establishments had one vital characteristic in common; they were designed specifically for the accommodation of people who traveled by automobile. It was absolutely essential that the motorist should have space for his car as well as himself, preferably in the immediate proximity of his room so that loading and unloading could be done with maximum convenience. As the business expanded, chains of motels came into existence, offering some assurance of standards of quality and the opportunity to make reservations from one stage of a journey to the next.

For those who preferred to eschew motels on grounds of cost or preference, there were camp grounds, although never quite enough during the vacation season for the crowds who sought them. More important, there was the trailer. Large house trailers, euphemistically termed mobile homes, became popular during the Second World War as a means of remedying housing shortages in the vicinity of newly built military installations and war plants, and they continued to be used by people affected with wanderlust. The biggest ones needed truck tractors to tow them, but there were smaller types that could be pulled by the ordinary passenger car, ranging all the way down to the simple units, sometimes homemade, that carried only goods. A variation of the trailer was the camper, a structure containing sleeping and cooking facilities and mounted on a small truck chassis. The house trailer and the camper extended the range of the vacationing motorist by enabling him to penetrate areas where commercial accommodations were either scanty or non-existent.

To serve these rambling millions the automobile service associations became organizations with greatly expanded functions. They provided emergency road service and legal assistance for their members, prepared maps and other guides for travel, kept track of road conditions, checked the quality of motels and restaurants, and frequently sold insurance. By far the largest group was the American Automobile Association, which included 750 member clubs and branches. As one sample of its activities, AAA garages were answering close to 70,000,000 service calls a year.

Not all the consequences of this mass movement on the highways were desirable. It was very easy to get the impression that the American landscape was being overrun by a horde of ignorant and wantonly destructive savages, whose idea of enjoying the beauties of nature was to line the roads with empty beer cans, litter the beaches with refuse, throw rubbish into the geysers of Yellowstone, scrawl obscene remarks on imposing rock formations, and toss burning cigarette stubs into woodlands. In justice to the American motorist these acts were the work of the inevitable irresponsible minority. Nevertheless it was physically impossible for millions of people to overflow scenic and recreational areas without changing them radically—in the eyes of purists, without spoiling the unspoiled. Regions whose charm stemmed in part from their inaccessibility were bound to lose some of their quality when concrete and asphalt brought visitors by the thousand. On Cape Cod, for instance, which had always been close to centers of population, the building of an express highway from the canal to Provincetown took on the proportions of a calamity. Nature lovers were deeply and rightly concerned about the preservation of the remaining scenic and wilderness areas of the United States. Apart from the problem of numbers, the planning and construction of superhighways was frequently done with an arrogant and arbitrary disregard both for property rights and the preservation of irreplaceable esthetic or historic features. Too often due process of law was replaced by a bulldozer.

At the same time it was difficult to deplore the social revolution which opened recreational travel to the many instead of the privileged few. Before the great expansion of paved road and automobile ownership, the Adirondacks and the White Mountains were vacation resorts only for the wealthy, the Great Smokies were an unknown region populated by a few primitive backwoodsmen, and for most persons seeing the Grand Canyon except in pictures was as unlikely as climbing Mount Everest. There was a great deal to be said for enabling the American people to enjoy their own country—to say nothing of visiting their neighbors, because automobiles ran just as well on the roads of Canada and Mexico as on those of the United States.

That some of the results were unfortunate is undeniable, but on balance the good appears to outweigh the bad. There is no reason to believe that the scenic beauties of the North American continent were intended to be reserved for a minuscule and favored minority, and there is strong reason to believe that it is eminently desirable for the members of an intensely urbanized society to be able, quite literally, to get out of town. There is even a variety of Newton's Third Law in operation. The threat of the expanding millions to the beauties of nature has stimulated energetic efforts to preserve those that are left. The response of public authorities at all levels to this mass movement on the highways has been—has had to be—expansion of recreational facilities, acquisition of sites for parks to meet the growing demand, and at least gestures toward the preservation of wildlife and scenic and national wonders. It may be that what has been done has not yet been enough. As with the building of roads, it has been inordinately difficult to keep pace with the multiplication of both people and cars. But it is worth something that the effort has been undertaken.

THE PASSING OF RURAL ISOLATION

The combination of motor vehicles and hard-surfaced roads, both in profusion, also brought about far-reaching changes in rural life. It was not the only agency to have this effect. Credit has to be given to the telephone, the radio, and television, and to the extension of electric power to country districts. But the motor vehicle was the agency of direct physical contact, the medium by which the farmer could take himself and his family to town for business or pleasure.

There was far more to the story than the mere facilitating of travel from country to city. From time immemorial the townsman had enjoyed all the advantages in social life, in culture, in education, in medical services. Even the language indicates the gap; the "urbane" individual came from the city. Although the automobile did not close this gap entirely, it certainly narrowed it. The country resident, especially the one who was remote from rail transport, was no longer cut off from the amenities of city life. He had the opportunity to seek them out, or to have them brought to him. By the 1950's it was becoming very difficult in the United States to distinguish on sight the farmer from the townsman. The badly dressed, unshaven individual who might be encountered on the street was more likely to be a college student than a "hayseed" come to town for the day.

In the field of education the motor vehicle, particularly the bus, made it possible for rural schools to approximate urban by allowing children to be transported over considerable distances to consolidated schools. The little red schoolhouse of American folklore was on its way to extinction during the 1950's, at the rate of ten a day. One can grow nostalgic about the barefoot boy making his way to the local one-room school, and perhaps something irretrievable was lost with its passing. Nevertheless the consolidated school had more to offer in educational resources; it could attract better-trained teachers for one thing, partly because the teachers themselves owned automobiles and therefore did not have to fear being lost in the "sticks" out of contact with their profession.

As with education, so with medicine. The old-fashioned country doctor is a cherished figure in American legend, and he represented values which are emphatically worth preserving. It was never necessary for his medical association to suggest, as was done in California in recent years, that he might display his caduceus on something less ostentatious than a Cadillac. Nevertheless it was undeniable that easy and rapid highway transportation made possible better medical service in rural areas. The country doctor delivering the baby or performing an appendectomy in the farmhouse by the light of kerosene lamps was a touching and often a heroic picture, but it was also a dangerous picture, no matter how great the dedication and skill. It was infinitely better that medical aid could be summoned by telephone and arrive rapidly by car and that in case of need the patient could normally be moved to a hospital in time to receive proper care.

Although no claim can be advanced that the motor vehicle provided a solution for the "farm problem," it did profoundly affect the economic pattern of farm life. Before the arrival of the automobile the economic limit of wagon transportation was fifteen to twenty miles. Beyond that the cost of moving goods by highway became so prohibitively high that a village or farm more than twenty miles from rail or water carriage was almost inevitably consigned to a subsistence economy. By contrast, in the middle of the twentieth century, nine-tenths of all farm commodities in the United States were carried to market by motor truck. No community had to be left out of the mainstream of the national economy. In purchasing, likewise, motor transport made the farmer independent if he so chose of the resources of the nearby village store.

This catalog of change could be carried through such specific details as traveling libraries or mobile highway post offices, analogous to railway post offices, in which the mail is sorted en route with resultant expediting of service to small towns and rural areas.

This system of handling mail was initiated in 1951 in response to the shrinking of rail facilities through the abandonment of branch lines and the curtailment of local main-line service.

There were some regrets at these patterns of change from those who saw local distinctiveness and individuality being submerged in a rising tide of monotonous sameness. It was certainly true that when the United States entered the latter half of the twentieth century there was a general uniformity in styles, tastes, and habits, and no doubt there were penalties attached. However, if we consider farm life of the preautomobile era in terms of Hamlin Garland's description of his mother's existence ("life" is too positive a term for it) in *A Son of the Middle Border*, it is possible to argue that the assets outweighed the liabilities. The farm woman of that period, with nothing to look forward to but unending drudgery and drabness, would cheerfully and enthusiastically have exchanged her contribution to local individuality for a uniformity that enabled her to get away once in a while. The automobile was removing the Middle Border and Sinclair Lewis's Gopher Prairie from the American scene, and there were few who could seriously mourn their departure.

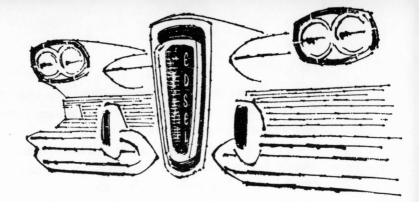

CHAPTER 12

Tail Fins and Compacts

The Korean War was merely a brief interlude in the growth of the American automobile industry. The automotive contribution to the conflict was impressive, to be sure, but there was no need for the all-out effort of the Second World War, and the curtailment of civilian production was minor. The worst obstacle was shortage of metal alloys, and this was overcome in part by substituting plastic components wherever possible. As soon as the war ended automobile manufacturing surged to new peaks of productivity, quite unmistakably carrying the economy with it. Business rose with the automobile industry to the crest of a boom in 1955, marked by the staggering production figure of more than 9,000,000 vehicles for the year, almost 8,000,000 of them passenger cars. This prodigious performance temporarily flooded the new-automobile market. Demand fell off by 2,000,000 a year later, with the result that the whole economy suffered a sharp recession in 1957.

This expansion in production was accompanied by improvements in assembly-line techniques that made it possible to keep retail prices of new cars in a stable relationship to the national price index. Between 1946 and 1955 the average retail price of a new automobile (f.o.b. Detroit) rose from $1,500 to $1,900, an increase of 27 per cent, which was less than the rise in both the general consumer price index and average weekly earnings of workers in manufacturing industries. At the same time the consumer was

199

getting more car for his money—sometimes more than he really wanted. The automobile of the 1950's was bigger than its predecessor, with a more powerful engine, running up to 300 horsepower even in the lower-priced makes. (The advertised figures were usually brake horsepower based on bench tests under optimum conditions, and so there could be a discrepancy between announced rating and actual performance.) By the middle of the decade the majority of all passenger cars were being sold with automatic transmissions, and the proportion grew steadily larger. Brake and light systems became more reliable, and power brakes and power steering came into more general use. Tubeless tires, including the punctureproof type, became available early in the 1950's, and there was a constant improvement in the quality of automotive fuels and lubricants.

The assembly of motor vehicles had come a long way since Henry Ford's pioneering days at Highland Park. The customer of the 1950's could choose among engines, body styles, colors for both exterior and interior, and even hubcaps. He could designate what he wanted in the way of accessories—radio, heater, air-conditioner, for instance—and the car combining his preferences would roll off the assembly line in company with others representing different assortments of choices. Punch-card control systems kept the variety of selections in order. Automatic controls were coming into extensive use throughout the manufacturing process, not only to keep production costs down but because they made for greater accuracy and quality.

TABLE 4

AVERAGE RETAIL PRICES OF PASSENGER CARS

1899	$1,559
1909	1,719
1919	1,157
1929	828
1939	845
1947	1,580
1955	1,910
1959	2,060
1963	2,310

SOURCE: Automobile Manufacturers Association.

The area in which the consumer appeared to have the least choice was price. The automobile manufacturers competed energetically with each other, but in technical features, styling, comfort, and safety rather than in price. In economic terms the industry was an oligopoly operating under a system of administered prices. As is usual in such situations, the largest producer, General Motors, set the price pattern to which the others generally conformed. There was no question of price-fixing; had there been, the lawyers of the Department of Justice's Anti-Trust Division would certainly have made a case of it. The automobile firms simply had too much investment at stake to engage in price wars that could result only in the participants' inflicting lasting injury on each other. General Motors was in a particularly difficult quandary. It could have cut prices for its own cars and still have earned respectable profits, but the effect would have been to ruin its competitors, except Ford probably, and this outcome would hardly have met with the approval of the Department of Justice.

There was, as a matter of fact, little public complaint about automobile price policies. Car prices, we have seen, had moved up no faster than the general price level, and if the improvements in quality are allowed for, the consumer's dollar was actually going farther than before. Besides, the buyer had more leeway than was apparent. He normally had the opportunity to bargain with the dealer on the trade-in allowance for his old car, which could be a considerable factor in the total payment, and although the dealer was expected to be guided by the manufacturer's list price, he was still an independent businessman with freedom to make adjustments. There was always, moreover, a check on any excessive rise in new-car prices: the enormous and uncontrolled used-car market. Consequently criticism of the automobile industry's price policies came mostly from sources that were not actually interested in unrestricted price competition but were using the charge of needlessly high prices either as leverage for higher wage demands, or to justify a greater degree of governmental intervention in the automobile industry.

The Triumph of Concentration

The oligopolistic structure of the automobile industry was further confirmed by shrinkage in the number of vehicle manufacturing firms. Among passenger-car producers, the Kaiser-Willys effort has been noted. Except for jeeps, it ended in 1955. The remaining independents, bearing historic names in American automobiledom, found themselves hard pressed and sought preservation in merger. In 1954 Nash-Kelvinator and Hudson joined forces as the American Motors Corporation, with all manufacturing operations concentrated at Kenosha, while Studebaker and Packard combined as the Studebaker-Packard Corporation.

Of the two, American Motors was to prove more successful by far, a result traceable primarily to the ability and persistence of one man. In 1950 Nash-Kelvinator had acquired as its general manager George Romney, the man who had distinguished himself as manager of the Automotive Council for War Production, and when American Motors was formed, Romney became its president. He was aware that merger alone would not be enough; if American Motors was to succeed it must offer something different that would attract business away from the Big Three. As early as 1950 he had revived the name of Rambler for a low-priced car, and he was convinced that there was a market for a smaller, lower-priced car than the producers in the United States were offering. So American Motors concentrated its effort on the Rambler, to the extent of discontinuing both the Nash and the Hudson in 1957. It was a gamble, and for several critical years it appeared that Romney would lose.

Studebaker-Packard seemed to have about the same prospects as American Motors at the time of its formation. The two groups started at the same level in total sales, approximately 100,000 in 1954. The Studebaker-Packard structure, however, was inherently weaker. Packard, never a large-scale producer, was struggling to hold a place in the luxury car field and was faring badly in competition with Cadillac as a prestige automobile. The Packard plant in Detroit was closed in 1956 and production transferred to the Studebaker factory in South Bend; two years later the Packard name passed into history. The Studebaker half of the combination had its own weaknesses, centering on the fact that the company had never come back to real financial health after its catastrophe in 1932.

Consequently this merger failed to achieve the hoped-for results. There was a time in the middle 1950's when the Curtiss-Wright Corporation was negotiating for the acquisition of Studebaker-Packard, mainly so that the latter's $35 million deficit could be used to offset Curtiss-Wright's profits for tax purposes. This plan, however, was eventually dropped. All it achieved was to provide a startling illustration of the effect of the tax structure on business policy; it takes some readjustment of customary economic ideas to realize that there are conditions in which a company can lose money on this scale and be a desirable acquisition. Studebaker production in South Bend lasted until 1964, when the company gave up the attempt to compete in the American market and moved its automobile manufacturing to Hamilton, Ontario.

The trend to concentration also appeared in truck manufacturing, with the White Motor Company as the focus. For White this development was an impressive performance for a company that had had a difficult time during the depression years of the early thirties and was under the constant pressure of competition from the automotive giants, including three General Motors divisions engaged in the manufacture of commercial vehicles (GMC Truck and Coach, Chevrolet, and Pontiac).

White's expansion began in the 1950's, the first major step being the acquisition in 1953 of the Autocar Company of Ardmore, Pennsylvania, one of the oldest of American motor vehicle manufacturers (1898) and one of the earliest (1908) to give up passenger-car production and concentrate on trucks. Next came Reo (1957), and Diamond T (1958), to make White by far the largest of the dwindling number of firms engaged in the manufacture of commercial vehicles. For this achievement credit goes principally to Robert F. Black, who became president of the White Motor Company in 1935 and successfully pulled it out of its depression difficulties—summed up in automotive circles as "Black took White out of the red." His success was based on a calculated realization that his company could not compete in mass production. He told the author in 1956, "If all trucks could be built like passenger cars, we would be out of business." It was necessary for White to lead the field in research and design of motor trucks and to manufacture to quality specifications. So the company pioneered with the cab-over-engine truck, the pancake bus engine, and other innovations. The results speak for themselves; when conditions were ripe, White was able to absorb its competitors. There is a certain irony in the techniques of motor-vehicle manufacturing. The passenger car, which has become a status symbol as much as a medium of transportation, is turned out in impersonal volume by the assembly line. It is the unglamorous, heavy-duty truck that is custom-built to specifications.

In the upper brackets of the industry the Big Three continued to fight for the passenger-car market, with General Motors easily in the lead. The Ford car and the Chevrolet staged a furious race year in and year out for leadership in sales, with Chevrolet usually having a narrow edge, but the full General Motors line outsold the combined Ford offerings by a substantial margin. General Motors had a secure hold on half the entire automobile market and sometimes went higher. It so dominated the industrial scene, indeed, that when its president, Charles E. Wilson, was nominated as Secretary of Defense by President Eisenhower, he could say with a clear conscience to the Senate committee which investigated his qualifications, "What's good for the country is good for General Motors and what's good for General Motors is good for the country."

General Motors' problems in this period came from the judiciary rather than from questions of production and sales. After prolonged investigation and litigation, the United States Supreme Court in 1958 finally ordered the Du Pont Company to divest itself of its General Motors holdings, which came to 23 per cent of the outstanding General Motors common stock, or 63,000,000 shares. It was a difficult decision for a layman to comprehend. There was no suggestion that Du Pont had ever exercised any improper influence over General Motors in their forty-year relationship. The decision was based on a section of the Clayton Act of 1914 prohibiting the holding of stock interests that might restrict competition. The majority of the court held that Du Pont's stock holdings might give it a preferential position in the sale of automobile paints and lacquers to General Motors. There was no evidence that Du Pont had ever acted in this way nor was there allowance for the fact that the Du Pont Company was the pioneer and principal American producer of quick-drying automobile finishes, so that under normal business conditions it would have had a preferential position anyway.

The decision produced consternation in the financial community. In the best of circumstances disposing of 63,000,000 shares of General Motors stock would have posed serious problems. In addition, because this stock had all been acquired between 1916 and 1921, there was a frightening capital-gains tax liability. A proposal that Du Pont place its General Motors stock in a non-voting trust was rejected by the court. Eventually a special act of Congress was required to remove some of the capital-gains liability and make possible the sale of the stock without crippling losses, and by 1964 the stock had been duly disposed of. Such penalties as were involved fell on the Du Pont stockholders and not on General Motors; its automotive supremacy was left unimpaired. In 1964, in fact, General Motors established an all-time record in profits of $1.7 billion.

The 1950's saw the Ford Motor Company firmly and profitably reestablished in second place among automobile manufacturers and energetically but unavailingly trying to narrow the gap between it and General Motors. The Ford weakness was, or seemed to be, in the middle price range, where the Mercury had to compete with General Motors' Buick, Oldsmobile, and Pontiac and Chrysler's

Dodge and De Soto. The Ford firm did not arrive at its conclusion hastily; if anything, it took too long. In the face of suggestions that what was really wanted was a smaller and cheaper car than was being offered, the company conducted an extensive market research, which concluded that there was insufficient demand for a small car but a bright prospect for one in the range between the Lincoln and the Mercury. The result was the Edsel, in which the Ford Motor Company invested $250 million, including whatever it paid the poet Marianne Moore to think up names for it that were never used. It was a well-engineered but rather awkwardly styled car, and it lasted just two years after it was put on the market in 1958. Its failure was due fundamentally to its timing; 1958 was a recession year, when the prospect for a new high-priced automobile was poor in any event, and somewhere between the planning and the unveiling of the Edsel public preference turned away from the big, ornate cars that had dominated the scene for several years. The experiment served to provide a vivid explanation of why the automobile industry had evolved into its pattern of domination by a few very large firms; only a big company could make a mistake costing a quarter of a billion dollars and live.

A brighter and definitely more momentous landmark in Ford history was the first offering of Ford Motor Company stock to the public. This event occurred in 1956 as the result of a decision of the Ford Foundation that it was unwise to have the Foundation's entire resources, enormous as they were, represented by common stock in the Ford Motor Company. The Ford Foundation dates back to 1936, when it was created in order to avoid the possibility that the family might be forced to sell control of the company in order to pay inheritance taxes. In view of the deaths of Edsel Ford and his father within four years of each other it proved to be a wise move. The Foundation was of minor importance for its first ten years, but then in consequence of those two deaths it came into possession of 90 per cent of the stock of the Ford Motor Company, and because of the successful rehabilitation of the company, the Ford Foundation suddenly found itself the world's largest private philanthropic enterprise.

The difficulty was that the stock was non-voting; the Foundation depended on the management of the company but could not control it. Hence the decision to diversify. A transaction of this magnitude naturally required delicate legal and financial handling. Among other things, it was necessary to reclassify the stock so that the purchasers could have an equitable voice in company affairs without sacrificing the proper interest of the Ford family. However, it was all worked out, and the offering of the stock demonstrated that the Ford name had lost none of its glamour. Brokerage houses were swamped with orders for the 10,000,000 shares that were available, and the issue, offered at $64.50, went as high as $70.00 a share in the first few days. Subsequent offerings left the foundation, in 1961, with half the total common stock of the Ford Motor Company, the family with a ninth, and the rest in the hands of the public.

Of the three giants, the Chrysler Corporation experienced the greatest difficulty in maintaining its position during the 1950's, for reasons that cannot readily be explained in terms of clear and tangible occurrences. There were errors of judgment in styling and there were managerial troubles, along with unaccountable shifts in consumer preferences. The visible evidence of Chrysler's troubles was that the company's bread-and-butter model, the Plymouth, lost the third-place position it had held comfortably for twenty years and was persistently outsold by one or the other of the General Motors medium-price lines: Oldsmobile, Buick, or Pontiac. The once-popular De Soto also lost its appeal and was discontinued in 1960.

The process of concentration applied primarily to the actual production of motor vehicles and not so much to the fabrication of parts. The independent supplier firms showed a remarkable capacity to survive in the automotive world. Even mighty General Motors went outside its own organization for half the components of its cars. The manufacturers retained this policy consciously. With some parts, cost calculations showed that it was cheaper to buy on the open market than to install facilities for making them; with others, the supplier company's experience and "know-how" were worth preserving. Moreover, although the automobile company might be making the item itself, it was desirable to keep competitors in existence as a check on the efficiency of one's own operations.

Consequently, while the industry was admittedly dominated by a handful of giant corporations, in the early 1960's there were almost three thousand companies in the United States classified as manufacturers of motor vehicles and parts, and after due allowance for subsidiaries of the big companies, there was manifestly still a multitude of small-scale independents. Outside the automotive industry there were many more suppliers. Tires, for instance, have always been made by rubber manufacturers, although some have been sold under the names of automobile companies. The Ford Motor Company reported in 1963 that it had thirty thousand separate suppliers scattered throughout the world who took fifty-six cents of each dollar the company earned and contributed products which, to quote the company's annual report, "may range from a lockwasher to an entire steelmaking furnace capable of producing seven thousand tons of steel a day."

Conspicuous Consumption

The Plymouth can fairly be described as a victim of the competition in power and glitter that characterized American automobile manufacturing in the middle 1950's. It continued a little too long to look like a low-priced car at a time when its rivals were trying to eliminate all differences in external appearance between automobiles of varying price ranges. The idea seems to have been that the decision on the purchase of an automobile was based as much on prestige considerations as on convenience of transportation, so that sales would be stimulated if every buyer of a new car could be given the feeling that he was getting something equivalent to a Rolls-Royce. The idea was valid enough, but the method chosen for its execution had the unfortunate effect of giving most new American automobiles an ostentatiously nouveau riche quality from which Rolls-Royce designers would have recoiled in horror—and probably did.

What happened was that lower-priced cars became big and gaudy, whereupon the vehicles in the higher price ranges felt compelled to compensate by becoming bigger and gaudier. Engine horsepower even on the standard models rose to new heights, and body designers were lavish with chrome and gleaming finishes to the point where the glare from car surfaces became a potential driving hazard. Body styles featured grandiose and eye-catching tail fins, justified on the ground that they were needed to house the complex of lights now installed at the rear of an automobile: tail, stop, back-up, and directional. There were even occasional claims that these elaborate fins had a stabilizing effect on the vehicle's motion—which might well have been so if the car had been airborne.

At the peak of the automobile boom of the 1950's, therefore, the American passenger car was exemplifying Thorstein Veblen's concept of conspicuous consumption on a scale never anticipated by him. Most of the trappings were purely for show and had nothing to do with improving the vehicle's qualities as a medium of transportation. The higher horsepowers were defended as providing a reserve of power for emergencies, and they did on occasion serve this purpose, but whether the availability of greater speeds prevented more accidents than it caused is debatable. The big cars had an advantage in riding comfort, especially on long trips. On the other hand, the profusion of big cars complicated traffic and parking problems, since fewer vehicles could be accommodated in a given area.

In a boom period with a high level of employment these vehicles seemed to be what the American people wanted, and so they were built. To be sure, sales of small foreign cars on the American

market were rising, and Chevrolet and Ford had been more successful than they had anticipated with their quasi sports cars, the
Corvette and Thunderbird, the former introduced by Chevrolet in
1953 and the latter by Ford in 1954. But this sector of the market,
the foreign and sports cars, was written off as purely prestige
buying on the part of a specialized group of consumers. Nor, in the
middle of the decade, did Romney's efforts with the Rambler seem
likely to bear fruit. It was this expansive mood that led Ford to
decide on bringing out the Edsel.

Even in labor relations there was a perceptible disposition to
emphasize external appearances. There were some contract negotiations in the early 1950's whereby cost-of-living increases were
incorporated permanently into base wage rates, a predictable revision of the original arrangement. But the grievances and hostility of
earlier years had at least temporarily subsided and the next major
round of negotiations in 1955 concentrated on Walter Reuther's
proposal for a guaranteed annual wage to offset the seasonality of
automobile manufacturing. Ford was the first company to reach an
agreement on this problem, and the terms of this settlement were
adopted generally throughout the industry. The company contributed five cents a worker for each hour of employment to create
a fund from which payments would be made to supplement state
unemployment benefits up to an agreed percentage of the worker's
normal earnings. Payments ran for a maximum of twenty-six
weeks, depending on the recipient's employment record and the
amount available in the fund.

This settlement was hailed as a great advance in industrial
relations, but it does not stand up under critical examination.
Although it would work well enough under the full employment
conditions in the automobile industry at the time, it required very
little calculation to make it evident that in a depression with
large-scale layoffs the fund would be depleted far more rapidly
than it could be replenished. One happily erudite Ford official
paraphrased Voltaire's description of the Holy Roman Empire and
observed (in private) that what the UAW had secured was neither

guaranteed nor annual nor a wage. Nevertheless it sufficed to keep labor peace in automotive circles for almost another decade.

The Coming of the Compacts

What came to be known as the great horsepower race was bound to end sooner or later. There was a useful limit to the size and power of the ordinary passenger automobile, and after the banner year of 1955 this limit was passed. Cars were becoming more and more expensive both to buy and to operate, much of the cost was manifestly in frills, and when humorists could remark, with enough accuracy to sting, that the buyer of a new car had to be able to afford not only the vehicle but a new and bigger garage to house it, the situation was palpably ridiculous. Yet consumer reaction was surprisingly slow. The manufacturers could protest with considerable justification that they were giving the customer what he seemed to want and offer in evidence the fact that their least luxurious models were their poorest sellers.

There were some straws blowing in the wind. Sales of small foreign cars were still climbing, although their total of 60,000 in 1955 was less than 1 per cent of the sales of motor vehicles in the United States. Nevertheless it was impossible to dismiss the standard Volkswagen, Hillman, Renault, or Morris as appealing exclusively to the sports car enthusiasts. At the time, however, they were explained away in terms of status-seeking or as second cars for the growing proportion of multicar families in the United States. It might have been considered significant that the Rambler sold 80,000 in 1955, double its previous record, but this too was disregarded, because everything automotive sold well in 1955 and American Motors was still losing money on Romney's experiment.

The awakening came when automobile production slid from its 1955 peak and the national economy slumped into the 1957–58 recession. As depressions go, this one was moderate, but it served to revive the neglected habit of looking at price tags and considering costs of upkeep and maintenance. So, paradoxically, an economic condition which troubled the major manufacturers saw American Motors prosper. Romney's persistence and faith finally had their reward as Rambler output went into six figures and continued up until it approached the half million mark in 1960. Simultaneously imports of foreign cars skyrocketed to 700,000 in 1959, which was about 10 per cent of the aggregate domestic production of motor vehicles for the year, or 12 per cent if only passenger cars are counted. Almost half the total came from West Germany, principally the highly popular Volkswagen. The United Kingdom ranked next, and then in order France, Sweden, Italy, and Japan. Of these, Swedish and Japanese automobiles were newcomers to the American scene.

TABLE 5

MOTOR VEHICLE IMPORTS IN 1963 BY COUNTRIES OF ORIGIN

COUNTRY IMPORTED FROM	TRUCKS, BUSES & CHASSIS		PASSENGER CARS NEW		PASSENGER CARS USED		AUTOMOTIVE PARTS VALUE
	Number	Value	Number	Value	Number	Value	
Belgium......	20	$ 354,000	17	$ 50,650	1	$ 2,000	$ 1,875,507
Canada......	1,665	1,225,043	921	680,537	169	124,815	18,961,974
Denmark.....	—	—	60	87,166	—	—	29,371
France.......	8	9,852	28,531	23,384,874	30	30,242	3,593,524
W. Germany..	13,873	15,427,080	274,105	276,291,422	14,151	17,332,057	33,140,818
Italy.........	1	1,280	12,973	17,012,369	20	60,935	1,777,400
Japan........	443	466,168	7,038	6,807,549	—	—	1,463,692
Netherlands..	—	—	311	277,785	3	3,200	331,878
Sweden......	1	16,396	16,901	23,993,675	15	16,267	2,155,990
United Kingdom...	216	493,236	68,092	96,366,837	268	337,980	18,298,202
Other........	1,407	530,501	75	100,963	12	24,235	1,006,317
Total....	17,634	$18,523,556	409,024	$445,053,827	14,669	$17,931,731	$82,634,673

SOURCE: U.S. Department of Commerce.

The domestic manufacturers met this challenge by themselves, without going to the government for aid. There was no suggestion that the influx of foreign cars should be curtailed by tariffs or otherwise; on the contrary, the automobile industry, through the Detroit Chamber of Commerce, openly advocated the removal of barriers to international trade. This position was arrived at by harsh experience. American automobile manufacturers had discovered that the restriction of trade was a game that could be played multilaterally, and that exports of American motor vehicles were the first victims of reprisals against United States tariff policies. Far from trying to prohibit the foreign invasion, the American companies joined it. General Motors and Ford had long been European producers and were perfectly willing to sell their European models on the American market, although neither actually did so on a scale comparable to the genuine foreign manufacturers. Chrysler moved into the picture by acquiring interests in the French Simca Company in 1958 and the British Rootes Group (Hillman, Humber, Singer, Sunbeam) in 1964.

The most effective response of the American manufacturers to the challenge of the small car, foreign and domestic, was to go into the compact business themselves—a reaction that had been pessimistically anticipated by the European producers. They had calculated, with commendable accuracy as it turned out, that when their American sales amounted to 10 per cent of the total number of motor vehicles sold in the United States, the threat would then be sufficient to bring the big American companies into the small-car field, with resources in economic strength and productive capacity beyond the ability of the Europeans to compete with. Events would disprove the gloomier forebodings of the Europeans. The high level of 1959 was not repeated in the ensuing years, but European firms retained a respectable volume of United States sales.

The late 1950's and early 1960's accordingly saw a dramatic shift in the pattern of American automobile production as a profusion of compact models was thrust before the buying public. Studebaker, under the pressure of necessity, hastened to follow the American Motors example, but without the same satisfying results. The Scotsman (1957) and the Lark (1958) gave Studebaker a temporary respite. But although the Rambler remained energetically in competition after the Big Three compacts appeared, the Studebaker entries faded rapidly.

From this time compacts came and went in bewildering variety. The more prominent included Chrysler's Valiant and Dart, Ford's

Falcon and Comet, and General Motors' Corvair, Tempest, and Chevy II. All featured economy and ease of operation, but all were bigger than the foreign cars they were meant to supplant. Occasionally claims for the compacts were carried to the point of absurdity (the same could be said of some of the advertising for standard automobiles). Corvair, for instance, was clearly inspired by the Volkswagen when it was designed with an air-cooled engine in the rear, but some of the Corvair advertising gave the impression that this was the first time in automotive history that anyone had thought either of building an air-cooled engine or of putting it at the rear of the car.

The compacts made more sense than some of the behemoths that had preceded them, but with all the fanfare that was lavished on them, their sales record revealed that the American preference for big cars was essentially unimpaired. The standard Chevrolet and Ford models easily outsold their smaller brothers. At Chrysler the Plymouth was still having its troubles in the early 1960's, but both it and the regular Dodge remained ahead of the Chrysler compacts. As far as it was possible to draw conclusions from a limited experience, the evidence indicated that although small cars had a firm hold on a segment of the American automobile market, it was a minor segment. Indeed, as the American-built compacts vied with each other for public approval, there was an observable tendency for each year's model to be a little larger and a little more ornate than before. If this trend continued there was an intriguing prospect that some enterprising manufacturer might copy Romney's example and this time come out with a compact compact.

THE AUTOMOBILE CULTS

The rise and fall of consumer preferences among the tail-finned models, the compacts, the foreign cars, and so on demonstrated that if the automobile had brought uniformity to many aspects of American life, the American people compensated by requiring diversity in their automobiles. There was not one automobile market; there were many, each with its own body of devotees. The largest single demand was for the conventional passenger car in varying sizes and prices, but there were communities in which eating with a knife would have been more acceptable than driving anything but a station wagon and others in which the convertible was a sine qua non.

Then there were the groups with special enthusiasms. There was a sports car cult, whose members enjoyed riding in small, high-performance vehicles, sometimes making a show of driving exposed to the elements in all weather. There were those who were addicted to foreign cars merely because of their snob appeal. They usually justified their perference by arguing that foreign cars were better built and did not have "planned obsolescence" incorporated into their design. The argument was valid for styling but not for performance or durability, because there is no convincing evidence that foreign cars last longer or run better than comparable American vehicles.

Among teen-agers there was a wide variety of automotive enthusiasms. There were those who delighted in "jalopies"—old cars, preferably as dilapidated as possible, whose continued functioning could be explained only in terms of the miraculous. In contrast to these were the customizers, who sought individuality in their cars by modification of the bodies. The changes could take such forms as reworking body lines, removing chrome or grill-work, lowering the front or rear end, or painting in unconventional patterns. Frequently the results showed artistry; sometimes they were grotesque. Lowering bodies was carried to such extremes that some states legislated against the practice. California, for example, stipulates that "no modified motor vehicles may be driven on the highway if any portion of their bodies other than the wheels are [*sic*] lower than the low point of any rim of the wheels." Another important group was the "hot-rodders," who took conventional cars and gave them extra power by reboring cylinders, installing extra carburetors or fuel-injection systems, and other methods. These "souped-up" vehicles were frequently used for drag-racing, which consisted of starting from a standing stop and trying to achieve maximum acceleration in a specified distance, usually a quarter of a mile. Since indulging in this sport on public highways was undesirable, many communities provided space for drag strips on which drag races could be held under controlled and orderly conditions.

Automobile racing retained all the popularity it had had since the days of the horseless carriage, but it had developed in a variety of different forms. The standard style of racing, with specially built racing cars, held its place although there was no longer a pretence that it was a method of testing cars. In addition, a multitude of small tracks came into existence for sports- and stock-car racing. The latter title was a misnomer. The vehicles entered in those contests were no more regular stock cars than those that ran in the Indianapolis 500 every Memorial Day. They were completely rebuilt for racing purposes, with high-powered engines and body structures remodeled for greater stability and safety at high speeds.

Finally, the automobile was acquiring a history. The fiftieth anniversary of the Duryea car came in 1943 and was overshadowed by the Second World War, but afterward there was a steady succession of golden jubilees: the first automobiles in Detroit (1946); the beginning of automobile manufacturing in Hartford (1947); Ford and Buick (1953); General Motors and the Model T (1958). It was now possible to cherish an automobile because it was old rather than because it was new; the lovers of antique cars, indeed, possessed a fervor that the owner of a gleaming new model fresh off the assembly line could never experience. Part of this enthusiasm manifested itself in the preservation of old cars in museums or in collections of private individuals or societies. The museums varied widely. Some were well organized and professionally managed. At the risk of seeming to discriminate, mention can be made of the Smithsonian Institution, which possesses the original Duryea, Haynes, and Winton cars, the Ford Museum in Dearborn, probably the largest of the collections, and the Thompson Products (now Thompson-Ramo-Wooldridge) Museum in

Cleveland. At the other end of the scale were numerous so-called auto museums along the highways, which were often simply tourist traps containing an assortment of junk.

There was also a substantial effort to promote study of automotive history. Much of this work was strictly antiquarian, performed by local organizations of automobile "buffs." There were societies of national scope, such as the Antique Automobile Club of America, which published magazines and promoted a certain amount of scholarly research. Recognition of the historical significance of the automobile was further emphasized when the Ford Motor Company opened its archives to students in 1951 through the medium of a department directed by a trained archivist, Henry E. Edmunds. At the same time the company sponsored a massive historical project covering the career of Henry Ford and the history of the Ford Motor Company, under the supervision of the distinguished American historian Allan Nevins. It was completed in three volumes in 1963. A further step on a broader scope was the designation in 1954 of the Detroit Public Library (certainly a logical choice) as the principal repository for materials on automotive history in the United States. The library's Automotive History Collection was assisted by the Automobile Manufacturers Association and has built up the most complete collection in the world of books, periodicals, and documents on the history of the American automobile and the automobile industry.

The true antique car enthusiast, however, was not interested in having his idols either mounted immobile in a museum or enshrined in the pages of a book. He wanted them out on the highway where they belonged. Most states by the 1950's made special provision for vehicles more than twenty-five years old to be registered as antique automobiles so that they could be legally operated. Enough of them were running so that the rubber companies unexpectedly found a profitable sideline in setting up sections of their plants to revive the manufacture of smooth-treaded, large-diameter, high-pressure tires.

For the antique-car devotees of the 1950's and 1960's a vehicle only a quarter of a century old was practically modern. The prized cars were early Model T's, curved-dash Oldsmobiles, Stanley Steamers, and others of comparable vintage. A surprising number of these were resurrected and rebuilt, and there were even new models built to the original design, to the accompaniment of anxious deliberations in antique automobile clubs concerning the authenticity for a particular car of artillery wheels or wire wheels, steering wheel or tiller, horn or siren, and innumerable other details. The clubs held meets to demonstrate the capabilities of their cars, at which the men were properly attired with long dust coats and goggles and the women wore the veils and scarfs of the horseless carriage era. The Glidden Tours were revived; at appropriate seasons one could see on American highways lines of colorful old cars chugging along on their prescribed routes. The big difference was that the participating vehicles usually reached the scene on trailers rather than under their own power. It was nostalgic, it was entertaining, and it underlined how in just over fifty years the automobile had implanted itself deeply in American culture.

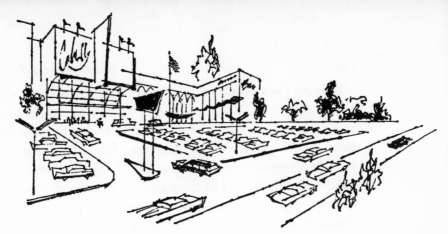

CHAPTER 13

Metropolis on the Freeway

The "average American" is a fiction of journalists, politicians, and social statisticians. But in the composite of characteristics that would make up this hypothetical individual, three would definitely emerge for the second half of the twentieth century: first, he lived in a metropolitan area and most likely in a suburb; second, he owned an automobile; and third, he and his family were almost completely dependent on their car for transportation beyond walking distance, or frequently within walking distance. The most important single supplement to the family automobile was another motor vehicle, the bus. After that, especially in large cities, came the taxicab.

The growth of the city is a well-documented aspect of modern life. In the United States the proportion of the population classed as urban—living in communities with more than 2,500 persons—rose from 40 per cent in 1900 to 70 per cent in 1960. Among urban communities the great metropolitan centers had a faster growth rate than the small towns, and their suburbs grew fastest of all. Suburban expansion began to outpace that of the cities as early as 1910. It mushroomed after 1920 until at midcentury one-fourth of the people of the United States lived in suburbs. By that time some central city areas were actually declining, and those that continued to grow did so at a rate never more than half as fast as that of their surrounding suburbs.

For this phenomenon the motor vehicle has been almost exclusively responsible. Modern Suburbia is a creation of the automobile and could not exist without it. It is true that with some American cities, notably New York, Chicago, Philadelphia, and Boston, suburban growth originally extended along a network of rail and rapid-transit lines, and in these metropolitan areas communication between city and suburb has remained heavily dependent on mass transportation by rail. Yet even in these four cities the great suburban expansion of the mid–twentieth century was accompanied by a shrinkage of rail commuter service, to the point where it was threatened with extinction. New suburbs grew with little reference to the mass transportation media. In any event the commuter, whether he lived in Wellesley Hills or Winnetka, Bala Cynwyd or Cos Cob, relied on a motor vehicle of some kind to get him to and from the railroad station. By comparison, a metropolis like Los Angeles, often and accurately described as a collection of suburbs in search of a city, grew up on highway transportation. Admittedly Los Angeles had an extensive electric interurban network in the early part of the century, but no one will seriously suggest that the Pacific Electric had much to do with the expansion of Los Angeles after 1925. The city was conspicuously a product of the automobile.

Los Angeles might be considered an extreme example but it was nonetheless an example of the fact that urban growth in the United States was predicated on motor-vehicle transportation. The extent of this dependence was not realized until the Second World War, when the critical shortages of rubber and gasoline stimulated investigation to determine the minimum possible use of private automobiles. The result was staggering. As of 1940, 13,000,000 persons, close to one-tenth of the population of the United States at the time, lived in suburban communities without access to any kind of public transportation system. In view of the accelerated expansion of Suburbia after the war, this proportion has become considerably higher. For good or ill the contemporary American metropolis is now so constituted that it could not live if movement by motor vehicle were to cease for any reason whatsoever.

TRAFFIC AND TRANSIT

Contrary to what is generally believed, the automobile did not create congestion on city streets. That is as old as cities themselves. Ancient Rome had ordinances restricting vehicular traffic for the convenience and safety of the citizenry. The effect of the automobile was to create a traffic problem much more complicated than had ever existed before.

The crux of the problem in the United States was movement between city and suburb. To the American motorist it must have seemed that congestion was a malignant and ubiquitous plague that pursued him wherever he went, but in fact if a method could be found for dealing with the flow into Metropolis in the morning and out again at might, other traffic difficulties would be considerably easier to remedy. A study of urban problems made in the 1950's by *Fortune* and published in 1957 under the title *The Exploding Metropolis* revealed that in the twenty-five largest American metropolises three-fifths of the people who entered the downtown business district every day did so by car. This average represents a range from 17 per cent for New York City to 78 per cent for San Antonio, Texas. Los Angeles, which might have been expected to lead the list, had a 66 per cent level; on the other hand, in metropolitan Los Angeles 95 per cent of all local passenger travel was by private automobile, the highest figure for any urban area in the world.

The New York situation is exceptional. The metropolitan region is elaborately equipped with rapid-transit lines and commuter railroads, and it would be a physical impossibility for the millions who enter and leave Manhattan Island daily to do so by automobile, both because of the restricted area of the island and the limited means of access. Yet it is safe to say that the difficulties of getting into New York by automobile and of finding a place to put the car after getting there are far more responsible for the low incidence of private automobile use than is the existence of the extensive mass transportation system. One item of evidence is that New York has fared no better than other large cities in the matter of declining patronage and revenue for the public transportation services. Another is that the low relative inflow of private cars is offset by extensive use of taxis, which comprise about half the motor vehicles in downtown Manhattan.

Whatever the variations from one metropolis to another, the traffic problem was there. The first obvious remedy was to improve existing streets, build new ones, and adopt various measures for expediting the movement of vehicles. These last took such forms as one-way streets, synchronized traffic lights, restriction of parking on main arteries, and techniques for reversing traffic lanes so that the flow would be inbound in the morning and outbound in the evening. Most ambitious—and expensive—was the construction of expressways. These, like the original Los Angeles freeways and the Detroit expressways, were principally designed to facilitate movement in and out of the central city. Some were built as bypass routes to keep through traffic out of the cities altogether, the classic being Massachusetts' Route 128, which swings in a great arc around Boston from Nantasket on the south shore to Cape Ann on the north and is, as far as is known, the only highway to have a railroad station named for it. Where it intersected the main line of the New Haven Railroad, a station called Route 128 was built at which all trains, express and local, stopped for the convenience of the heavily populated southern suburbs of Boston. The great advantage of the station was that it was easy to reach by automobile and had ample parking space.

About fifteen hundred miles of metropolitan freeways existed in 1955, mostly in California. The cost, never less than a million dollars a mile, and the complexities of building through urban areas made state and local authorities hesitate to undertake such projects except where there was compelling need. When Illinois decided to construct an express belt line around Chicago, it made it a tollroad. The Interstate Highway Act of 1956 removed the financial barrier by including provision for an additional five thousand miles of urban expressway, and a marked increase of activity ensued.

To the weary motorist inching along in rush hour traffic it must have appeared that all this expenditure on new highways and traffic control systems was simply being poured into a bottomless rathole, and he would have found widespread concurrence among traffic experts. No matter how fast or on what scale improved facilities were provided for getting into Metropolis, they could never keep up with the volume of vehicles using them. It was common for a new section of Los Angeles freeway to be opened and have its first traffic jam within twenty-four hours. The pressure on urban arteries came from two sources. First, there were just many more motor vehicles; between 1950 and 1963 total automobile registrations in the United States rose by a factor of two-thirds, from 49,000,000 to 82,000,000, or at the rate of 5 per cent per year. This increase was calculable and could be allowed for in highway planning. The unknown variable was the number of existing vehicles that would be attracted into the cities by more and better roads. Surveys of the New York traffic problem in the middle 1950's indicated that only one-fourth of the potential total of cars in New York's Suburbia were driven into the city. Even if no more cars were added, the main effect of building more express routes into New York City would be to draw an unpredictable flow of automobiles from this enormous reservoir of the remaining three-fourths.

Was it worth while even trying to keep up with the insatiable demands of the automobile? There was a substantial body of opinion that held that it was not; that the automobile was an inordinately wasteful and expensive method of providing for the transportation needs of Metropolis. Traffic surveys of major cities have shown with a striking consistency that car occupancy in rush hours averages between 1.4 and 1.8 persons. Elementary common sense seemed to dictate that the billions being spent on freeways would be better employed in creating really adequate systems of mass transportation. The appeal of this position was strong enough so that when the 1960's arrived, nearly all major American cities were discussing plans either for developing new rapid-transit facilities or rehabilitating those that they had.

It was an attractive solution to traffic woes, but it was not as simple as it looked. Existing urban transportaion systems were in poor condition physically and financially; they were used from necessity and not from choice. By and large they were not competitive in any way with the private automobile. According to the findings of *The Exploding Metropolis*, in the middle 1950's automobile traffic had a definite advantage over public transportation in speed. In every city of more than half a million population private cars moved during rush hours in the most congested sections at an average rate of twenty miles an hour, a figure not only astonishingly uniform but undoubtedly higher than would generally have been guessed. The average for all media of public transportation was thirteen miles an hour. The comparison is unfair to the public transportation systems, since these include streetcars and buses, neither of which is as maneuverable on crowded streets as the private car. Bus service came out slightly ahead of the automobile in Detroit, where express buses have definite traffic lanes assigned to them, and rail travel on separate rights-of-way had a clear advantage. The New York subway did slightly better than the automobile at rush hours, and commuter trains went almost twice as fast—thirty-six miles an hour for the much abused Long Island Railroad. Since these speeds are for peak congestion periods, allowance has to be made for the fact that at other times the automobile would do considerably better than twenty miles an hour, and the performance of the bus would improve also. The commuter train and the rapid transit, on the other hand, would show no appreciable gain and might even have a lower average speed for off-peak hours because there would be fewer express runs.

There are valid and compelling reasons for trying to replace the endless lines of motor vehicles on city streets and expressways with efficient mass transportation, but experience so far has made it manifest that the automobile will be an extraordinarily difficult contender to eliminate. Its disadvantages as a means of commuting between city and suburb can be freely conceded; nevertheless no existing or proposed system of mass transportation offers any real promise of dissuading the inhabitant of Metropolis from using his car if he possibly can. Whether the trip in town is made to go to work or to shop or for entertainment, the automobile allows flexibility of schedule, it avoids the nuisance of getting to and from stations or bus stops, and it is invariably pleasanter than riding in crowded, uncomfortable, and usually dingy public vehicles. The out-of-pocket cost, which is all that most motorists take into consideration, is unlikely to be enough higher than that of public transportation to offset the convenience of the automobile, and if two or more people ride in the car, the cost factor is normally in its favor. Exact figures are unavailable, but the *Fortune* study referred to estimated that even with a generous allowance for depreciation and highway taxes the cost of commuting by car in 1955 was six cents a mile as compared with an average of four cents for public transportation.

To compete effectively with the private automobile a transit system would have to be capable of scheduled speeds that would get a passenger to his destination in less time than he would require to make the trip in his own car on a freeway under favorable traffic conditions. Movement by rail on a separate right-of-way is the best existing method of achieving this goal, although a possible alternative might be high-speed buses operating on traffic lanes reserved exclusively for their use. Such service, whether by rail or bus, would also have to be frequent, convenient, comfortable, and attractive, and it would have to be offered at a price low enough to make it worthwhile for people to leave their cars at home. Transit facilities meeting these standards do not now exist but they are attainable if communities are prepared to face the cost; a system incorporating the qualities just described is technically feasible but it cannot be expected to pay its own way. In essence, metropolitan populations must choose between paying taxes to provide up-to-date mass transportation and paying them to build more express highways and parking facilities for their automobiles. The first choice may be the better one on several grounds, but the notion that it will be less expensive is illusory.

Another suggested remedy for urban traffic congestion is to keep automobiles out of the downtown business district altogether. Some cities, of which the best examples are Toledo, Ohio, and Pomona, California, have established central "malls" accessible only to pedestrians, with encouraging results both esthetically and commercially. But neither Toledo nor Pomona is of metropolitan size; the latter in fact is part of the greater Los Angeles metropolis. Neither, therefore, has to deal with the problem of moving enormous masses of people in and out every day. In the case of the Pomona mall, with which the author is familiar, the provision of generous parking areas immediately contiguous makes it evident that the patrons are expected to come by car. A major city would have to tear down a large part of its downtown section to provide parking space on a comparable scale. Indeed, proposals of this kind for the metropolitan centers have assumed that at least half the people coming into the mall area would use public transportation, so that implementation of the idea becomes contingent on resolving the larger question of providing adequate transit facilities. The concept of the central mall has its own indubitable merit, but it offers no quick and easy cure for crowded city streets.

MOTORIZED SUBURBIA

If the automobile brought blight to the inner city, it gave life to Suburbia. Besides being the principal means of transportation between suburb and city, it accounted for practically all movement within suburban communities themselves. Figures cannot tell the whole story, but it is an eloquent testimony to the automotive character of Suburbia that it has the highest incidence of automobile ownership in the United States; 87 per cent of suburban families own cars, as compared with just under 80 per cent for the nation as a whole. It is an interesting commentary on the structure of Metropolis that it has the low figure on the scale; in cities with more than half a million population the percentage drops to 61 within the city limits. This discrepancy can be explained on the ground that the higher-income families move to the suburbs while the low-income groups stay in the central city, but there is more to the story. Apartment dwellers in sections like Manhattan or in-town Washington, D.C., may be able to afford a car. But with ample taxi service or public transportation available for local travel, automobile ownership can well be dispensed with in order to avoid the nuisance and cost of parking and garaging.

The head of a suburban family might use an automobile to get to his job in the city, or he might drive his car to the railroad or bus station and park it there. If he used public transportation, there was a strong probability that his wife drove him to the station and met him on his return, meanwhile using the car for other family activities. (Since the husband and father spends most of his day elsewhere, Suburbia is definitely a matriarchy. This social phenomenon may be ranked as one of the major consequences of the automobile.) Suburban children go to school in motor vehicles, either driven in the family car or riding in school buses. When they are old enough they may and frequently do use their own cars, although studies have shown an inverse correlation between academic performance and the amount of time devoted to an automobile. The housewife drives to supermarket and shopping center and to civic and social activities. When the family is reunited in the evening, the car is available for visiting friends, going to the movies, or attending the meeting of the P.T.A., unless it has been taken by a younger member of the family to go on a date.

Considering their multifarious requirements for automotive transportation, it is understandable that suburban families should have not only the highest percentage of car ownership but also the highest percentage of multiple-car ownership. In 1963 one-fifth of all suburban households owned two or more automobiles, and these constituted two-fifths of all the multiple-car households in the United States.

There is a discernible relationship between suburban growth and the increase in two- and three-car families. Whereas the expansion of suburbs has been proceeding at an accelerating pace for most of the twentieth century, the real explosion of Suburbia occurred after the Second World War. During this same period multiple-car ownership at least doubled. For the ten years between the beginning of 1954 and the end of 1963 the total number of households in the United States with more than one car rose from 4,000,000 to almost 9,000,000. In percentage terms this was an increase from 9 per cent of all households in 1954 to 15.6 per cent in 1963, or from 12 to 20 per cent of car-owning households. If more than one car was needed only occasionally and multiple ownership was too much of a financial burden, rental agencies existed to fill the gap. These were not exclusively a suburban phenomenon; the larger agencies functioned on a nationwide scale. They reflected, however, the growing number of families, predominantly suburban, whose living conditions demanded that one car be available for family activities while another was in use for business.

The primary outward thrust of Metropolis was one of people seeking room and a community to live in rather than the mass impersonality of the great city. The automobile was the instrument that made it possible for millions, for the many rather than the few, at least partially to realize these desires. The "suburban sprawl" that surrounds every large American city, the acres upon acres of monotonously uniform "developments," could be accused of turning a dream into a nightmare; yet whatever the deficiencies of the rows of "ranch houses" and synthetic Cape Cod cottages, the occupants were certainly better off than as if they had been jammed into city tenements.

The mass movement to the suburbs naturally carried with it the various business enterprises necessary to provide for these vast numbers. There was nothing unusual about business moving to where its customers could best be found; the distinctive feature of this migration was that it had to accommodate customers who preferred to do their shopping by automobile. Until the 1940's suburban retail stores were either strictly local establishments or minor branches of downtown department stores. It then became increasingly evident that the suburban housewife would shop by preference where she could drive and park conveniently rather than face a tiring and time-consuming trip in town either by car or by public transportation. If the customer was not going to come to the store, the store of necessity had to go to the customer.

The answer was the suburban shopping center, located where there was plenty of room and easy access by road—preferably close to an express highway. The typical shopping center was built around a large, fully-equipped branch of a major department store or mail-order house. If the center was very big it might have two or more of these establishments. Around the core were ancillary enterprises: specialty shops, drug stores, restaurants, and so on. Surrounding the whole complex was the ample parking lot, the element on which the rest of operation depended, because the customers would come by car or not at all. There were 1,800 of these shopping centers in 1955, and their number was growing fast as both Metropolis and Suburbia continued to expand. A supermarket might or might not be part of a shopping center such as has been described; it was more usual for a supermarket to be the nucleus of a separate center of its own. In any event the supermarket was also a creation of the automobile. It could easily outmatch the corner grocery store in price and variety of selection, but to do so it had to be able to operate on a large scale. It had to draw customers in numbers from a considerably wider area than could be covered on foot, and they had to buy in quantity. These conditions presupposed shopping by car. The parking lot was an essential adjunct to the supermarket also. The total effect was a revolutionary redistribution of retail business in Metropolis. Before the Second World War less than 5 per cent of the retail purchases in large city complexes were made in suburban outlets. As early as 1950 this proportion had risen to a third, and it was still going up.

The vehicular orientation of suburban life was reflected in a development of business enterprises which went beyond the provision of parking space and were organized so that the patrons need not get out of their automobiles at all. The drive-in theater and the drive-in restaurant are not, strictly speaking, suburban phenomena, since they can now be found in every kind of community. They first appeared on the outskirts of urban areas, however, and the heaviest concentrations continued to flourish in Suburbia. There were more than 4,000 drive-in theaters in the United States in 1964 and about 30,000 drive-in restaurants. The latter total fluctuated markedly because many of the drive-ins were hamburger stands operating on a shoestring and with a very short life expectancy. The drive-in business technique has been widely adopted. Even the traditionally staid banking community has yielded to the domination of the automobile by installing drive-in tellers' windows, most frequently in suburban banks.

Freeway Industry

The suburban exodus was originally exclusively residential and long remained so. It was a migration of people looking for homes where they could live under better conditions than the cities could offer. The retail business enterprises that accompanied the movement did not affect its character; they were manifestly needed to serve the residents of Suburbia. Industry was in a very different position. In the initial stages of suburban expansion industry was emphatically not wanted, and it had little incentive in any event to move to places where the local labor supply was negligible and transportation facilities for moving freight were poor.

The advent of metropolitan expressways brought a marked change. For an industry whose hauling requirements could be adequately taken care of by truck, there were now distinct advantages to locating on the freeway in an outlying area. Land was cheaper and taxes lower than in central city industrial districts, and shipments by road could be made faster and more dependably since they did not have to contend with crowded city streets. The work force likewise had easy access to the plant by automobile.

Consequently, the 1950's saw a noticeable tendency for light industry—for instance, electronics plants or firms engaged in research and development—to spring up along the outer sections of metropolitan expressways. Besides residential tracts and shopping centers, Suburbia began to sprout "industrial parks," choice sites in which a variety of small factories could be placed. To make them acceptable to their communities, the industrial parks were carefully designed and landscaped; many of them, indeed, were esthetically superior to adjoining subdivisions of identical tract houses. Some of these suburban industrial centers had rail transportation available, but for the most part they, like Suburbia itself, depended on the motor vehicle.

This industrial expansion into suburban areas was welcomed, within limits. Living in Paradise Estates might be all that was expected of it, but providing schools of the desired quality and other public services, such as sewers, where none had existed before, had an inflationary effect on tax rates. If the community could include some nice respectable industrial plants, the kind that did not make loud noises or emit vast quantities of smoke and fumes, these could assume some of the tax burden that would otherwise fall on residential property. Preferably they should also be industries that either required a small labor force or could draw it from some other community, so that Paradise Estates would not have a welfare burden if business was bad. There was thus a happy meeting of minds. The light industries and the "think tanks" could benefit most from locations on suburban freeways, and they were also the type preferred by suburban residents.

It is clear enough that the motor vehicle is primarily responsible for the pattern of development of suburban life in the United States, in both its social and economic aspects. There is a less conspicuous reciprocal effect, whose implications have not yet been fully realized. This is the likelihood that this movement of commerce and industry into the suburbs is anchoring the automobile still more firmly on Metropolis. The suburbanite's need to travel into the downtown business district for shopping purposes was approaching a possible vanishing point. If the rise of freeway industry meant that the commuter movement between home and work was to change in significant volume from its accustomed suburb-to-city flow to a flow from suburb to suburb, then much of the case for subsidized mass transportation would lose its meaning. In fact, no conceivable public transportation system could provide for the necessary travel as efficiently or as economically as the private automobile.

THE TROUBLED CENTER

The same forces that stimulated growth and vitality on the out-skirts of Metropolis threatened the middle with rot and decay. This condition applied both to population and to business activity. Plans for arresting this downward trend invariably and necessarily devoted much attention to the automobile. It could hardly be considered the sole cause of urban troubles, but no twentieth-century American city was going to make much progress with its other problems until it had figured out what to do with the motor vehicle.

The questions of traffic control and the relief of congestion that have been discussed previously were only part of the story, although the major part. For most American cities the prospect of replacing automobiles with rapid-transit facilities was a distant and uncertain one if it existed at all. Meanwhile, if people were to come into the downtown area to do business, they were going to come by car, and provision had to be made to accommodate them. Along with arrangements for expediting traffic, parking had somehow or other to be made available. A traffic study of Boston in the middle 1950's showed that a daily average of 150,000 motor vehicles entered the business district, an area in which, counting all garages, parking lots, and curbside space, there was room for 110,000 cars, including those that parked illegally. For Boston, one remedy was to follow the example of other large cities and go underground. To the horror of Proper Bostonians, a parking garage was built beneath Boston Common, matching the one built on the other side of the country beneath Pershing Square in Los Angeles. Enlarged parking facilities, however, had precisely the same effect as improved traffic arteries: they encouraged more people to drive into the downtown section and were overcrowded almost as soon as they opened.

Freeway construction in metropolitan centers also presented problems similar to those encountered in the building of express highways in rural areas. Highway departments had the same regrettable propensity to regard the bulldozer as the appropriate means for settling disputes over rights-of-way and the preservation of historic or artistic sites. They had their defense; their job was to build highways as economically as possible. There were signs that public opinion was beginning to react against indiscriminate destruction for the sake of building superhighways. San Franciscans, for example, revolted in the early 1960's against the desecration of their cherished Embarcadero. The result is that the motorist who drives into San Francisco by the route that was at one time unflatteringly nicknamed Bloody Bayshore finds that after passing an impressive six-level interchange at the civic center and then the exit to the Bay Bridge, the magnificent freeway suddenly comes to a dead end. The growing strength of this attitude was reflected in a supplemental piece of federal highway legislation passed in 1962. This act required among other things that planning for federally-aided urban expressways should provide for the preservation of "social and community values."

Finally the automobile posed for Metropolis an acute and intensifying problem of atmospheric pollution. It was not the first offender in this matter. Industrial operations and domestic heating plants were blanketing cities with smoke and waste gases long before automotive exhausts added their contribution. Pittsburgh's reputation as the Smoky City was established in the nineteenth century. What the motor vehicle did was make a bad matter worse by intensifying the formation of "smog," a word coined to combine smoke and fog. Although it has other components, by far the greatest part of the smog that now plagues many American cities consists of hydrocarbons and nitrous oxides emitted from motor-vehicle exhausts. Smog from this source first appeared in critical volume in metropolitan Los Angeles during the 1940's and was for long considered to be a peculiarity of the Los Angeles area, because conditions there are unusually conducive to atmospheric pollution. The Los Angeles basin is enclosed on the land side by high mountain ranges. Since the prevailing winds blow off the Pacific Ocean with an average velocity of less than ten miles an hour, the smog-laden air does not get dispersed laterally, and it is often prevented from rising vertically by a distribution of atmospheric layers known as temperature inversion, whereby a layer of warm air at high levels keeps the low-level air masses down. The situation has nothing to do with the automobile. The Los Angeles basin was identified as the "valley of the smokes" by the first Spanish explorers to visit it. When, however, the world's most intense concentration of motor vehicles began pouring exhaust gases into this atmospheric dead end, the result was critical.

Los Angeles met the difficulty by creating an Atmospheric Pollution Control Board, which had a fair amount of success in curtailing pollution from non-automotive sources such as industrial gases and backyard incinerators. Against automobile exhausts, however, the best the APCB could do was fight a stubborn rear-guard action. All non-essential motor vehicle traffic was supposed to stop during major smog alerts, but this regulation was an unenforceable pious wish. Pressure was exerted on the manufacturers to install smog-control devices on their cars, and in the early 1960's these were required by law on new cars. The results were not satisfactory. The manufacturers were criticized for procrastinating, but they were in reality victims of the traditional American assumption that any technical problem can be solved just by inventing a gadget. Actually only two methods of controlling exhaust emissions gave promise of working, and neither was wholly effective. One went in the crankcase and the other on the exhaust manifold. Their purpose was to consume more of the hydrocarbons in the fuel, but they did not consume all; they had no effect whatever on nitrous oxides, and they required frequent expert servicing. If they were improperly installed and maintained, they were likely to cause serious motor damage. It was worth accepting the limitations of these devices in order to alleviate the smog situation, but it was clear that no easy technical remedy was in sight.

Although the Los Angeles experience was the most extreme and difficult case of atmospheric pollution traceable to the automobile, most other metropolitan areas found themselves wrestling with similar conditions. The massing of large numbers of motor vehicles in a limited area created smog, and barring some new breakthrough either in automotive fuels or in exhaust control, the only guaranteed way to get rid of the smog was to get rid of the motor vehicles. Some cities made encouraging progress in reducing atmospheric pollution, Pittsburgh being an outstanding example, but Pittsburgh was almost as much a special case as Los Angeles. An unusually heavy proportion of its atmospheric troubles consisted of industrial gases, and industrial smokestacks are far more easily controlled than automobile exhaust pipes.

It would be possible, and extremely obvious, to summarize the whole situation by stating that Metropolis can live neither with the motor vehicle nor without it. It is not that simple, although urban planners probably wish that they had this choice. Under present-day conditions Metropolis must live with the automobile and somehow in the process reduce traffic congestion and atmospheric pollution. Without automotive transportation for people and goods by private car, bus, and truck, Suburbia would disintegrate; there is no alternative. The inner city problem is more complicated, but although a reduction of highway traffic may be conceivable and desirable, its elimination is wholly impractical. What the urban center needs to achieve is a balance between utilizing the automobile and being smothered by it.

CHAPTER 14

Retrospect and Prospect

The story of the automobile in the United States begins effectively with appearance of the Duryea car in 1893; the first seventy years of the tale was therefore completed in 1963. The anniversary went generally unnoticed, but it was appropriately marked by further evidence of phenomenal growth. In 1963 the total number of motor vehicles built in the United States since the days of the Duryea brothers reached and passed 200,000,000. About as phenomenal was the fact that 80,000,000 of these were in active use. It took until 1948, fifty-five years, to produce the first 100,000,000; the second took just fifteen years. The figures are impressive enough by themselves, but they contain only a fragment of the epic of the American automobile.

Behind the tables of statistics is a production achievement unparalleled in the history of the world, from which came drastic transformations in the economy and the society of the United States. Whether these changes were beneficial or not remains undetermined. Some were and some were not; it is arguable that on balance the advantages have outweighed the disadvantages, but the final verdict has still to be returned. These effects have extended beyond the United States to give the motor vehicle a vital part in the shaping of contemporary civilization. Admittedly the automobile was neither originally nor exclusively an American creation. It

237

TABLE 6

U.S. PRODUCTION SINCE 1900

CAL-ENDAR YEAR	PASSENGER CARS		MOTOR TRUCKS AND BUSES		TOTAL	
	Number	Value (000)	Number	Value (000)	Number	Value (000)
1900..	4,192	$ 4,899	. . .	. . .	4,192	$ 4,899
1905..	24,250	38,670	750	1,330	25,000	40,000
1910..	181,000	215,340	6,000	9,660	187,000	225,000
1915..	895,930	575,978	74,000	125,800	969,930	701,778
1920..	1,905,560	1,809,171	321,789	423,249	2,227,349	2,232,420
1925..	3,735,171	2,458,370	530,659	458,400	4,265,830	2,916,770
1930..	2,787,456	1,644,083	575,364	390,752	3,362,820	2,034,835
1935..	3,273,874	1,707,836	697,367	380,997	3,971,241	2,088,834
1940..	3,717,385	2,370,654	754,901	567,820	4,472,286	2,938,474
1945..	69,532	57,255	655,683	1,181,956	725,215	1,239,210
1950..	6,665,863	8,468,137	1,337,193	1,707,748	8,003,056	10,175,885
1955..	7,920,186	12,452,871	1,249,106	2,020,973	9,169,292	14,473,844
1960..	6,674,796	12,164,234	1,194,475	2,350,680	7,869,271	14,514,914
1963..	7,637,728	14,427,077	1,462,708	3,076,184	9,100,436	17,503,261

NOTE: A substantial proportion of the trucks and buses consists of chassis only; therefore the value of the bodies for these chassis is not included. Value is based on vehicles with standard equipment. Federal excise taxes are excluded.
SOURCE: Automobile Manufacturers Association.

TABLE 7

REGISTRATIONS SINCE 1900

YEAR DECEMBER 31	PASSENGER CARS	BUSES	TRUCKS		TOTAL
			Number	Percent of Total	
1900...............	8,000	—	—	—	8,000
1910...............	458,377	—	10,123	2.2	468,500
1920...............	8,131,522	—	1,107,639	12.0	9,239,161
1930...............	22,972,745	40,507	3,518,747	13.3	26,531,999
1940...............	27,372,397	72,641	4,590,386	14.3	32,035,424
1950...............	40,333,591	223,652	8,604,448	17.5	49,161,691
1960...............	61,558,847	272,129	11,937,589	16.2	73,768,565
1963............... (Prelim.)	68,452,000	13,606,000			82,058,000

NOTE: Registrations shown here are not synonymous with vehicles in use since the latter implies a count of vehicles in operation on a specific date or an average for a period of time, while registrations are a count of trans-actions (with transfers eliminated) during a specified period. Buses are not segregated from passenger cars or trucks in earlier years. Also included are municipally owned buses engaged in public transit. Due to new method of counting buses in 1959, the bus data for earlier years are not strictly comparable. The addition of Alaska and Hawaii to the registration counts in 1959 accounted for increases in the U.S. totals. Data for the years 1950 to date have been revised to exclude farm trucks registered at a nominal fee in certain states and restricted to use in the vicinity of the owners' farms. Figures for 1950 and following years exclude military vehicles.
SOURCE: U.S. Bureau of Public Roads.

was not, however, the automobile by itself that exerted these profound social and economic influences, but the automobile linked with mass production.

The growth of the American automobile industry is therefore

the heart of the entire story. The industry found the secret of producing complicated mechanisms like motor vehicles in quantity, at low unit cost, and in variety—as expressed in the General Motors slogan of "a car for every purse and every purpose"—and from this discovery flowed all the far-reaching economic and social consequences of the automobile. The breakdown of rural isolation, the explosion of Suburbia, the construction of superhighways, the traffic congestion, the smog, the revision of social habit patterns, and the geometrical increase in productivity resulting from the adoption of the assembly-line technique all came about because the automobile in the United States was seen as a commodity for general and multipurpose use, rather than as an item of luxury. The term "carriage trade" had economic significance when carriages were drawn by horses and only the wealthy could afford them; the mass-produced automobile made it a meaningless expression.

This transformation was brought about by a group of identifiable personalities: Ford, Durant, Leland, Sloan, Olds, Chrysler, Chapin, Knudsen, Nash, Kettering, Packard, Winton, Willys. This list is neither complete nor in an intentional order of priority, although Henry Ford has to come first in any rating of automotive leaders, but it will do as a sample. As individuals they varied widely, but as a group they were forceful, hard-driving, and willing to accept the rough-and-tumble of energetic business competition, and above all completely dedicated to the automobile. This quality can be seen vividly in the less successful men like W. C. Durant or Benjamin Briscoe, whom no amount of discouragement could keep from coming back to the automobile business.

It has been pointed out that the automobile industry in its early days approached the classical concept of free competition. Similarly the men who founded and directed the automobile companies can be taken as case studies in entrepreneurship. They were individuals who saw an opportunity in a technological innovation and accepted the risk of attempting to exploit this opportunity, usually with their own scanty resources or with funds that were very definitely venture capital. If the rewards for successful entrepreneurship were high, they were commensurate with the risks. The incidence of failure as very heavy—not necessarily the spectacular failures like Durant but the forgotten men like David D. Buick and hundreds of others who appeared briefly on the scene and then vanished. One qualification should be made. The automobile men deviate from the theoretical model of the entrepreneur in that they do not seem to have been exclusively profit-motivated. They had a firm respect and desire for profits to be sure, but with Durant and Briscoe again as examples, most of them appear to have been so constituted that they would be happier losing money trying to manufacture and sell automobiles than making it anywhere else. Some of the losers gave up immediately; the commoner procedure, however, was for the defeated party to nurse his wounds briefly and charge back into the competition at the earliest opportunity.

The era of unrestricted competition ended with the establishment of large-company domination during the 1930's, a condition that developed as an inevitable consequence of mass production and mass marketing. Any assumption, however, that the industry went to the other extreme and became non-competitive would be erroneous. There was a tendency to stabilize prices, a propensity common to large-scale industrial enterprises with a heavy fixed investment to protect. The rise of the UAW accentuated this trend by introducing an element of inflexibility into wages. Nevertheless there was energetic and continuing competition on other grounds—new models, styling, technical features. There was ample leeway. The automobile manufacturers were producing for a market consisting of millions of unidentified customers, who had complete freedom of choice and whose tastes and preferences were unpredictable and uncontrollable, no matter how persuasive the advertising might be. The experience in the 1950's of the market turning from big cars to foreign imports and compacts showed that even the big companies had to be constantly alert for changes in consumer attitudes.

An important consequence of the struggle for markets was that the product was steadily improved. From the clumsy horseless carriage of the 1890's to the modern automobile there has been a constant advance in quality, although the fundamental engineering principles have remained essentially unchanged. Through the years engines, transmissions, fuels, brakes, lights, and tires have all been made more efficient and more dependable—basically because the surest way to sell more cars was to keep making them better. The mass use of the motor vehicle in the United States could not have developed on the scale it did, with all the attendant consequences, if the cars had not achieved progressively higher standards of reliability.

Moreover, contrary to general impression, travel by automobile became safer. Statistics of highway accidents on holiday weekends might seem to belie this claim, but it can be substantiated. Deaths from traffic accidents rose by 12,000 in thirty years, from 31,000 in 1933 to 43,000 in 1963, a factor of about 40 per cent. Meanwhile motor-vehicle registrations went from 24,000,000 to 80,000,000, an increase of 233 per cent. The rate of highway fatalities for this period declined from 15.6 to 5.4 for every 100,000,000 vehicle-miles traveled, or, calculating it another way, from 13.2 to 5.2 for every 100,000 motor vehicles. The meaning of these figures is that as far as automotive and highway engineering can achieve it, the possibility of accident from causes other than human error has been reduced to a minimum, and the likelihood of death or injury in the event of accident has also been lessened.

No one was happy about traffic accidents, least of all the insurance companies who found themselves in a race between premiums and damage claims. If the possibility of personal injury was statistically less, the costs of medical and hospital care were higher, and repair bills went up geometrically as automobiles became bigger and more complicated. The financial and legal consequences of highway accidents were an increasingly burdensome problem. Court dockets were badly overloaded with accident claims. Some states tried to resolve the question of liability by compulsory insurance laws, others by requiring financial responsibility. None of them could claim to have found a fully satisfactory solution.

RESEARCH AND DIVERSIFICATION

Charles F. Kettering is supposed to have dismissed the study of history on one occasion by remarking that no one could make progress by looking in his rear-view mirror. The historian's obvious retort is that the motorist who never looks in the rear-view mirror is inviting trouble, but that is beside the point. It is understandable that so young an industry should be more concerned with its future than its past. As a matter of fact, concern even with the future is a fairly recent phenomenon. Until midcentury the automobile industry lived very much in the present. Development consisted of working on next year's model, and research was thinking of what to do for the year after that.

There were exceptions. The Sloan reorganization of General Motors included a General Motors Research Corporation. Its purpose at first was principally to make a place in the structure for Charles F. Kettering, where he could pursue his own individualistic way. Subsequently it grew into a full-scale research organization, renamed General Motors Research Laboratories. In addition, in the 1920's the more important automobile companies began to equip themselves with elaborate proving grounds to test their products. This in itself was testimony to the advancement of the automotive art. The motor vehicle had become too sophisticated a mechanism to be tested adequately on a convenient stretch of vacant road, to say nothing of the fact that stretches of vacant road were becoming harder to find, and the notion that the racetrack could function as a proving ground had been discarded.

The greatest growth of research activity occurred after the Second World War, which brought into being or into prospect of realization several technological changes that had hitherto been remote. The automobile industry was deeply enough involved in the development of these technologies to be aware that the motor vehicle of the not distant future could be very different from the automobile as it then existed, and it behooved the manufacturers to study carefully the likely directions of change. There was much talk at the end of the war about nuclear power for motor vehicles, based mostly on ignorance of the problems of utilizing nuclear energy. The potentialities of the gas-turbine engine came closer to immediate practicality. It was obvious at the end of the war that the piston engine for aircraft was on the way out, although in commercial as distinct from military use the piston engine displayed a greater tenacity than might have been expected. Nevertheless, the automobile companies needed to keep abreast of gas-turbine technology.

There was scope for consideration of the future of the motor vehicle itself. The great expansion of aviation during the war revived speculation about the replacement of the family automobile by some kind of aircraft, perhaps a helicopter, but once again this prospect failed to materialize, despite a substantial increase in private flying. The technical and production problems were difficult but not impossible if the market existed; the insuperable obstacle was just that flying any kind of aircraft requires a much higher degree of skill and training than is required to drive an automobile. Thus the motor vehicle was likely to survive, but it could still face radical changes. It might, for instance, give up its wheels and ride on a cushion of air; both Ford and Curtiss-Wright demonstrated experimental models of such a vehicle in 1959.

In the early 1960's several of these possibilities, and others, were under serious investigation in automotive research laboratories, and some were approaching the testing stage. The Chrysler Corporation actually built and sold a limited number of prototype cars with gas-turbine engines in 1963. Another radical change that appeared to be within reach was an electric automobile with current supplied by fuel cells, or possibly by a completely novel type of battery. Either of these developments held prospects of major social and economic consequences. First, there would be repercussions in the petroleum industry, since the gas turbine uses simpler fuels than the piston engine, and the electric motor needs no petroleum products except lubricants. Second, the problem of atmospheric pollution would be markedly reduced, because a gas-turbine engine effects more complete combustion than a piston engine, and the electric motor discharges no waste products into the atmosphere.

The advance of electronics offered other prospects. By 1960 experiments were being made on a device whereby a car could be steered automatically by a current in the highway and on radar systems that in conditions of poor visibility would show where the edge of the pavement was or if there were obstacles in the vehicle's path. As with most new technologies, time was needed to sort out these various ideas and determine which of them might be really practical. It is one thing to test under laboratory conditions but quite another to put the results into a form that is both economical and feasible for day-to-day operation by the millions of people who drive automobiles. A radically new power plant may have conspicuous technical superiority over the standard gasoline engine, but it cannot be put into general use if it is too complicated for the ordinary motorist to operate or for the local garage to service and repair.

An alternative method of hedging against future change was to diversify, but in view of the mixed experience of automobile firms in venturing out of their field, it was pursued with understandable caution. General Motors, which had to function with the uncomfortable sensation that the Department of Justice was constantly peering over its shoulder looking for monopoly, stayed close to automotive operations, among which it included diesel locomotives, aircraft engines, and earth-moving equipment, this last added by the purchase of the Euclid Road Machinery Company in 1953. In addition, the electrical equipment divisions were drawn by military contracts into missiles and electronics. Through its acquisition of Frigidaire the corporation eventually moved into the manufacture of other household appliances such as electric ranges, washing machines, dryers, and dishwashers. American Motors inherited the Kelvinator Division from Nash and remained in the refrigerator business also.

The Ford Motor Company made the boldest step toward diversification early in the 1960's by moving into electronics and astronautics. The principal move in this direction was the purchase in 1961 of the Philco Corporation, manufacturer of television, radio, and other electronic equipment. Philco also enabled Ford to join General Motors and American Motors as a producer of household appliances. The company moved into missile and space work through its Aeronutronics Division, which was consolidated with Philco in 1963. In addition, Ford, despite its unhappy experience with the Ferguson tractor patents in the 1950's, remained securely established as one of the world's largest manufacturers of wheeled tractors. The White Motor Company also entered the farm machinery business through the acquisition of the Oliver Corporation (1961) and Motec Industries (1963).

There were therefore some indications that the automobile and the automobile industry might be on the threshold of major changes, but that these changes would be made slowly and cautiously. There were valid reasons for avoiding precipitancy, quite apart from the enormous investment represented by the facilities for building, servicing, and supplying existing types of motor vehicles. During its first three-quarters of a century the American automobile had evolved into something much more than a convenient medium for getting from here to there. It is transportation, it is prestige, it is recreation. In one way or another it supports one-sixth of all the business enterprises and one-seventh of all the wage earners in the United States. It has become almost indispensable as an adjunct to courtship. It has enabled people by the million to move about more freely than has ever before been possible, with both good effects and bad. In short, the American automobile has become a way of life, and whatever happens to it must profoundly affect the economy and the whole culture of the United States.

Important Dates

1769   First self-propelled highway vehicle built in France by Nicholas Joseph Cugnot.

1805   Oliver Evans ran the *Orukter Amphibolos* through Philadelphia.

1879   George B. Selden applied for U.S. patent on "road engine."

1893   Duryea car ran in Springfield, Massachusetts.

1895   Selden patent issued.

1896   Henry Ford built his quadricycle.

1897   Commercial production of motor vehicles begun by Pope Manufacturing Co. in Hartford, Connecticut, and Winton Motor Carriage Co. in Cleveland, Ohio.

1901   Curved-dash Oldsmobile introduced.

1902   American Automobile Association organized.

1903   Ford Motor Company founded.
Selden patent suit started against Ford and others.

1905   Society of Automobile (later Automotive) Engineers founded.

1908   Model T Ford put on market.
General Motors Company organized by W. C. Durant.

1911   Final decision in Selden patent case: "valid but not infringed."

1912   Electric starter introduced on Cadillac by Charles F. Kettering.

1914   Complete moving-assembly-line production begun by Ford Motor Company.
Ford instituted five-dollar day.

1915   Agreement for cross-licensing of patents adopted.
1916   Federal Road Aid Act passed.
1921   W. C. Durant left General Motors; founded Durant Motors.
        Federal Highway Act provided for "primary" routes.
1923   Ethyl gasoline developed by Charles F. Kettering and
        Thomas Midgley.
        Alfred P. Sloan, Jr., made president of General Motors.
1925   Chrysler Corporation founded.
1927   Manufacture of Model T Ford discontinued.
1935   United Automobile Workers chartered.
        Federal Motor Carriers Act passed.
1937   General Motors accepted UAW as bargaining agent.
1940   First section of Pennsylvania Turnpike opened.
        Prototype of jeep demonstrated.
1942   Production of civilian vehicles halted.
        Gasoline rationing instituted.
1945   Civilian production resumed.
        Gasoline rationing ended.
1947   Henry Ford and William C. Durant died.
        Fiftieth anniversary of commercial automobile production
           celebrated in Hartford.
1950   Tubeless tires introduced.
1954   Nash and Hudson combined as American Motors.
        Studebaker and Packard merged.
1955   Record production year—more than 9,000,000 motor ve-
           hicles.
1956   Interstate Highway Act passed.
        Ford Motor Company stock offered to public.
        Tollroad system from New York to Chicago completed.
1959   Foreign cars accounted for more than 10 per cent of sales on
           American market.
1963   Gas-turbine cars put on market by Chrysler.
1964   Studebaker transferred all automobile production to Hamil-
           ton, Ontario.

Suggested Reading

There is an extensive body of literature on the American automobile. The following list is intended to be selective rather than inclusive, indicating where the interested reader might profitably start on some of the varied aspects of the history of the automobile.

GENERAL WORKS

R. E. Anderson, *The Story of the American Automobile* (1950) is a good survey of early development. R. M. Cleveland and S. T. Williamson, *The Road Is Yours* (1951), D. L. Cohn, *Combustion on Wheels* (1944), and M. M. Musselman, *Get a Horse!* (1950) are all written in popular style but are sound historically. Merrill Denison, *The Power to Go* (1956) is frequently superficial but also has shrewd insights; it is especially good on the history of trucks. J. B. Rae, *American Automobile Manufacturers: The First Forty Years* (1959) concentrates on the history of the industry.

Several older works remain well worth reading: R. C. Epstein, *The Automobile Industry* (1928); C. B. Glasscock, *The Gasoline Age* (1937); E. D. Kennedy, *The Automobile Industry* (1940); T. F. Mac-Manus and Norman Beasley, *Men, Money, and Motors* (1929); and L. H. Seltzer, *The Financial History of the American Automobile Industry* (1928).

On the chatty, personal reminiscence side are E. W. Lewis, *Motor Memories* (1947), by an official of the Timken Roller Bearing Company, and C. G. Sinsabaugh, *Who, Me?: Forty Years of Automobile History* (1940), by an editor of automotive magazines.

Automobiles of America (1962), compiled by the Automobile Manufacturers Association, is an indispensable reference.

HISTORIES OF COMPANIES

The great classic in this field is Allan Nevins' and F. E. Hill's three
volumes: *Ford: The Times, the Man, the Company* (1954); *Ford:
Expansion and Challenge 1915–1932* (1957); and *Ford: Decline and
Rebirth 1933–1962* (1963). They are detailed and authoritative. The
only history of General Motors is Arthur Pound, *The Turning Wheel*
(1934). The Studebaker centennial produced Stephen Longstreet, *A
Century on Wheels: The Story of Studebaker* (1952). K. S. Smallzreid
and D. J. Roberts, *More Than You Promise* (1942) is more detailed on
the Studebaker family. *The Pope Manufacturing Company: An Industrial Achievement* (1907), compiled by the company, is now rare,
but it is almost the only detailed account of this important pioneer automobile manufacturer.

BIOGRAPHICAL

Henry Ford has naturally been given detailed attention by biog-
raphers. His own autobiography, *My Life and Work* (1922) written
with Samuel Crowther, is a useful book, presenting Henry Ford as
he wanted to appear rather than as he was. The Nevins and Hill
volumes give a complete life story and a sympathetic but scholarly
appraisal. Roger Burlingame, *Henry Ford: A Great Life in Brief* (1955)
is a really excellent short study. Keith Sward, *The Legend of Henry
Ford* (1955) is an unfriendly study by a former UAW organizer, useful
as an antidote to the aura of hero-worship surrounding Ford. Harry
Bennett, *We Never Called Him Henry* (1951) has little to offer. J. K.
Galbraith's essay "Was Ford a Fraud" in *The Liberal Hour* (1964 ed.),
117–37, gives well-deserved credit to James S. Couzens as a builder of
the Ford Motor Company, but the denigration of Ford in order to
glorify Couzens is overdone.

Walter P. Chrysler and Boyden Sparks, *Life of an American Work-
man* (1937) is a lively account of Chrysler's career. There is a similar
volume on Alfred P. Sloan, also in collaboration with Sparks, *Adventures of a White Collar Man* (1941). Sloan's later autobiography,
My Years with General Motors (1964) has useful information but the
presentation is formal and pedestrian. J. C. Long, *Roy D. Chapin* (1945)

is unfortunately a limited edition. Norman Beasley, *Knudsen: A Biography* (1947) is worth reading as is T. A. Boyd, *Professional Amateur: The Biography of Charles F. Kettering* (1957), written by a close associate of Kettering.

No one should miss Hiram Percy Maxim's delightful *Horseless Carriage Days* (1937), now in paperback. F. L. Smith, *Motoring Down a Quarter Century* (1928) is also an enjoyable tale by an early president of the Olds Motor Works. Charles E. Sorensen, with S. T. Williamson, *My Forty Years with Ford* (1956) is a revealing story, probably more so than its author realized or intended. There are no good biographies of Nash or Durant. Margery Durant, *My Father* (1929) is a work of filial piety. R. E. Olds, after a long period of neglect, has been given an adequate biography in G. A. Niemeyer, *The Automotive Career of Ransom E. Olds* (1963).

INDUSTRIAL ORGANIZATION

There are two good, well-written surveys of mass production. Christy Borth, *Masters of Mass Production* (1945) focuses on the automobile industry and the personalities who were responsible for mass production there; Roger Burlingame, *Backgrounds of Power* (1949) is a broader survey by an outstanding student of the history of technology.

The authority on the Selden patent case is William Greenleaf, *Monopoly on Wheels* (1961), although there is a tendency in this book to exaggerate the threat of monopoly.

For the development of business organization in the automobile industry, especially the General Motors contribution, the conclusive studies are A. D. Chandler, Jr., *Giant Enterprise: Ford, General Motors, and the Automobile Industry* (1964) and *Strategy and Structure: Chapters in the History of the Industrial Enterprise* (1962). Paul F. Douglass, *Six upon the World* (1954) and Peter Drucker, *The Concept of the Corporation* (1946) explore the same topic with a different but equally effective approach. H. C. Vatter, "Closure of Entry in the American Automobile Industry," *Oxford Economic Papers, New Series*, IV (1952), 213–34, is a scholarly and penetrating study of the evolution of oligopoly and is especially informative on the Kaiser-Frazer experiment.

The marketing of motor vehicles, particularly the franchised dealer system, is spelled out in detail in Federal Trade Commission, *Report on the Motor Vehicle Industry* (1939). A more analytical approach is

B. P. Pashigian, *The Distribution of Automobiles: An Economic Analysis of the Franchise System* (1961).

The subject of technical standardization is brilliantly analyzed in G. V. Thompson, "Intercompany Technical Standardization in the Early Automobile Industry," *Journal of Economic History*, XIV (Winter, 1954), 1–20.

LABOR RELATIONS

Sidney Fine, *The Automobile under the Blue Eagle* (1963) is a thorough and fascinating account of the tangled labor situation in the automobile industry at the beginning of the New Deal. Selig Perlman, *Labor in the New Deal Decade* (1945) is a useful survey, and Benjamin Stolberg, *The Story of the CIO* (1938) has a good deal of detail on the rise of the UAW. Ely Chinoy, *Automobile Workers and the American Dream* (1955) takes an unusual approach to the problems of the assembly-line worker.

HIGHWAY TRANSPORTATION

Neither highways themselves nor commercial highway vehicles have received the attention their importance warrants. The Public Roads Administration of the Department of Commerce issues much informative material on highways. Special mention can be made of *Highways in the United States* (1954). An economist's view appears in C. L. Dearing, *American Highway Policy* (1941).

The same author also collaborates on a study of highway and other forms of transportation in C. L. Dearing and Wilfred Owen, *National Transportation Policy* (1949). It is less inclusive than Harold Barger, *The Transportation Industries, 1889–1946* (1951).

For the general reader the best sources are two pamphlets written for the Automobile Manufacturers Association by F. M. Reck, *A Car Travelling People* (1958) and *From Horses to Horsepower* (1954). They are concise, well written, and informative.

SOCIAL CONSEQUENCES

The social revolution brought about by the automobile was vividly described for the 1920's in R. S. and H. M. Lynd, *Middletown* (1929). The community selected as "Middletown" was Muncie, Indiana. The best general survey can be found in F. L. Allen, *The Big Change*

(1952). *The Exploding Metropolis* (1958), by the editors of *Fortune*, had a lucid and complete analysis of the role of the motor vehicle in metropolitan growth and its attendant problems. It can be supplemented by Wilfred Owen, *The Metropolitan Transportation Problem* (1956) and *Cities in the Motor Age* (1959). Both these books explore methods of drastically reducing automobile traffic in urban centers. No one has done anything comparable on the effect of the automobile on rural life in the United States. A promising foundation for study of this whole topic has been laid by the Public Roads Administration in *Highways and Economic and Social Changes* (1964). It is an invaluable and somewhat overwhelming compilation of data. There is some interpretation, but much more needs to be done.

Acknowledgments

My indebtedness for assistance in the compilation of this book is substantial. Individuals and organizations have given time, effort, information, and materials freely and generously; without their contributions this book could not have been produced. The responsibility for the way in which their contributions have been used, however, is entirely mine. The selection of information, the views expressed, and the errors are to be charged to me alone.

The Automobile Manufacturers Association has provided much in the way of data and illustrations. I wish particularly to thank Robert C. Lusk, Director of Educational Services, and Miss Louise Rose of the Public Relations Department for their patience and goodwill in complying with endless and frequently unreasonable requests. In addition, willing cooperation in providing illustrations has been extended by Governor George Romney of Michigan; the Community Affairs Department of the Chrysler Corporation; John P. Breeden, Jr., Public Relations Assistant, Office of the Vice President, Product Planning and Styling, Ford Motor Company, through whom I also received permission to use material from *The Ford Book of Styling;* Jack Harned, William M. Adams, and Edward T. Breslin, Public Relations Staff, General Motors Corporation; the Public Relations Department, Studebaker-Packard Corporation; Joseph Walsh, Director of Public Relations, International Union, United Automobile, Aerospace and Agricultural Implement Workers of America—UAW; and the Press Relations Department, Sears, Roebuck and Co. I am indebted to the Indiana Toll Road Commission for the data on tollroad travel in Table 3 and to the United States Bureau of Public Roads for the map of the Interstate highway system.

In the preparation of the manuscript I have also had invaluable assistance. My wife, Florence, prepared the index; my daughter Helen typed my drafts with patient devotion; and my son James gave me the benefit of his extensive knowledge of modern cars. I am especially grateful to Jerome W. Hall, who made two excellent studies of highway development while he was a senior at Harvey Mudd College and who was of major assistance in collecting material on this subject. Arnold Ruskin of the Department of Engineering at Harvey Mudd College gave me some very useful suggestions on sources of information. Finally, Mrs. Glenn E. Thompson, secretary of the Department of Humanities and Social Sciences at Harvey Mudd College, typed the final manuscript with a skill and promptness which greatly facilitated the completion of the work. Some chapters were typed by Mrs. Edith Davies, also of Harvey Mudd College.

My friend Henry E. Edmunds, director of the Ford Archives, has been his usual helpful self in a variety of ways. Chilton Books generously gave permission to use material from my previous work, *American Automobile Manufacturers: The First Forty Years* (Philadelphia: Chilton Co., 1959).

Index